Conversations with Gloria Naylor

Literary Conversations Series

Peggy Whitman Prenshaw
General Editor

Photo credit: Lynda Koolish

Conversations with Gloria Naylor

Edited by Maxine Lavon Montgomery

University Press of Mississippi
Jackson

Books by Gloria Naylor

The Women of Brewster Place. New York: Viking Penguin, 1982.
Linden Hills. New York: Ticknor and Fields, 1985.
Mama Day. New York: Vintage Book, 1988.
Bailey's Cafe. San Diego: Harcourt Trade Publishers, 1992.
The Men of Brewster Place. New York: Hyperion Press, 1998.

www.upress.state.ms.us

The University Press of Mississippi is a member of the Association of American University Presses.

Copyright © 2004 by University Press of Mississippi
All rights reserved
Manufactured in the United States of America

12 11 10 09 08 07 06 05 04   4 3 2 1
∞
Library of Congress Cataloging-in-Publication Data

Naylor, Gloria.
  Conversations with Gloria Naylor / edited by Maxine Lavon Montgomery.
    p. cm. — (Literary conversations series)
  Includes index.
  ISBN 1-57806-632-8 (cloth : alk. paper) — ISBN 1-57806-633-6 (pbk. : alk. paper)
  1. Naylor, Gloria—Interviews. 2. Novelists, American—20th century—Interviews.
3. African American women in literature. 4. African Americans in literature.
  I. Montgomery Maxine Lavon, 1959– II. Title. III Series.

PS3564.A895Z465 2004
813'.54—dc22
                                                    2003061307

British Library Cataloging-in-Publication Data available

Contents

Introduction

Gloria Naylor appeared on the literary scene in 1982 with *The Women of Brewster Place* and one year later garnered the American Book Award for Best First Novel. Her debut work of fiction, which would become a television miniseries, was a critical and commercial success, and its publication heralded what was to be a stellar literary career.

The interviews assembled in this collection coincide with Naylor's steady book production since the publication of this first novel. In keeping with her assertion that "you're no better than your next work," Naylor has remained unswerving in her mission to write a series of novels reflecting the richness, complexity, and diversity of the African American experience.[1] Her expanding œuvre now includes five novels, an edited collection of short stories, two theater projects, and numerous articles, essays, and notes.

The many interviews she has granted over the course of her career reveal not only her productivity, but also her accessibility to scholars, teachers, creative writers, and journalists eager for insight into her life and art. At times charming and witty, always engaging and profoundly astute, Naylor exhibits a raw honesty to self that allows a rare glimpse into her private and public life. The selections included in this volume range from two 1983 newspaper pieces appearing after the publication of *The Women of Brewster Place* to a dialogue with Charles E. Wilson, Jr., in 2000 after the publication of *The Men of Brewster Place*. Because interviewers frequently pose the same questions, repetition and overlap are an inevitable consequence. Throughout the course of the interviews assembled in this volume, Naylor expands upon her answers rather than contradicting earlier remarks. But the evolution of Naylor's opinions and views manifests itself in her willingness to take up a broader range of issues and delve more deeply into topics such as her relation to the upcoming generation of African American novelists. Therefore, the evolution from *The Women of Brewster Place* to *The Men of Brewster Place* is one of maturation and clarification rather than revolution.

It is interesting to note the manner in which the selections mime the intertextual play present in Naylor's fictional cosmology. Repetition is central to

Black oral and literary forms of expression, as Henry Louis Gates, Jr., and others have persuasively argued.[2] Black authors often read and revise earlier works and the result of this tendency is a formal pattern of repetition among texts. Through recurrent mention of character and place Naylor engages in this same kind of textual play by creating a fictional universe in which a novel both echoes one of her previous works and anticipates a subsequent one. For instance, as she points out in her conversation with Toni Morrison, she began the emotional trek to her second novel, *Linden Hills*, before completing *The Women of Brewster Place*. Kiswana Browne, Brewster Place's zealous community activist, hails from neighboring upper middle-class Linden Hills, the focus of Naylor's second novel. Willa Prescott Nedeed, to whom readers are introduced in *Linden Hills*, is grandniece to Miranda Day, the feisty Willow Springs matriarch in the third novel, *Mama Day*. George, whose birth occurs in the culminating scene in the fourth novel, *Bailey's Cafe*, is the same individual who journeys south to the Sea Islands in *Mama Day*. And, of course, with the publication of *The Men of Brewster Place*, after a sixteen-year hiatus, Naylor returns, in a figurative sense, to the site of her first novel. The result of this creative intertexual configuration is the formation of a fictive universe in which textual boundaries are fluid and redrawn with the publication of a following work.

In a similar fashion, the interviews included in this volume may appear seamless in nature, resembling a lengthy conversation over an extended period of time more so than a series of disconnected, self-contained discussions. Prevalent throughout many of the pieces is Naylor's expressed determination to write a quartet of novels that would lay the foundation for a career, a point she first mentions in her conversation with Toni Morrison. Only after the publication of *Bailey's Cafe*, which is the last text in the tetralogy, did Naylor summon the courage to label herself as an author. In accordance with her mother's cautionary advice about not allowing others to define the self, Naylor found it important to form an authorial identity apart from the pronouncements of the literary establishment. As Naylor names the precursory influences on her art, she tells Morrison about an exposure to classical texts in the western literary traditions—one dominated by whites and men—and laments the absence of works by and about Black women in the English curricula at Brooklyn College and Yale University. "Was there no one telling my story?" she queries. She then credits Morrison's insistently lyrical *The Bluest Eye* as being the watershed text that inspired her to write.

In the interview with Pearl Cleage, Naylor clarifies her position regarding the relation between art and propaganda. To the question, "Do you feel a responsibility to propose solutions?" Naylor is quick to point out that her work is not about giving answers; she poses problems, not solutions. Naylor's retort thus brings to mind a key issue in Black literary and cultural studies—one harking back to the Harlem Renaissance and the notion that Black creative artists bear an obligation to their community. Black authors were under a tremendous burden to present socially acceptable portraits of the race. In other words, African American literature was not to be solely aesthetic in nature, but had to promote the goal of racial uplift.

Naylor's stance regarding this issue is one that aligns her with Langston Hughes, spokesperson for a host of creative artists who declared independence from the stifling dictates of the literati. His landmark essay "The Negro Artist and the Racial Mountain" served as a manifesto for an emergent generation of artists intent on boldly expressing "their individual dark-skinned selves without fear or shame."[3] By no means, however, does the response to Cleage's question suggest that Naylor is apolitical. On the contrary, Naylor, who came of age during the turbulent 1960s and 1970s, is politically aware and situates her texts within the various social and political moments defining twentieth-century America. She positions herself squarely within the ideological camps of cultural nationalism and feminism. Unlike multiethnic Harlem Renaissance writer Jean Toomer, whose frustration with the practice of racial categorization prompted a disassociation from a specifically Black cultural past, Naylor openly names the political space from which she writes. As she reveals in the interviews collected in this volume, she embraces her unique Black, female, and working-class-background self, even as she draws upon that rich heritage in giving form and essence to her fictional works. Rather than reifying essentialist notions of race that Toomer and some contemporary literary and cultural critics decry, however, Naylor uses symbolic acts of Black religion, speech, and music in her novels to challenge, not affirm, fixed notions of race.

Repeatedly, Naylor mentions the profound influence that her parents' southern sharecropping background has had on her life and art. As she explains to Kay Bonetti, she was conceived in Robinsonville, Mississippi, and the home that she grew up in, although located in the urban North, was particularly southern. Naylor attributes the communal voice in her work to the storytelling she heard from her parents and other southern relatives.

   With Bonetti, Naylor also delves deeply into what has become a leitmotif not just in interviews but in critical studies of the author's work: the intertextual relation between Naylor's writing and canonical texts in the western and Black literary and oral traditions. Hers is an indebtedness not only to the storytelling mode, but to, among others, Dante, William Shakespeare, Gabriel García Márquez, and foremother Zora Neale Hurston. Hurston's classic text *Their Eyes Were Watching God* influenced Naylor in crafting the magical storm scene in *Mama Day*. In this interview Naylor also articulates her views on magical realism, a form eschewed by some Black authors, and offers valuable insight into the ways she incorporates that mode into her work.

   By the time Naylor reaches her forties she is more self-assured and, consequently, more outspoken than she was at the beginning of her career. Naylor moves from being a self-professed bookish introvert to a mature, confident woman carving out a significant place for herself in the world of belles lettres. The passing of time also bears witness to the author's expanded artistic and political vision. The range of topics taken up in later interviews includes religion, gender concerns, global issues, and the future generation of Black women writers.

   Virginia Fowler interviews Naylor one year after the publication of *Bailey's Cafe*, the book that marks the end of one phase of the author's career and the beginning of a new one. In that conversation Naylor talks at length about her seven-year stint as lay minister with the Jehovah's Witnesses, a group the author severed ties with shortly after the assassination of Dr. Martin Luther King, Jr. The group's belief in a coming theocratic government that would eradicate social ills proved to be illusory at best. What Naylor did not abandon, however, is the call to be a witness, with writing as her mission. She describes the craft of writing in patently religious terms: "If you want to know about religion, my novel-writing is sacred territory. It's another place, you see, because I know how my sanity was saved that way. And I'm going to protect that." Throughout her work she relies heavily upon the Bible, critiquing the text by use of a careful re-visionary process involving parody and pastiche. Ever ambivalent about her religious affiliation and beliefs, Naylor maintains that even though she has no allegiance to any one faith, she is nonetheless a very spiritual being.

   The interview with Charles Rowell takes place one year before the publication of *The Men of Brewster Place*. In this conversation Naylor tells Rowell that she is "a very different woman from the woman who wrote *The Women of Brewster Place.*" Not only does she talk at length about the intriguing and often controversial male characters who people her fictional world, she anticipates her fifth novel's focus on the Black male dilemma. Perhaps more than any other interviewer, Rowell probes deeply into the subject of Naylor's relation to the southern literary tradition, and he allows Naylor an opportunity to amplify comments she made in earlier interviews with regard to the legacy that the South bequeaths to Black novelists. The southern experience is by no means monolithic, Naylor asserts, and is as complex as the authors whose works reveal an engagement with the region. Here, for the first time, a mature Naylor hints at an end to her lengthy apprenticeship to the authors whose work influences hers and suggests that she is a likely foremother to a new generation of women writers.

The interviews, conversations, and dialogues assembled for this volume best represent the full range of Naylor's interests, attitudes, and opinions over the course of her literary career. Together, the selections included shed light on the woman behind *The Women of Brewster Place* in all of her wit, wisdom, and candor. Naylor refers to her work as "a peeling away of layers to discover what already exists" (Epel) and this metaphoric description applies to these interviews as well. Here, established notions of who Naylor is are stripped away to reveal the private and public life of the woman whose accomplishments have assured her a lasting place within a literary tradition once dominated by whites and men. By all assessments, Naylor has fulfilled her aspiration of doing what James Baldwin achieved with his exceptional career: to "leave behind a moral vision, right or wrong, and a very long and prolific career, and a courageous one" (Fowler).

These interviews are arranged chronologically according to the date the interview was conducted, not the date the piece was published. For those interviews published previously, both the date and place of publication are noted. Transcripts have been edited for readability, and typos in published pieces have been silently corrected. Otherwise, these interviews are reproduced in their entirety.

I would like to acknowledge those individuals who played a role bringing this project into fruition. First of all, I am especially grateful to Gloria Naylor who so graciously consented to the publication of this work and granted permission to include a number of selections. Her interviews have been as enriching and inspiriting as her works of fiction. Jeneen Surrency, Sheryl Davis, and David Bluth assisted with the location, collection, transcription, and assembly of the selections. Fred Standley and Hunt Hawkins are valued colleagues who offered enthusiastic encouragement and advice. Florida State University's committee on Black Faculty Research and Support provided financial assistance. Last, but certainly not least, I want to thank my family for their love, patience, and emotional support: my husband, Nathaniel Crawford; my daughter, Samantha Crawford; and my brother and sisters, Patrick Nyaga-Ireri, Mikki Nyaga-Ireri, and Juanita Montgomery Hale.

Chronology

1950	On 25 January Gloria Naylor is born in New York City, to Alberta (McAlpin) and Roosevelt Naylor.
1954	Family moves to housing project in upper Bronx.
1960	Family moves to apartment buildings in Harlem on West 116th Street (owned by maternal grandmother, Lucielia McAlpin).
1963	Family moves to Queens.
1963–64	Mother joins the Jehovah's Witnesses.
1967	Fire destroys grandmother's apartment buildings.
1968	Naylor graduates from high school and becomes a Jehovah's Witness minister.
1968–74	Naylor works as a switchboard operator at various places in New York; continues to live with parents.
1974	Moves to Dunn, North Carolina, and then to Jacksonville, Florida, preaching as a full-time minister for the Jehovah's Witnesses; works as a switchboard operator and in fast-food restaurants.
1975	Leaves the Jehovah's Witnesses; moves back to parents' home. Attends Medgar Evers College, then transfers to Brooklyn College of CUNY to study English.
1976	Moves out of parents' home.
1977	Reads Toni Morrison's *The Bluest Eye*, which inspires her to write about the experiences of black women.
1980	Marries.
1981	Receives B.A. in English from Brooklyn College; completes *The Women of Brewster Place*; divorces; travels to Spain and Tangiers; begins *Linden Hills*; begins graduate work in African American studies at Yale University.
1982	*The Women of Brewster Place* is published; works on *Linden Hills*.
1983	Receives M.A. in African American studies from Yale University; receives American Book Award for Best First Novel; writer-in-residence at Cummington Community of the Arts and a visiting lecturer at George Washington University; receives Distinguished

Writer Award, Mid-Atlantic Writers Association (MAWA); travels to Guadalajara, Mexico; begins work on *Mama Day*.

1985   *Linden Hills*, which had been her master's thesis at Yale, is published; receives National Endowment for the Arts Fellowship.

1986   Receives Candace Award of the National Coalition of One Hundred Black Women; scholar-in-residence at the University of Pennsylvania; visiting professor at New York University; visiting lecturer at Princeton University.

1987   Visiting professor at Boston University.

1988   *Mama Day* is published; receives Guggenheim Fellowship; Fanny Hurst Visiting Professor at Brandeis University and senior fellow in Society for Humanities, Cornell University; becomes member of the Book-of-the-Month Club Selection Committee.

1989   Receives Lillian Smith Award; begins work on *Bailey's Cafe*.

1990   Establishes One-Way Productions, a multimedia production company.

1991   Visiting writer at University of Kent, Great Britain, under the auspices of the British Arts Council.

1992   *Bailey's Cafe* is published; travels in Senegambian region of Africa, lecturing and conducting research for next novel, "Sapphira Wade"; father dies on September 17; travels to Oslo to continue research for novel; stage reading of *Bailey's Cafe* at Lincoln Center.

1993   Stage production of *Bailey's Cafe* by Hartford Stage Company, 28 March–30 April.

1996   Edits *Children of the Night: The Best Short Stories by Black Writers, 1964 to the present*; writes *1996* based on experiences in South Carolina.

1998   *The Men of Brewster Place* is published; appointed Ferrol Sams, Jr. Distinguished Chair of English at Mercer University.

2000   One-Way Productions is dismantled.

Adapted from *Gloria Naylor: In Search of Sanctuary* by Virginia C. Fowler, copyright © 1996 Twayne Publishers, by permission of the Gale Group.

Conversations with Gloria Naylor

A Talk with Gloria Naylor

William Goldstein / 1983

From *Publishers Weekly* (9 September, 1983), 35–36. Copyright © 1983 Reed Business Information. Reprinted with permission.

In a marketplace not particularly kind to either black writers or first novels, books rarely achieve the kind of success that has been building around *The Women of Brewster Place* by Gloria Naylor. Good reviews of the hardcover novel when it was published last year by Viking spurred only two printings totaling 7,610 copies, but the book, winner of the TABA prize for best first novel of 1982, has become very popular of late. After four printings, there are 42,500 copies of the Penguin paperback in print and *Brewster Place* spent the last several weeks bubbling just below the bottom end of *PW*'s trade paperback bestseller list. Booksellers canvassed in our Summer Survey frequently mentioned Naylor's novel as one of their better sellers, reporting that many copies have been sold together with Alice Walker's *The Color Purple*, this year's *other* prize-winning novel by a black woman writer.

Brewster Place is a novel of seven chapters chronicling the fates of seven black women of different backgrounds brought by confusion and circumstance to live on a decaying, yet emotionally vibrant walled-off street just out of sight of a highway filled with sunshine. The setting is an unnamed Every-city somewhere in urban America. Each woman has her dream, and each story is the tale of "a dream deferred just a bit," says Naylor, "which is the problem of the black female experience in America."

Naylor speaks of her own experience out of a background of religious faith and expresses, in both her work and conversation, deeply felt convictions. She is "just a girl from Queens who can turn a sentence," by her own light-hearted definition, but, for seven years between high school and matriculation at Brooklyn College, Naylor was a Jehovah's Witness missionary and most recently a graduate student in Afro-American literature at Yale University. She will begin teaching creative writing and American literature at George Washington University in Washington, D.C. in the fall.

"It was a gradual movement from the Witnesses to black literature," Naylor explains. In the wake of Martin Luther King's death, she had decided

3

that it was not the right time to go on to college. "After the assassination, one of my teachers in high school cried in front of the class and said, 'You know there's a cancer spreading in this country and I want you to go home and think about what that means.' I went home and I did that. And I said, the cancer's not only in this country, that cancer is in the world."

What the Witnesses offered, Naylor says, was a focus; through their platform of theocratic government, "they offered me a picture of how there will be this government ruled by God. That was what I needed to hear at that time and why I threw myself into that religion full force—I wanted to work for better world conditions and for seven years I thought I was doing that by proclaiming the arrival one day of this government."

She slowly realized that she could take her talents into other areas and still work for the same goals. She studied nursing at Medgar Evers College until she found herself spending more time with her English courses. After transferring to Brooklyn College to study literature, Naylor went onto an Afro-American literature masters at Yale. "I had cut my literary teeth, so to speak, on the English classics—and I am still an admirer of the *style* of Faulkner though we can talk about his ideology *another* time," she injects with a sly laugh. "But what I wanted to see, with all my background in literature and the *thousands* of books I had read up until that time, were reflections of me and my existence and experience." She took courses in both the Afro-American studies department and in women's studies because "I hoped that by combining the two, I could find out what black women had been doing."

What Naylor discovered, however, was a rich vein of literature left largely unexplored—an academic dilemma, she stresses, of great cultural and historical proportions. She mentions the belated recognition of writers like Zora Neale Hurston, last year's discovery of Harriet Wilson's *Our Nig*, the recent acclaim for Alice Walker's work, as examples of the fact that "blacks have been writing in this country since this country has been writing and have a literary heritage of their own. Unfortunately, they haven't had encouragement or recognition for their efforts." There is, she points out, "a historical tendency to look upon the output of black writers as not really *American* literature. What's happened—what *had* happened," she amends herself, "was that when black people wrote, it wasn't quite serious work—it was race work or protest work. And often very gifted writers died unrecognized for that reason—and for other reasons that many other gifted writers have died unrecognized.

"So I think," she concludes, "that what I am personally benefiting from are all those graves. All those doors that had been knocked upon and been unheeded. Now that we're getting a revitalization of our lost authors in this country. . . . Well, if anything, maybe people have knocked and somebody's listening."

The underlying racism that Naylor feels still subtly permeates American society is symbolized in *Brewster Place* by the wall that makes the street a dead-end: "It was put up to keep apart the people who are down and out," Naylor says. "And despite the differences of their backgrounds, all of the women in the novel share the fact that they all live with this wall. And for me, that wall symbolized, simply, racism in this country. For that is the reductive experience for all blacks, regardless of their status. Now, it is not something you dwell on every day of your life, but it is something you know is part and parcel of your existence. Yet you go on doing the things you do, like these women did: they raised their children, they had their sorrows, their happinesses—but it is always there."

Beyond racism, or perhaps even before it, Naylor believes, the women of Brewster Place—Etta Mac Johnson, Mattie Michael, Kiswana Browne, Lucielia Louise Turner, Cora Lee and The Two (Lorraine and Theresa)—face the problem of womanhood in a society where women are undervalued and abused. Their alienation is ameliorated by what Naylor points out is "the networking or nurturing by women you can see throughout the novel—sometimes it is very violent and a life is saved, sometimes it is less dramatic and there is a kind of cultural awakening from one woman reaching out to another." But, she continues, such a make-shift network often fails, and in *Brewster Place* this situation is dramatized by a particularly violent rape perpetrated upon one of "The Two" (the chapter about them is so named by Naylor because they are lesbians and looked upon by the others as "not individuals, or even as women, but as some alien social situation").

"In the case of Lorraine [the rape victim] there was no woman on that block willing to help her and she *was* in trouble—there were tensions in her own home that come as part of the human experience, just living with another individual. And she had no one to go to. . . . It was her alienation from the other women that put her in that alley," Naylor states emphatically. "The thing is, Lorraine wasn't raped because she is a lesbian, they raped her because she was a woman. And," she continues, raising her voice and her hand, and striking the desk with each phrase, "regardless of race, regardless of social status, regardless of sexual preference, the commonality is the female experience. When you reduce that down in this society even to something as abysmal as rape, there is no *difference* between women."

The repercussions of Lorraine's being cut off from a female network, Naylor believes, "didn't only stay with her. They came back and affected the entire black community, male and female. I feel very strongly that we as black people have to be there as nurturing agents for each other, male and female, female and female. And when that broke down in 'The Two,' I wanted to show how that could *destroy* the community".

"The women are women I never knew personally," the author says. "But I have known that *spirit*, I have definitely known that *life*. That's how those characters were born. But they lived for me as characters with their own personalities and I let them have it. I wanted to immortalize the spirit I saw in my grandmother, my great aunt and my mom." The two house numbers that are mentioned in the novel are the addresses of two buildings Naylor's grandmother owned in Harlem.

Naylor grew up in a middle-class area, and her next novel will be "another neighborhood microcosm, this time of the black middle-class, a suburb. It's called *Linden Hills* [a middle-class area alluded to in *Brewster Place*]." The novel comprises seven sections—an opening chapter and one for six days of the week. Its structure is based, Naylor explains, on that of Dante's *Inferno* and features two young street poets who live on a suburb on a hill. "As they move down the hill, what they encounter are individuals who have 'moved up' in American society, among these crescent-shaped drives until eventually they will hit the center of their community and the home of my equivalent of Satan." Of course, Naylor says, laughing again, "the working out of the symbolism is easier said than done. Although it's an ambitious thing, and perhaps a bit cerebral, primarily it is a *story*."

Her work, Naylor says, attempts to "articulate experiences that want articulating—for those readers who reflect the subject matter, black readers, and for those who don't—basically white middle-class readers." For the latter, "hopefully, *hopefully*," she says, "there will be some glimpse of understanding. But for the first group," Naylor emphasizes, "the book will, perhaps, be an artifact in and of itself and there will be, I hope, some sense of pride."

The Painful Salvation of Gloria Naylor

Jacqueline Trescott / 1983

On this morning Gloria Naylor has put aside the love, bickering, and violence of her stories. Instead she offers herself, a tranquil still life of the writer-in-residence. The fall sun blushes gold on the worn walnut desk in her small quarters at George Washington University. The bookcase is almost bare, a signal of indefiniteness.

Naylor has brought little of herself into the room. She blends in, rather than disturbs. In time she will probably be a more confident possessor of space, but right now it's her words that have made people move to the edges of their chairs.

Her combustible portraits in *The Women of Brewster Place* have prompted songs of praise. The book won the important imprimatur of the American Book Award committee this year for the best first novel. Next year it will become a segment on public television's *American Playhouse.*

Naylor is grateful, but the attention isn't as satisfying as the solutions she found in writing. She smiles slightly, a warm rod through a serious face. The moment she saw her book for the first time, that was a moment of justification. "I wonder if I will never feel that way again. I knew what it meant to me as a process, how that writing actually sort of almost saved my life. Here was the evidence. I was complete then, totally complete," says Naylor.

"It pulled me out of a severe depression," she continues, moving slightly in a wooden chair and lighting a cigarette. "I was doing things physically to my body. I was one hundred pounds overweight. Not that the writing made me lose weight, but it was just what it symbolized. It symbolized me finally taking hold of myself and attempting to take my destiny in my own hands. All the other things came."

Kiswana Browne, Mattie Michael, Etta Mae Johnson, Lucielia Louise Turner, Cora Lee, Lorraine and Theresa—the vivid occupants of her book—live on a poor dead-end street, physical captives of its wall but free to laugh, quarrel, and destroy beyond its bounds. Everyone knows a street like this. Bryant Street, NE bumps into a wall. So where is it? She laughs deeply. "It is purposely nowhere. I wanted to create a metaphysical situation. The women shared racism and sexism; to put it somewhere would have introduced connections I didn't want."

The characters share portions of Naylor's thirty-three years of emotional barriers, some self-pitying, some defiant, some dreamy. "People . . . are being laudatory when they say, 'Oh my God, the way you can write about pain.' You sort of want to tell them, 'No, baby, I was feeling that pain.' I would love to take credit for being a genius, but no, I was letting out what was in a form I could deal with, another woman's life."

"Then she opened her eyes and they screamed and screamed into the face above hers—the face that was pushing this tearing pain inside of her body. The screams tried to break through her corneas out into the air, but the tough rubbery flesh sent them vibrating back into her brain, first shaking lifeless the cells that nurtured her memory."

When she started writing, Naylor was putting back her own broken pieces. She grew up in New York, a deliberate circumstance. Her mother, who was barred from the public libraries in her childhood Mississippi, saved money from her field work so she could send for books, and promised herself her children would be born in the North. Naylor's mother is a telephone operator and her father a motorman for New York Transit and she has two younger sisters, one a nurse, the other a homemaker.

The daughter-to-be-the-writer sat in classes for gifted children in public schools and read Brontë, Dickens, Faulkner, and Hemingway. She cried over the passion of *Jane Eyre* and didn't cry over a book again until *Native Son.*

When Naylor was a high school senior, the Rev. Martin Luther King Jr. was assassinated and she sought order to her own confusion. For the next seven years, she was a Jehovah's Witness missionary, traveling through New York, North Caorlina, and Florida. "I wanted a solution to the chaos. Many of my peers joined the hippie movements or became black nationalists. This way seemed right," she says. When she was twenty-five, she quit because she found the life, especially the celibacy, confining. "I began to feel ill at ease."

In the next seven-year phase, Naylor made up for what she now considers lost time. Nursing was a brief option. She replaced pessimism with skepticism. Even of love. Ten days was all she could give to a marriage.

When her luck changed she was in her mid-twenties, attending Brooklyn College, working at a hotel switchboard at night and having her reading world opened by Joan Larkin, a professor. On her first try, Naylor had a story published by *Essence Magazine* in 1980. Then, ironically, given her past disappointments, she didn't hesitate when a friend who was a secretary to the president at Viking said she would show her short stories around. "To us that was close enough," she says of her fearless naiveté. The secretary circulated four short stories in January 1981. Two weeks later Naylor had a contract and the secretary a promotion to editor. "Now, looking back, it's like, 'How did that happen?' That just does not happen," she says.

It was that crossroads when her optimism finally bumped her despair. "Maybe it was because I had so much bad luck. Maybe it was just the time. I believe that if we walk across the street, it can change the whole direction of our life, truly." The relief helped her to write: "*Butch had a laugh like the edges of an April sunset—translucent and mystifying. You knew it couldn't last forever, but you'd stand for hours, hoping for the chance to experience just a glimmer of it once again.*"

The writing of the next four stories and a prologue that emerged as a book, hoover, was another low time. "I went through the frozen stage for a time. Then, as always, I did what I had to do," she says. Disappointment is now determination, sometimes it's too much of a whirl. "It's dislocation. You get sort of dizzy, thinking about how my life has changed," she says. After Brooklyn, she earned a master's degree in Afro-American studies at Yale University.

Until the spring, when she finishes teaching at GW, she has an apartment on 16th Street. She rises at dawn to face a December deadline for her second book, *Linden Hills*, and keeps working at that powerful spareness that gives *Brewster* its edge.

Mattie Michael knows she has lost a son: "*She walked up the street and saw that his car wasn't parked out front and the house was dark. . . . Normally she would have gone through the front door, taken off her coat, and hung it in the front hall closet. . . . She took off her coat and laid it on one of the kitchen chairs. There was an extra jacket of his in the front hall closet that would not be there.*"

A Conversation

Gloria Naylor and Toni Morrison / 1985

From *Southern Review* 21 (1985), 567–93. Copyright © Gloria Naylor. Reprinted with permission.

Hudson, river, c. 315 mi. long, rising in NE New York in L. Tear of the Clouds near Mt. Marcy in the Adirondacks and flowing generally S., forming N.Y.-N.J. line for c. 17 mi. near its mouth in Upper New York Bay. . . . At New York City Holland and Lincoln tunnels, railroad tunnel, subways, ferries, and George Washington Bridge link N.Y. and N.J. Above New York City river widens at Tappan Zee. On W bank Palisades stretch N from N.J. Catskill Mts. descend to Hudson Valley. First explored by Henry Hudson in 1609. Major highway for Indians and early settlers. Has many historic, literary, and artistic associations.

(The Columbia Viking Desk Encyclopedia)

There is a blue house that sits on this river between two bridges. One is the George Washington that my bus has just crossed from the Manhattan side, and the other is the Tappan Zee that it's heading toward. My destination is that blue house, my objective is to tape a dialogue between myself and another black American writer, and I stepped on this bus seven years ago when I opened a slim volume entitled The Bluest Eye. *Where does the first line of any novel—like any journey—actually begin? . . . Quiet as it's kept, there were no marigolds in the fall of 1941 . . . I encountered those words, crystallized from the stream of a lifetime where they had been flowing through experiences seen and unseen, felt and unfelt, heard and unheard. That sentence was the product of a thousand tributaries before it would ultimately swell with an existence of its own, flowing off to become yet another source to uncountable possibilities.*

From grade school I had been told that I had potential, while I only knew that I felt most complete when expressing myself through the written word. So I scribbled on bits of looseleaf and in diaries—to hide it all away. I wrote because I had no choice, but that was a long road from gathering the authority within myself to believe that I could actually be a writer. The writers I had been taught to love were either male or white. And who was I to argue that Ellison,

10

Austen, Dickens, the Brontës, Baldwin, and Faulkner weren't masters? They were and are. But inside there was still the faintest whisper: Was there no one telling my story? And since it appeared there was not, how could I presume to? Those were frustrating years until I enrolled in a creative writing seminar at Brooklyn College. My instructor's philosophy was that in order for us to even attempt to write good literature, we must read good literature. And so her reading list included Tillie Olsen, Henry James—and Toni Morrison. I have tried hard but I can't remember if we read The Bluest Eye *at the beginning, middle, or end of the semester. Time has been swallowed except for the moment I opened that novel because for my memory that semester is now* The Bluest Eye, *and* The Bluest Eye *is the beginning. The presence of the work served two vital purposes at that moment in my life. It said to a young poet, struggling to break into prose, that the barriers were flexible; at the core of it all is language, and if you're skilled enough with that, you can create your own genre. And it said to a young black woman, struggling to find a mirror of her worth in this society, not only is your story worth telling but it can be told in words so painstakingly eloquent that it becomes a song.*

Now that I saw it could be done, the question was, who had done it? Intellectually, I accepted that the author of The Bluest Eye *was a black woman, and it gave me a measure of pride that we had been here all along, creating American literature. Yet, I stared at the name, Toni Morrison, on the book's cover and it seemed as far removed from me as the separate universe I assumed all artists moved in—they were "different" people. Then a newspaper clipping, announcing that Toni Morrison would be reading from her latest novel,* Song of Solomon, *gave me my first opportunity to see this ethereal creature. When I walked into that room the striking resemblance between this writer and my second cousin jolted me.* She looked like Jessie. *The caramel skin, wide full mouth, the liquid eyes capable of lightning jumps from an almost childlike vulnerability to a piercing assessment of the surrounding climate. The round head that would tip sharply to the side just before a burst of laughter. I didn't approach her after that first reading, but then and several times afterwards, I would simply sit and watch intently—every movement, every gesture. I knew all of her novels practically by heart then, but I was waiting—perhaps a bit fearfully—for some evidence that would shatter the growing revelation that she was a real person. It never came. And that refrain kept playing itself over and over in my mind until it shrieked itself along with her into reality—She looked like Jessie. I knew without a doubt that Jessie and I shared the same blood. And so that meant, somehow, the writer who could create a "Bluest*

Eye" was just like me. I went home one night after one of her readings, stared into my bathroom mirror, and I began to cry . . . After the funeral the well-meaning came to console and offer their dog-eared faith in the form of coconut cakes, potato pies, fried chicken, and tears . . . Where does the first line of a novel actually begin and end? Through these experiences, so many before and after them, my own sentence was crystallized.

That had been my encounter with the work and the writer. But now two books later as my bus pulls up in back of her home, I am finally going to meet the woman. How can I possibly begin? What do you say to someone who has played this type of role in your life?

Well, first, you say, "Hello" . . .

It is now many hours later. Across the Hudson, the New York shore is becoming a hazy blue-gray as evening approaches. The river moves against her grounds with a hypnotic rhythm that seems to suspend you a touch above time and place. I settle back into a deep, wide lounge that accepts my body as the view from her windows receives my spirit and gently expands it over the waves. It is a peaceful moment. While I am in the midst of the contentment most guests experience with attentive hosts, there is an added facet to my comfort: I have come to the realization that I like this woman. I had no guarantee of that before today, knowing that the artist and her art, while inextricably tied, are still two separate entities. And I had prepared myself so there would have been no harm done had I left there acknowledging her genius, but now aware that she was someone I would not voluntarily spend another afternoon with. So I considered it a gift that I would leave with more than an absence of harm—a newly possessed acquaintance with a good human being.

Through the day I have seen that there is so much that is different about us: I'm at the beginning of my career, she's at the height of hers; I am reticent and cautious, she is open and dramatic. We are from two generations, city and small town. I am childless and she is a devoted parent. But we are, after all, women; and so as I turn the tape recorder on, we continue talking as any two women might who happen to be fiercely proud of their identities and dedicated to their work.—GN

Gloria Naylor: So I took the advance from _Brewster Place_ and treated myself to a graduation present. First I went to Algeciras, which is in southern Spain, because I had read that Hemingway had sort of made Barcelona his and Baldwin had made Paris his. I even carried along a copy of _Nobody Knows My Name_, expecting to see Europe the way these writers had seen it. After all I'd just written _a_ book—you know, I was ready to be continental. But the experience was so different for me. I was harassed a lot on the streets because I was a woman traveling alone. In southern Spain the women don't walk alone. So the men assumed I was a prostitute or that I wanted them to approach me, and it was really difficult. And the freedom that Hemingway and Baldwin experienced I didn't have. Sure, I had it when I sequestered myself away in that boarding house in Cadiz and started working on *Linden Hills*—I was free to write as much as I wanted, but not to roam the streets. And I'm going to be honest— I resented that; I was bitter that I couldn't have the world like they had the world.

Toni Morrison: It is such an incredible thing to know that in a very strong way, geographically, it is their world because they alone can walk up and down certain places.

GN: But now you said you went to Paris, and I personally didn't have the same type of problem there. Did you?

TM: No. But I never went anywhere to do what you did. I have never had that courage and I have a tough time even now trying to. I guess because I should have done it much younger. My interior life is so strong that I never associate anything important to any other place, which makes me very parochial in that regard. The only reason I never went to Africa was because I didn't have anything to do over there. I didn't want to just go and look. Before I got married I used to go anywhere at the drop of a hat—overnight, I didn't go long distances; but after that I had other things to take into consideration. But I could do it now I guess.

GN: I wasn't married that terribly long to know that there was a difference between B.M. and A.M.—"before marriage" and "after marriage." I didn't have that, so I always loved to go. I met him because I was on the go.

TM: How old were you when you got married?

GN: Thirty. I was twenty-nine when he proposed. I was going to turn thirty in January. Then he proposed over the telephone—long distance *collect* when I was twenty-nine and eleven months old. I was making that twenty-nine to thirty transition, saying to myself, "Well, what have I done with my life? I better go on and get married." It was really fear. Do you know Marcia Gillespie? I met her that November of 1979 because I sent *Essence* one of my short stories and her secretary called me and set up a luncheon appointment—my first literary luncheon. And she just sat down and said, "Sister, if you do anything, keep writing." And that scared me. And so his proposal coming on the heels of that statement sort of gave me a way out of my fear. I didn't have to face the terror of the dream I had lived with all my life coming true—that was untraveled terrain. But marrying somebody—anybody—was very traveled terrain, because I grew up feeling somehow that that was how you made your definition. Although Marcia had offered me the hope of another way to make a definition, his was safe—it was conventional.

TM: That's what I want to explore in this new book. How we choose to put ourselves someplace else, outside, rather than in here, inside.

GN: But don't you think men do it too? I think they do but their sacrifices aren't as pronounced. But almost every human being, I think, has a problem saying, "Well, who in the hell am I? And what is it that nurtures me, and who is that me?"

TM: Men can hide easier because they can always be men. They can be abstract, in a crunch, and they seem to know what maleness is. They have a posture for that. They have a job for that. They have an idea of how to be male and they talk about it a lot. I'm not sure that they talk to each other about the other thing, personal identity. Have you ever heard men talk to each other?

GN: Well, they don't talk to me about such things—or in my presence.

TM: Well, I have heard them when they talk among themselves, and they don't talk about the vulnerable "me." It must be hard for men to confide in one another, not incidents that happen to them, but to confide that other life that's not *male*. That's hard for them, because they are trained out of it so early in life. When I was growing up, I listened to my brothers talk to one another and other men when they thought they were talking outside my hearing, and they don't talk to each other the same way that I would hear my aunts and my mother. Only when they get very much older, then they can stop posturing. . . . It's a terrible burden, because they want to know—when they're little kids, of course, they say, "Who am I?" And then somebody says, "Well, you're a man." And they try to figure out what that is. That's what they shoot for. But if somebody says, "Well, you're a woman," what does that mean? Well, that usually means somebody's handmaiden. If you pass the test of being a woman, as far as a man is concerned, that's something quite different from what I would mean. And when you think of who are the women that you admire and what do you admire about them as women, it would never be what men would think. So many things just go out the window.

It doesn't mean they don't admire it in some sense; they just don't want to be in its company day after day.

GN: I know what you're saying, but when someone asks me what women I admire, they're normally women who have turned their backs on the world; they're women who have been selfish to some degree, who have gone against the grain. Zora Neale Hurston is an example. She defied so many of the acceptable conventions for women during her time, and I never had the courage to do that. I hope more young women will, but not go about their lives in a destructive way so they are socially abrasive, but to do it where it's just self-confirming.

TM: And that's different from what men want when they're defining you. It's special and it's true that those are the things that cause other women to admire, not envy, admire, really get a kick out of each other. I was trying in *Tarbaby* to suggest that quality. It's neither up nor down, or socially acceptable or unacceptable. It's original. The woman that Jadine sees in the supermarket (the one with no eyelashes) is somehow transcendent and whatever she really was, what she was perceived as by Jadine, is the real chic. The one that authenticates everything. The one that is very clear in some deep way about what her womanhood is. And it can happen at any moment and any woman might do it. For Jadine it was that particular woman who looked that particular way. But she can appear at any moment. And when you see it, it does stay with you even though you may surrender to whatever your culture's version of you is supposed to be. Still, the memory of that one is somehow a basis for either total repression or a willingness to let one's true self surface. I went through a period of thinking that such women were not only selfish, but narcissistic. And the line between those two became difficult to see. When is it vanity and narcissism and being a spoiled brat, and when is it clarity? Self-affirmation? That's the problem. Sometimes when you see a certain woman you know she is not coherent. She may be a person who has all the accoutrements of *self-centeredness*, but is not centered at all. She may be really just piling stuff on—more jewels, you know, sort of a costume idea of a woman. But that is the search. And I think that in these days and these times, black women, if they don't know what it is, then nobody may know what it is at all.

GN: I had such a character in *Linden Hills*. And when I put Willa in that basement my overall idea was to have this very conservative upper-middle class black woman through her discovery of all those remnants from the past wives who'd lived in that house, just get up, walk out of there and say, "No, this is shallow. This is not for me." I wanted her to learn from those lessons in history. But what eventually evolved through all the pain that she went through was the discovery that she liked being where she was—a conventional housewife. And there is this moment when she says not only to the reader, but to *me*—"I was a good wife and a good mother. And I'm not going to apologize to anyone for that." That was a real surprise to me; I hadn't planned on the character doing that. But what her self-affirmation became was acknowledging her conventional position. You see, I used to believe that self-affirmation meant you had to be totally aconventional. But to keep a house, especially the way my mother kept her house—against all odds—is really a creative statement. So a woman's affirmation doesn't have to be an executive chair at IBM or something like that.

TM: Well, those are class differences. That was, I think, some of the major criticism earlier in the women's movement. Did everybody have to want to be the vice-president? What about the typist who really wanted to type? There's a class conflict. It seemed to suggest that you could only feel as though you had come into your own if you walked in the corridors of power in some capitalist mode. That's another one of those unreal, I think also fraudulent, conflicts between women who want to be mothers and women who don't. Why should there be any conflict with that? You could, first of all, do both. And why should I denigrate somebody who wants to stay home and have a garden?

GN: If that's their choice. Maybe the fight was that we didn't think at one time that there was an alternative. But if you realize these are the alternatives and that is what I choose to do, then that's fine.

TM: If that is the choice. . . . You see, the point is that freedom is choosing your responsibility. It's not having no responsibilities; it's choosing the ones you want. So many women have been given responsibilities they don't want. A lady doctor has to be able to say, "I want to go home." And the one at home has the right to say, "I want to go to medical school." That's all there is to that, but then the choices cause problems where there are no problems because "either/or" seems to set up the conflict, first in the language and then in life—as though you can't do two things or do one and then stop it and go do something else.

As though there is a schedule somewhere. That's what's happened with the twenty-nine and thirty. "Now I'm thirty: thirty and not married; that's critical."

GN: But then you get married and realize that you didn't want to be married, you just wanted to get married. And after that you just go on.
TM: The romance thing is a little bit of a problem. Being in love with some- body, it's such a fine, fine feeling. It just turns everything up so nicely. The feeling of being in love, whether it's a successful love affair or not, is almost irrelevant. It's just that you're up. Like the volume of a radio turned up.

GN: Everything becomes a lot clearer in the world; if not clearer, it's filtered through a different kind of light.
TM: Our sensibilities are alive. I love love. I like the feeling of it. And I like the way the world looks, the way things sound, the way food tastes. I like that heightened sensibility. Of course you have to distinguish between that and marriage, which is another kind of sensibility. It's nice when it's all in the same thing. But sometimes you just put everything in marriage like that was the entire solution. There are a lot of other things to love, but none of them have currency these days. Loving God, now that's fanatical. Loving your country, your school, your children. It all has some sort of taint that's Freudian. So the only one that's sort of untainted, the one that everybody thinks is strong and self-important, is loving the other person. And very seldom can that other person bear the weight of all of your attention.

GN: Toni, about *Song of Solomon* in that marvelous scene when Guitar is driving Hagar home after she tried to destroy Milkman and she realizes that she can't kill him. . . . You know, I called one of my girl friends and read that to her over the phone saying, *"Hear this—"* I've read more of your books over the phone to girl friends—Guitar was taking her home and she was going on about, "Well, I can't live. I'm nothing without him." And he says to her, "Hagar, if you say to someone, 'I am nothing without you' what is there in you for them to want?" So being in love is fine, but only when there's a self there who's doing the loving.
TM: Yes, when there's somebody there doing the loving.

GN: Exactly.
TM: You don't think you're nothing without him. He doesn't think so either. That comradeship, that feeling of working with a partner is what's nice in a

marriage, when two people are doing something together. And then of course something shifts. Somebody is running it; somebody is calling the shots. Somebody has to give or make it look like he's giving. Then the play or the battle is about power.

GN: And the responsibility to give way seems to always fall on us. I remember the transformation I went through almost immediately after I was married. Unconsciously, I felt as if I needed to ask permission to do something, and I started to get scared when I really listened to myself. And this was a woman who normally never asked anybody about anything when she wanted to do something. But now being married, somehow, I felt I should do that.
TM: That happens even afterwards. Later you realize that you are the one who tells you "no" or "yes."

GN: Eventually I will reach that point—if I'm with a man or not—when I can just say, "Well, *I* am the authority and I am asking myself." I mean, I want to be able to say that to myself inside. Because now I can do it verbally, but I don't believe a word of it. What I guess I really want to do is be a man; that would make it easy. I used to fantasize about that, you know—I guess a lot of women do.
TM: It wouldn't be easier if you were a man, but what would be easier is if you had all the rights and the authority that are male and the adventure, what we equate with adventure, that is male. And to not, as you say the character in your book does not, have to apologize for that. The history of your women and your family and mine has a lot of different colors in it. A lot of different adventures. But, for example, I tried hard to be both the ship and the safe harbor at the same time, to be able to make a house and be on the job market and still nurture the children. It's trying to make life enhanced by additional things rather than conflicted by additional things. No one should be asked to make a choice between a home or a career. Why not have both? It's all possible. Like women doing nine things since the beginning and getting to the end of the row at the same time.

GN: But you know, I think that whole sense of adventure and authority tied into maleness has a lot to do with how books are created and who's creating them—and in what numbers. I had told you before about how you

influenced me and how *The Bluest Eye* sitting there gave me a validity to do
something which I had thought was really male terrain. And all of my education had subconsciously told me that it wasn't the place for me.
TM: Only men did that.

GN: Yes, men wrote—because what was I reading? When I hit college what was
I reading in the Afro-American studies department? Fine, black, male writers.
What had I read in high school? White male writers. Sure, there were a few
women then, but they were white women and in another century to boot. But
for me, where was the *authority* for me to enter this forbidden terrain? But then
finally you were being taught to me. But you've told me, Toni, there was no *you*
there when you were in school. So how did you get the courage to just say, "Well,
yes, I will pick up this pen."
TM: I wonder . . . I think that at that moment I had no choice. If I had had
some choices such as the ones we are talking about, I wouldn't have done it.
But I was really in a corner. And whatever was being threatened by the
circumstances in which I found myself, alone with two children in a town
where I didn't know anybody, I knew that I would not deliver to my children
a parent that was of no use to them. So I was thrown back on, luckily, the
only thing I could depend on, my own resources. And I felt that the world
was going by in some direction that I didn't understand and I was not in it.
Whatever was going on was not about me and there were lots of noises being
made about how wonderful I was— "black woman you are my queen." I
didn't believe it. I thought it sounded like something I had heard when
I was eleven, but the vocabulary was different. There was something in it
I just didn't trust. It was too loud. It was too grand. It was almost like a wish
rather than a fact, that the men were trying to say something that they didn't
believe either. That's what I thought. And so it looked as though the world
was going by and I was not in that world. I used to live in this world, I mean
really lived in it. I knew it. I used to really belong here. And at some point
I didn't belong here anymore. I was somebody's parent, somebody's this,
somebody's that, but there was no me in this world. And I was looking for
that dead girl and I thought I might talk about that dead girl, if for no other
reason than to have it, somewhere in the world, in a drawer. There was such a
person. I had written this little story earlier just for some friends, so I took it
out and I began to work it up. And all of those people were me. I was Pecola,

Claudia. . . . I was everybody. And as I began to do it, I began to pick up
scraps of things that I had seen or felt, or didn't see or didn't feel, but imagined. And speculated about and wondered about. And I fell in love with
myself. I reclaimed myself and the world—a real revelation. I named it.
I described it. I listed it. I identified it. I recreated it. And having done that, at
least, then the books belonged in the world. Although I still didn't belong.
I was working hard at a job and trying to be this competent person. But the
dead girl—and not only was that girl dead in my mind, I thought she was
dead in everybody's mind, aside from my family and my father and my
mother—that person didn't exist anywhere. *That* person. Not the name, but
the person. I thought that girl was dead. I couldn't find her. I mean, I could
see her on the street or the bus, but nobody wrote about her. Which isn't
entirely accurate. People had done that. But for me at that time that was
them, that was not me. People ask, "Is your book autobiographical?" It is not,
but it is, because of that process of reclamation. And I was driven there, literally driven. I felt penned into a basement, and I was going to get out of it.
I remembered being a person who did belong on this earth. I used to love my
company and then I didn't. And I realized the reason I didn't like my company was because there was nobody there to like. I didn't know what happened. I had been living some other person's life. It was too confusing. I was
interested primarily in the civil rights movement. And it was in that flux that
I thought . . . I guess it was right there. It was my time of life also. The place
where those things came together. And I thought that there would be no me.
Not us or them or we, but no *me.* If the best thing happened in the world and
it all came out perfectly in terms of what the gains and goals of the *Movement*
were, nevertheless nobody was going to get away with that; nobody was going
to tell me that it had been that easy. That all I needed was a slogan: "Black is
Beautiful." It wasn't that easy being a little black girl in this country—it was
rough. The psychological tricks you have to play in order to get through—and
nobody said how it felt to be that. And you knew better. You knew inside better. You knew you were not the person they were looking at. And to know that
and to see what you saw in those other people's eyes was devastating. Some
people made it, some didn't. And I wanted to explore it myself. But once having done that, having gone to those places, I knew I'd go there again. So when
I said every now and then, "Well, I don't care if they published it or not," I
cared, but I didn't care enough to not do it again. If they had all said, as they
did, that they couldn't publish that book for various and sundry reasons . . .

GN: You mean *The Bluest Eye* was turned down before it was finally published?
TM: Many times. You know the little letters you get back from the editors.
They wrote me nice letters. "This book has no beginning, no middle, and no
end"; or, "your writing is wonderful, *but*. . . ." I wasn't going to change it for
that. I assumed there would be some writing skills that I did not have. But
that's not what they were talking about. They thought something was wrong
with *it* or it wasn't marketable. I guess I do know what they thought, but it was
just too much to think about at that time. And so after I finished that book
I was in some despair because several months passed and I didn't have another idea. And then I got to thinking about this girl, this woman. If it wasn't
unconventional, she didn't want it. She was willing to risk in her imagination
a lot of things and pay the price and also go astray. It wasn't as though she was
this fantastic power who didn't have a flaw in her character. I wanted to throw
her relationship with another woman into relief. Those two women—that too
is us, those two desires, to have your adventure *and* safety. So I just cut it up.

GN: You had *a Nel and* a Sula.
TM: Yes. And then to have one do the unforgivable thing to see what that
friendship was really made out of.

GN: When I taught *Sula* the second semester, we had a huge fight about that
in class. When I talked about Sula and Nel being two faces to the same coin
and that was the epitome of female bonding, the kids were with me. And they
even hung in there when I explained that their relationship, while falling
short of a physical bonding, involved a spiritual bonding that transcended
the flesh and was much superior than a portrayal of an actual physical bonding would have been anyway. But then we got to the scene where Sula and
Jude are on the floor together; the kids rebelled—"How could Sula have been
Nel's *best* friend if she took Jude from her?" But then I tried to make them
think about how important Jude really was—which was Sula's point. "We
shared everything else, so he should be low now on the priority of things we
won't share." At first that really shook my students up, then it made them
begin to think—"Yeah, exactly how important is it?"
TM: You see, if all women behaved like those two, or if the Sula point of view
operated and women really didn't care about sharing these things, everything
would just crumble—hard. If it's not about fidelity and possession and my
pain versus yours, then how can you manipulate, how can you threaten, how

can you assert power? I went someplace once to talk about *Sula* and there were some genuinely terrified men in the audience, and they walked out and told me why. They said, "Friendship between women?" Aghast. Really terrified. And you wouldn't think anybody grown-up would display his fear quite that way. I mean you would think they would maybe think it. But it was such a shocking, threatening thing in a book, let alone what it would be in life.

GN: But it's always been there to a great degree—in life. We do share our men. We may not like it very much, but there is a silent consensus about that and it hasn't really torn us apart as women. I believe that woman have always been close to women. It's much like that universe you had mentioned before among black women writers, but it's not only the writers; black women have always had each other when we had very little else. But what we didn't dare do was to put it in black and white like you did in *Sula*. And when that's done—when it's printed—it's threatening. Maybe what was so threatening about it too was that you didn't rant and rave; you made your point very subtly. The same way you did in *The Bluest Eye*; it wasn't a fist stuck up into heaven—"Black Power." But how much more powerful could that statement be than to say, "Look at what happens when society makes a little girl invisible." And just to whisper. . . . that's what I wanted to tell you about your work. You know how you can be in a room and the person that talks in a whisper is the one you always lean toward. Your books just whisper at the reader and you move in, you move in, and then you finally hear what's being said, and you say to yourself, "Oh, my God." You did it with *Sula*. Very quietly you move the reader in until we get to that line, "All along I thought I was missing Jude." The impact is then tremendous. And I believe writing is at its best when it's done that way. I just don't agree with some people that books should make a statement. And often when I'll go somewhere to read or lecture, someone will inevitably ask, "Well, what were you trying to *say*?" in this part or that part. And my response is, "Nothing at all." I don't think art should be didactic. My art, as I see it, involves a certain honesty to the world that I'm creating on that page and a measure of integrity to myself. And if the readers want to extrapolate a message, then they can do it on their own; I haven't put one in there for them. That's not my responsibility as a black or as a black woman.

TM: Well, you're absolutely right. There's no question about it. For two reasons. One, some of these people have been taught to read very badly. That is, they have been given even great books and then trained to think of them as resolutions and solutions and then to put them to uses that are nefarious, as though they are reading a "How To" column. They go to a book the way you go to a medicine cabinet. They're not going to it at all the way I go into a book. The other thing is that I think, really and truly, for a black writer to be didactic is really a cardinal sin because the last thing that I would do with black people, if they're anything like I am or like all the black people that I have respect for, is to be that pompous and tell them what to do. They have never taken direction well; they've always participated in whatever it was. Whether it was political or blues singing or jazz or whatever, you have to share that with them. You don't hand out these little slips of paper and say, "You will do the following; this is the message."

GN: But on the other hand, there was something that I was very self-conscious about with my first novel; I bent over backwards not to have a negative message come through about the men. My emotional energy was spent creating a woman's world, telling her side of it because I knew it hadn't been done enough in literature. But I worried about whether or not the problems that were being caused by the men in the women's lives would be interpreted as some bitter statement I had to make about black men.
TM: You open a section of *Women* with his [Eugene's] conversation.

GN: Yes, I did it purposely there. I wanted the reader to see that that young man did care about the death of his child, but he had been so beaten down he couldn't come through for his family. But I'm wondering if that should have been my worry. The chapter still worked well with that section up front, but it *was* my way of making a statement. Showing that side of Eugene helped creatively because it made him a full-fledged character, and if you want your characters to live—to be human—there must be complexity. But, Toni, I'm talking about something else—there was also a pull there to want there to be no doubt about the *goodness* of these male characters. And I just wonder if I should have that pull?
TM: Yes, you should.

GN: But then it was only because they were black male characters and I was a black woman writing it.
TM: That's right. You should have that pull. You should wonder. Am I doing them justice? Is anybody going to misread this?

GN: That's what I ask myself a lot and especially for *Linden Hills* because a huge number of the major characters are male. Do you think other writers go through that? Did you ask yourself that at first, too?
TM: I didn't ask myself. I just loved them so much.

GN: For me, the love had to grow. I eventually began to love the two boys in *Linden Hills*, and as they went along I could applaud them or cry about whatever they did. You know, at first I actually introduced myself—not, "Hi, Willie and Lester, here's Gloria." But, "Hey guys, now here's a woman and I really don't know what it's like to be twenty years old, at that threshold of manhood, but I'm going to try awfully hard." Do you start with that process as well? That introduction of you to them?
TM: Yeah. You have to introduce yourself and you have to know their names. They won't behave if you don't know their names.

GN: I used to write letters to Willie at first. Before we got going together really well. Before he moved into my apartment, I had to sort of court him. And so I wrote him letters.
TM: You have to know who those people are in order to get that information from them. You have to be worthy and they have to have the trust. You can't go plopping in there talking about somebody's interior life from the position of a stranger.

GN: And therefore we can't worry if "x" months down the line, someone gets up in the audience and says, "Well, you didn't have it right."
TM: They have not written those letters to Willie. They do not know what they're talking about. You know.

GN: You know that you've tried. That's all you can say, "To the best of my ability and with all love and good intentions, I tried."
TM: The love shows. That's one thing that's unmistakable. The only time I never did that and didn't even try was in *The Bluest Eye*. That girl, Maureen Peal. I was not good with her. She was too easy a shot. I wouldn't do that now with her. I mean we all know who she is. And everybody has one of those in his or her life, but I was unfair to her. I did not in that book look at anything from her point of view inside. I only showed the façade.

GN: Because a Maureen Peal suffered as much as a Pecola Breedlove did in this society.
TM: That's right. And I never got in her because I didn't want to go there. I didn't like her. I never have done that since. I've always regretted the speed with which I executed that girl. She worked well structurally for the girls and this and that, but if I were doing that book now, I would write her section or talk about her that way plus from inside.

GN: But that was your first novel, and we learn from the first. When your second book was finished—*Sula*—did you begin to really feel like a writer then? Because now after *Linden Hills*, I feel there's a certain validity about what I do if for nothing than the fact that I can say, I write books with an "s." Was creating *Sula* like that for you, too? You felt really legitimate then, or had you felt it all along?
TM: I felt it after I finished *Song of Solomon*. After I did *Song of Solomon*, I thought, "This is what I do."

GN: You know, it takes a lot to finally say that. That "Yes, I write. No, Mama, I'll never have a regular job for more than a year. This is what I do."
You know, there are moments with my work when I can achieve the type of atmosphere that's permeating this house and our conversation now. It's as if I've arrived in a place where it's all spirit and no body—an overwhelming sense of calm. But those moments are rare. Usually, I vacillate between an intense love of my work and "What in the hell am I doing this for?" There has to be an easier way to get the type of pain that I'm inflicting upon myself at this desk. But I guess I keep at it because of those times when I can reach that spiritual center. It's like floating in the middle of that river, and waves are all around you. . . . I actually begin to feel blessed.
TM: It is a blessing. Any art form that can do that for you is a special thing. People have to have that sense of having moved something from one place to another and made out of nothing something. Having added something to something and having seen a mess and made it orderly or seen rigidity and given it fluidity. You know, something. And writing encompasses for me all there isn't.

GN: Do you ever think that you've been chosen, knowing that you're always going to do this? Because I really feel as if it's sort of like a calling. Not a calling meaning anything special or different, because the men who come up there to clean your road perform a service to this planet just like an artist performs a service. But I really feel that for me it goes beyond just a gift to handle words, but that it was *meant* for me to be writing as opposed to other things that I'm talented enough to do and can do well when I put my mind to it. For example, I do teach and I enjoy it. But there's not the same type of pull—I think I would self-destruct if I didn't write. I wouldn't self-destruct if I didn't teach.

TM: You *would* self-destruct if you didn't write. You know, I wanted to ask you whether or not, when you finished *The Women*, did you know what the next book was? Did you have any idea about it or did you go through that depressed period, postpartum, of wondering whether or not you would have a new idea, or were you sort of serene about it? What was that period like? I'm not talking about the publication date of the book. When you finished *The Women of Brewster Place*, what was the time period and the emotional trek to *Linden Hills*?

GN: Well, two things were going on, Toni. One was that I wanted there to be a *Linden Hills.*

TM: Even before you finished . . .

GN: Yes, because I had a character in *Brewster Place* named Kiswana Browne who lived in Linden Hills. And my next dream—you know, the daydreams about what you want to do, the easy part of writing any book—was that I would love to do a whole treatment of her neighborhood. And at about that time, I was taking this course at Brooklyn College, "Great Works of Literature." And we had read *The Inferno* and I was overwhelmed by the philosophical under-pinnings of the poem as well as the characters that Dante created. Then the idea came to me that I could try to sketch out this neighborhood along the lines of *The Inferno*. But it was a while before I could actually sit down and work on the book because there was fear, a little, because this was going to be a *real* novel. *Brewster Place* was really interconnected short stories and that type of work demands a shorter time span, a different emotional involvement. So it was in the summer of 1981 when I began to seriously sketch out what I might like to do with *Linden Hills* and it was a year later when I literally sat down and said, "Here is the emotional involvement. I have the idea and I'm going to go for it."

TM: I can see how you would know because you can see little pieces. Can't you see the trees or a little bit of the brook from Brewster Place? There's a little bit of it sticking up.

GN: But for you yourself?

TM: Well, I've had different kinds of things. I remember after *The Bluest Eye* having an extremely sad six or eight months. And I didn't know what it was because that was the first time I had ever written a novel. And I wasn't even sure when I could write another one because I wasn't thinking about being a novelist then. I just wrote *that* and I thought that would be *that* and that would be the end of *that* 'cause I liked to read it and that was enough. But then I moved from one town to another, for one thing, and I was feeling, for this very sustained period, what can only be described now as missing something, missing the company I had been keeping all those years when I wrote *The Bluest Eye*, and I couldn't just write because I was able to write. I had to write with the same feeling that I had when I did *The Bluest Eye*, which was that there was this exciting collection of people that only I knew about. I had the direct line and I was the receiver of all this information. And then when I began to think about *Sula*, everything changed, I mean, all the colors of the world changed, the sounds and so on. I recognized what that period was when I finished *Sula*, and I had another idea which was *Song of Solomon*. When I finished *Song of Solomon*, I didn't have another idea for *Tar Baby* but by then I knew that it arrives or it doesn't arrive and I'm not terrified of a block, of what people call a block. I think when you hit a place where you can't write, you probably should be still for a while because it's not there yet.

GN: Even a block with an idea itself? That doesn't frighten you?

TM: It doesn't bother me. And that brings me to the book that I'm writing now called *Beloved*. I had an idea that I didn't know was a book idea, but I do remember being obsessed by two or three little fragments of stories that I heard from different places. One was a newspaper clipping about a woman named Margaret Garner in 1851. It said that the Abolitionists made a great deal out of her case because she had escaped from Kentucky, I think, with her four children. She lived in a little neighborhood just outside of Cincinnati and she had killed her children. She succeeded in killing one; she tried to kill two others. She hit them in the head with a shovel and they were wounded but they didn't die. And there was a smaller one that she had at her breast. The interesting thing, in addition to that, was the interviews that she gave. She was a young woman. In the inked pictures of her she seemed a very quiet, very serene-looking woman and everyone who interviewed her remarked about her serenity and tranquility. She said, "I will not let those children live how I have lived." She had run off into a little woodshed right outside her house to kill them because she had been caught as a fugitive. And she had made up her mind that they would not suffer the way that she had and it was better for them to die. And her mother-in-law was in the house at the same time and she said, "I watched her and I neither encouraged her nor discouraged her." They put her in jail for a little while and I'm not even sure what the denouement is of her story. But that moment, that decision was a piece, a tail of something that was always around, and it didn't get clear for me until I was thinking of another story that I had read in a book that Camille Billops published, a collection of pictures by Van der Zee, called *The Harlem Book of the Dead*. Van der Zee was very lucid. He remembered everybody he had photographed. There was this fashion of photographing beloved, departed people in full dress in coffins or in your arms. You know, many parents were holding their children beautifully dressed in their arms and they were affectionate photographs taken for affectionate reasons. In one picture, there was a young girl lying in a coffin and he says that she was eighteen years old and she had gone to a party and that she was dancing and suddenly she slumped and they noticed there was blood on her and they said, "What happened to you?" And she said, "I'll tell you tomorrow. I'll tell you tomorrow." That's all she would say. And apparently her ex-boyfriend or somebody who was jealous had come into the party with a gun and a silencer and shot her. And she kept saying, "I'll tell you tomorrow" because she wanted him to get away. And he did, I guess; anyway, she died. Now what made those stories connect, I can't explain, but I do know that, in both instances, something seemed clear to me. A woman loved something other than herself so much. She had placed all of the value of her life in something outside herself. That the woman who killed her children loved her children so much; they were the best part of her and she would not see them sullied. She would not see them hurt. She would rather kill them, have them die. You know what that means?

GN: I do, yes.

TM: And that this woman had loved a man or had such affection for a man that she would postpone her own medical care or go ahead and die to give him time to get away so that, more valuable than her life, was not just his life but something else connected with his life. Now both of those incidents seem to me, at least on the surface, very noble, you know, in that old-fashioned sense, noble things, generous, wide-spirited, love beyond the call of . . .

GN: . . . of a very traditional kind of female . . .

TM: That's right. Always. It's peculiar to women. And I thought, it's interesting because the best thing that is in us is also the thing that makes us sabotage ourselves, sabotage in the sense that our life is not as worthy, or our perception of the best part of ourselves. I had about fifteen or twenty questions that occurred to me with those two stories in terms of what it is that really compels a good woman to displace the self, her self. So what I started doing and thinking about for a year was to project the self not into the way we say "yourself," but to put a space between those words, as though the self were really a *twin* or a thirst or a friend or something that sits right next to you and watches you, which is what I was talking about when I said "the dead girl." So I had just projected her out into the earth. So how to do that? How to do that without being absolutely lunatic and talking about some medical students that nobody wants to hear about. So I just imagined the life of a dead girl which was the girl that Margaret Garner killed, the baby girl that she killed.

GN: How old was the child?

TM: Less than two. I just imagined her remembering what happened to her, being someplace else and returning, knowing what happened to her. And I call her Beloved so that I can filter all these confrontations and questions that she has in that situation, which is 1851, and then to extend her life, you know, her search, her quest, all the way through as long as I care to go, into the twenties where it switches to this other girl. Therefore, I have a New York uptown–Harlem milieu in which to put this love story, but Beloved will be there also.

GN: Always Beloved being the twin self to whatever woman shows up throughout the work.

TM: She will be the mirror, so to speak. I don't know, I'm just gonna write and see what happens to it. I have about 250 pages and it's overwhelming me. There's a lot of danger for me in writing it, which is what I am very excited about. The effort, the responsibility as well as the effort, the effort of being worth it, that's not quite it. The responsibility that I feel for the woman I'm calling Sethe, and for all of these people; these unburied, or at least unceremoniously buried, people made literate in art. But the inner tension, the artistic inner tension those people create in me; the fear of not properly, artistically, burying them, is extraordinary. I feel this enormous responsibility in exactly the way you describe the ferocity you felt when somebody was tampering with a situation that was gonna hurt...

GN: My people...
TM: Your people. Exactly. I have to have now very overt conversations with these people. Before I could sort of let it disguise itself as the artist's monologue with herself but there's no time for that foolishness now. Now I have to call them by their names and ask them to reappear and tell me something or leave me alone even. But it does mean that I feel exactly the way you do about this. They are such special company that it is very difficult to focus on other people. There is a temptation to draw away from living people, people who are extremely important to you and who are real. They're in competition a great deal with this collection of imagined characters. But these are demands that I can meet, and I know I can because they would not have spoken to me had I not been the one.

GN: Had you not been somehow worthy. I consider it being worthy to be used as that medium.
TM: They won't talk to you otherwise.

GN: No, I understand. Just before the women who lived on Brewster Place had faded back to from wherever they came, I had gotten a bound copy of the book—which I really call a tombstone because that's what it represents, at least for my part of the experience—and those women wrote me a little epigraph which I recorded in the front of the book. They told me that I must always remember them, remember how they came to be, because they were the ones who were real to me and they were the ones I had to worry about. They wanted me to know that they cared about me and that they understood that I had cared deeply about them. And having said that, they just sort of faded on off.... A lot of people don't think that our characters become that tangible to us.
TM: Some people are embarrassed about it; they both fear and distrust it also; they don't solidify and recreate the means by which one enters into that place

where those people are. I think the more black women write, the more easily one will be able to talk about those things. Because I have almost never found anyone whose work I respected or who took their work that seriously, who did not talk in the vocabulary that you and I are using; it's not the vocabulary of literary criticism.

GN: No, it's not.

TM: And it's not taught. People speak, of course, of the muse and there are other words for this. But to make it as graphic a presence or a collection of presences as I find it absolutely to be, it's not even a question of trying to make it that way—that's the way that it appears. There are not a lot of people to whom one speaks that way. But I know that that's what it is. It isn't a question of searching it out. It's a question of my perceptions and in that area, I know.

GN: They become so tangible that not only do you deal with them affectionately, but sometimes you deal with them very irately. Listening to you talking about the self, I can remember with *Linden Hills* the woman who was imprisoned in that basement. I actually invented a mirror, if you will, for her after she had gone through all her experiences. After she had dug up the remnants of the other Nedeed women, I created a way for her to see her own reflection in a pan of water because she had no self up until that moment. And when she realized that she had a face, then maybe she had other things going for her as well, and she could take her destiny in her own hands. But the point of all that was what was going to happen step by step once she discovered herself—she was going to barge up out of that basement, etc.—and I had *my* ending all set. But when this character who had lived with me now for two years finally discovered her face in that pan of water, she decided that she liked being what she was. She liked being a wife and a mother and she was going upstairs and claim that identity. And I said, "Oh, Lord, woman, don't you know what the end of this book has got to be? You've gotta tear that whole house down to the ground, or my book won't make any sense." Obviously, she didn't care. And I was angry with her for a good week—I just stopped writing and ran around the house cursing her. But then again that was *her* life and her decision. So the ball was thrown back into my lap—my job was to figure out a way for this woman to live her life and for me to end that book the way I wanted to.

TM: Break her arm and make her . . .

GN: Exactly. But it's marvelous, Toni. There's something so wonderful about being and even grappling with those things and being in the midst of just watching them coming to fruition.
TM: Oh, yes.

GN: You know, when I finished *Linden Hills,* I said to myself, of course, the first day or two days after, "Never again! I must have been crazy!"
TM: "This had been too hard!"

GN: And just last week, I was thinking, "God, you know, that was fun!" Truly! And I can see it reflected in your eyes—the fun of it, now the challenge of it.
TM: It's truly amazing. And the wonderful thing is when I go and sit down and try to write—maybe I need a color, I need the smell, I need something, and I don't have it. And as soon as I get concave, a small thing comes and when I pick up that yellow lined tablet, Gloria, it is always there; not necessarily when you call it, not even when you want it, but always when you need it. And, as they say, "right on time."

GN: But do you ever wonder, since we have no control over when it comes, if we have no control over when it will leave—forever?
TM: Well, I thought after *Tar Baby* I would just quit. I had written four books. You know, I would just stop and do nothing and then I got involved in filming them which I had always stayed away from. I don't want to see it in another form; besides, I can't think that way. But then little by little, some people whom I respect bought *Tar Baby* and I got involved in producing *Song of Solomon,* and in both instances there were people who wanted fidelity, wanted faithfulness in the film to the book. As I got more involved in that, I had some conflict with the novel I've just described. But what happened was that—you see, the mercy of these people is incredible because when you get in their lives, other things happen also so you don't have to decide *whether* you'll do the novel—all of it surfaced at the same time. One idea shot up another and another and another. So I didn't find these projects in competition with each other. But I think, at the moment, that I won't write anything after *Beloved.*

GN: I know you said that before.
TM: That's exactly what I said. But I thought that about each book so no one pays any attention to me on that score. This is the one. This is it. Maybe I'll

write a play or maybe I'll write a short story. Maybe I won't. At any rate, what's gratifying is that—see, this is going to sound very arrogant, but when I wrote *The Bluest Eye*, I was under the distinct impression, which was erroneous, that it was on me, you know, that nobody else was writing like that, nobody, and nobody was going to.

GN: Well, you were right about that. Yes, you were!

TM: And I thought, "No one is ever going to read this until I'm dead. No one's going to do this." I really felt that—you know, I kept it sort of tight, but I thought, "Nobody's going to write about these people that way."

GN: That's not arrogant. That's the truth.

TM: They're going to make them into some little comic relief or they're going to sap it up. No one is going to see what I saw which was this complex poetic life. And it was as grand and as intricate and as profound as anybody had walked this earth. That's what I thought. And no one is going to write from the inside with that kind of gentleness, not romanticizing them, but knowing that whatever happened to them, there was that heartbeat, that love, that understanding. That's what I thought.

GN: Also, because your unique signature would have to be on that since the story was filtered through you. Whatever may have happened in the past and future . . .

TM: Well, I don't feel that way anymore.

GN: You don't feel that . . . no, I don't think—it could have, yes, the subject matter; I don't want to argue with you. I think the subject matter could have been tackled and, if we go back, we can look at it having been tackled in various ways. Wallace Thurman, *The Blacker the Berry*. Same subject matter, two different texts. The sensibilities were different. No, you're saying that no one could have done it that way, quite true. Arrogance would be to say no one could have done it that well and that's up to us to say that, that's not up to you to say that. Not well, but that way.

TM: But now I feel that, thank God, some things are done now. I used to think it was like a plateau; now there are these valleys, if you will, full of people who are entering this terrain, and they're doing extraordinary things with novels and short stories about black women and that's not going to stop; that's not going to ever stop.

GN: No, no, because one is built on another.

TM: And there won't be these huge gaps, either, between them. It's possible to look at the world now and find oneself properly spoken of in it.

GN: Because oneself spoke up for oneself.

TM: That's the point. It wasn't anybody else's job. I'm sitting around wondering why A, B, or C didn't tell my story. That's ridiculous, you know. This is *our* work and I know that it is ours because I have done it and you know it is because you've done it. And you will do it again and again and again. I don't know. It's a marvelous beginning. It's a real renaissance. You know, we have spoken of renaissances before. But this one is ours, not somebody else's.

GN: But being the pioneer of that renaissance within the contemporary time period, how do you feel about that, about watching the black women writers who have now come up after you. In a sense, Toni, you were the first widely accepted black woman writer.

TM: No. Paule Marshall, whom I had not read at that time, had written that incredible book before me.

GN: *Brown Girl, Brown Stones.*

TM: Yes, stunning, in the fifties. And, of course, there was Zora Neale Hurston and, you know, there were women before, so that's what I meant when I said—I was just ill-read, that's all, because I had gone to those schools where . . .

GN: Ill-taught.

TM: Ill-taught. And they didn't have those books in my libraries so it was a long time before I had a thrill of being introduced to such women. It was a double thrill for me because I was introduced to them after I had written, you see. And many people who are trying to show certain kinds of connections between myself and Zora Neale Hurston are always dismayed and disappointed in me because I hadn't read Zora Neale Hurston except for one little short story before I began to write. I hadn't read her until after I had written. In their efforts to establish a tradition, that bothers them a little bit. And I said, "No, no, you should be happy about that." Because the fact that I had never read Zora Neale Hurston and wrote *The Bluest Eye* and *Sula* anyway means that the tradition really exists. You know, if I had read her, then you could say that I consciously was following in the footsteps of her, but the fact that I never read her and still there may be whatever they're finding, similarities and dissimilarities, whatever such critics do, makes the cheese more binding, not less, because it means that the world as perceived by black women at certain times does exist, however they treat it and whatever they select out of it to record, there is that. I hadn't read Jean Toomer either. I didn't read him until I came into publishing and was . . . well, that was the time when there was the sort of flurry of reprints so people could get things. I was reading African novels and things like that, but, you know, all sorts of things that were just unavailable to me. They weren't at Cornell and they certainly weren't at Howard University in the days that I was there.

But your question about how I felt—it's like, there's nothing quite like seeing, for me there's nothing like reading a really, really fine book; I don't care who wrote it. You work with one facet of a prism, you know, just one side, or maybe this side, and it has millions of sides, and then you read a book and there is somebody who is a black woman who has this sensibility and this power and this talent and she's over here writing about that side of this huge sort of diamond thing that I see, and then you read another book and somebody has written about another side. And you know that eventually that whole thing will be lit—all of these planes and all of the facets. But it's all one diamond, it's all one diamond. I claim this little part, you did this one, but there's so much room, oh, my God. You haven't even begun and there's so much room and each one is another facet, another face of this incredible stone, this fantastic jewel that throws back light constantly and is constantly changing because even the face that I may have cleaned or cleared or dealt with will change. It looked like it was saffron light to me, but maybe twenty years later it looks blue. That's the way I feel about it. Geometrically all those things touch in a way, but each person has his own space, his own side of the diamond to work on. That's so gratifying, so exciting. That eliminates the feeling I had at the beginning—that of solitude. That my work doesn't have anything to do with life as it goes on, but as though there were something secret in my head when I was writing the book.

Is that so? Is that the way it was? I read the conversation between Gloria Naylor and me again; remember it again; listen to tapes of it. It's all there—not so orderly or so exact, but right nevertheless. Still, is that so? What am I missing and why do I care? It's okay to print whatever in any newspaper, magazine, or journal from the college weekly to Vogue, *from* Il Tempo *to the Cleveland* Plain Dealer. *I never comment on the interview; never write letters correcting errors or impressions. I am content to read proof and content not to see proof at all. So what's missing from this one that made me want to add to it and made Gloria want to preface it? Neither of us wanted an interview and we hope this is not one. An interview is my trying to get to the end of it; an interview is my trying to help the reporter or student fill in the blank spaces under the questions so she or he will believe he or she has some information; it is my saying eight or ten things eight or ten times into a tape recorder in precisely the same way I've said them before. And my mind drifts so when I am being interviewed that I hardly remember it. For while I am talking (about my work, the state of one thing, the future of another), the alert part of my mind is "interviewing" the interviewer: Who are you? Why are you doing this? This is not the way to find out anything; an hour? Why do you want to be good at it?*

I see them select or make up details to add to the fixed idea of me they came in the door with—the thing or person they want me to be. I sense it and, if I am feeling lazy, I play to it—if not I disappear—shift into automatic and let them have my shadow to play with, hoping my smoke will distract them into believing I am still there.

Because an interview is not an important thing.

But a conversation—well now—that's something. Rare and getting more so. And this meeting between Gloria Naylor and me was going to be that. Not one but two people present on the scene, talking the kind of talk in which something of consequence is willing to be revealed; some step forward is taken; some moment or phrase flares like a lightning bug and both of us see it at the same time and will remember it the same way. We didn't care how we "came off" or if we said something useful or memorable to anybody else—or whether what we said was good copy. In fact, we would use the good offices of the Southern Review *assignment to meet and see if we liked each other or not. No observers.*

She brought a tape recorder which we treated like a nuisance—which it was—so much so we forgot to turn it on all morning. Until the afternoon it lay on the table like an envelope addressed to "Occupant" that we were going to get around to opening in a minute, in a minute—when we had time. She had no list of questions; took no notes. Whatever would be missing from the "piece"; that what-was-so, we would provide. I would say what I was thinking when

I said————. What I thought when she said————. When we laughed. Or were interrupted by telephone or one of my children or something on the stove. But are these the things that make up a conversation: What happens between and around what is said? the silence after one word? the frown after another?

I meant to be ready, of course. She followed my directions and arrived when she said she would. I have never found a reliable way to be on time. Either I sit in airports two hours before flight time or stand perspiring at gates whose little signs have been taken down. But I meant to be dressed at least. I'd been up since five o'clock getting all sorts of things done, none of which included putting on shoes or street clothes. That tickled her and she laughed about it off and on the whole day. That was good because her smile really is one, and it's hard not to join in with one of your own.

She says my work was critical to her decision to write prose. She believes that, but I know my work may have figured in when she would write a novel but not whether.

She is troubled about political and/or vs. aesthetic responsibility; about whether having children would hurt or derail her work; about the limits of her obligations to the community.

She is amazed by the joy it gives her—writing. Fiercely attentive to the respect it demands of her.

She is angry and hurt by deceptions in publishing—its absence of honor. She is amused by her self; pleased by her triumphs. In short, worried about all the right things. Pleased about all the real things.

I look at her and think for the thousandth time how fine it is now. So many like her and more coming. Eyes scrubbed clean with a Fuller brush, young black women walking around the world who can (and do) say "I write is what I do. I do this and that too—but write is what I do, hear?" Women who don't have to block what they know; keep secret what they feel; who welcome their own rage and love because it has voice, place, point, and art—and the art is hers, not somebody else's. She wears on her head the "hat" she made—not one she bought made by somebody else.

She likes my chair. The river. The warm bread. "Do you ever leave this place? What for?"

I remind her of someone and she likes that. A link. I am not alien.

It was a conversation. I can tell, because I said something I didn't know I knew. About the "dead girl." That bit by bit I had been rescuing her from the grave of time and inattention. Her fingernails maybe in the first book; face and legs, perhaps, the second time. Little by little bringing her back into living life. So that now she comes running when called—walks freely around the house, sits down in a chair; looks at me, listens to Gloria Naylor and anybody else she wants to. She cannot lie. Doesn't know greed or vengeance. Will not fawn or pontificate. There is no room for pupils in her eyes. She is here now, alive. I have seen, named and claimed her—and oh what company she keeps.—TM

An Interview with Gloria Naylor

Kay Bonetti / 1988

Kay Bonetti: Ms. Naylor, I read somewhere that you were conceived in Mississippi and born in New York City where you grew up.

Gloria Naylor: Yes. That is quite true. My parents were born and raised in the South: my dad, in Arkansas and my mother, in Mississippi. But they both grew up together in a little sharecropping town in the northwest corner of the state called Robinsonville. And they married there. And my dad was keeping the promise that my mother made him make when he took her north a month before I was born, because she was adamant about the fact that she would not have any children born in the South.

KB: And I thought that it was interesting that Tupelo Drive is the very bottom of the hill in *Linden Hills*.

GN: That was total circumstance. The street in *Linden Hills* was no reference about that. As a matter of fact, Tupelo in *Linden Hills* was really a plain over two pillars because there were two pillars that you entered to go into lower hell.

KB: Oh.

GN: That's what I'm reading in Tupelo.

KB: I see. Well, that's very interesting because there's a lot of Black history tied up in the town of Tupelo, Mississippi.

GN: Oh, yes. I was down there when I was in college participating in a march against the Klan. I had gone down to the national march in Tupelo.

KB: Well, while growing up in New York, did you go through the public school system?

GN: I did. We were poor people. There was not a boarding school in my past. We went through the public school system—my two sisters and myself did,

39

and later I went to Brooklyn College. And then I received a scholarship and went to Yale.

KB: And you took a history degree in African American Studies?
GN: That's right.

KB: At what point in all of this rigmarole did you start writing?
GN: I have been writing basically since the third grade. I started writing poetry because I was always a very quiet child. And when I had entered puberty, it had reached a point where I was just painfully shy. And when I was around twelve or thirteen years old my mother noticed that I wasn't talking. When I say I wasn't talking, you know I would speak to people and say, "Good morning— How are you? Pass the cereal." But I basically was not talking about how I felt about things. And at that age, you know the hormones are going crazy in your body and also the world was going a tiny bit crazy, and I was a precocious child. And I had been reading the newspapers since the sixth grade, so I was reading about the Cold War. See, we felt like the Russians were coming. What people don't realize is that about every thirty years we get a red scare and the Russians start coming again. They never quite arrive here. But that's something else. But this is the Cold War Era—that time in the fifties. And so I was reading all these things and confused about them and confused about my own internal landscape, and I would not talk to her. And being a very wise woman, she saw that. So she gave me a diary—a little white plastic diary. She said, "Gloria, I know that there are things going on that disturb you. Perhaps there are things in our home, things in the world that you can't seem to talk to your father and I about. Why don't you write your feelings down in here?" So, it was from that point when I was about twelve or thirteen years old that I began to associate the written word with the unspoken emotion. And writing became a way for me to make order out of chaos, internal chaos—chaos that I saw externally as well. So I had been writing since I was thirteen. And so I have a hard time and I will only try to differentiate when I am asked in a situation like this. But I personally do not make a difference between what I started writing in that diary when I was twelve and what I do with my fiction. For me, it's all one continuum—my trying to seek order out of disorder, out of emotions or out of facts, statements—that kind of thing.

KB: You said someplace that in finishing *The Women of Brewster Place* you felt that it made you whole and for you art has a very important, private function.

GN: It does. My art is ninety-nine and one quarter percent private beyond a doubt because of what I have just said to you. At an early age I became accustomed to saying on the page what I literally could not say verbally. But more than that even, I write to myself primarily. Secondarily, I write to those characters that have emerged and come to me to have their stories told. I try very hard to maintain a level of integrity to that individual and to that individual's life. And because they have now arrived and I am there as sort of a stenographer, if you will, of those lives. All of that is personal. With *The Women of Brewster Place*, specifically, I had not up until that point ever started something that I had completed. And I was a great starter that never finished. But I was one of those people who have a very low threshold for pain. So when the going would get rough in anything, I would just get going. I literally would. You know I had begun a career as minister that I never finished. I had begun a marriage, which I didn't finish. I had started school, started school late. I was twenty-five years old when I first went to Brooklyn College. I didn't know whether or not I would finish that even. I was in there plugging away but I didn't know, given my history, if I would finish that. *Brewster Place* is the first thing that I began and finished. And I did that totally for myself. I wasn't living for anyone else or through anyone else. There was Gloria making a statement for Gloria. And so there was an incredible amount of accomplishment, personal accomplishment, in that work for me. And when it was indeed done, I can to this day visualize that bedroom in that little dumpy place in Brooklyn. When it was totally done, I said, "Yes, this is good," if you will, parodying the whole creation. This is good because I had done it. And anything that happened after that had a certain distance, emotional distance, from whatever good or whatever bad was about to happen after that because I knew what it had done for me personally. And that is how it is now with each thing I do. I grant you that my life is more complicated now. The perceptions grow tremendously about me, you know, one way or the other. People approach me now as a writer. So there is more padding to scrape away in order to reach what really counts.

KB: To what extent, in your opinion, does art have a public function?

GN: Well, I think there is a function involved in the broadening of the consciousness of those individuals who may pick up a work of art. We'll talk art in the sense of literature for individuals to enter worlds that they would not be privy to, to enter a form of language that they would not normally come across in secular texts, like a magazine or newspaper or something of that nature. I do not see artists as being an instrument for any sort of change as far as political change or social change is involved. And I often get into disagreements with friends about this. Because I do have some friends who believe art can bring change. I think that particular belief is true only in a personal landscape but not in a public landscape, because we have to be honest that literature is a very bourgeois activity. It comes out of the middle class and is read primarily by the middle class. So you are preaching to the converted. Any true social change, and especially if you are talking about revolution, won't necessarily come through the arts. And this small cloistered world of the arts will not bring about true revolution. I do not believe that. It does not have some kind of public function. It can enlighten, however. I can grant you this: that you can pick up a work that will open your mind to a world that you thought never existed. You can perhaps go and seek out that world and then try to better understand what is there and inevitably you may go to change something that is concrete, if you see a need for change.

KB: Growing up in New York City, where did you get that wonderful voice for the Willow Springs community, as you were reading today?
GN: My folks. My folks were from the South, like I said, and I was conceived there. I am the oldest of the three girls. So I was born in New York, but I grew up in a very southern home. They had their children early on in the marriage and the first seven years they had the three children. So, therefore, we grew up with young parents, young southern parents. Our foods were from the South and our codes of behavior as well. The speech that I heard during my formative years was southern speech. It would take them many years to lose their accents, if you will. They've never quite lost their socialization and their world view. That's totally southern. Our sense of family—how you're brought up to think about the family and the importance of it—well, it's from the South. Storytelling was important. Well, since I was the quietest of the three, I'd be the one in the corner of the kitchen when mom and dad would be reminiscing about Mississippi. And I would hear these things, and I had aunts and cousins, and that sort of thing, who had been from the South. So that's where that comes from.

KB: The stereotype of Black experience in this country is one of a fractured family and, in fact, it has a grain of truth in it, and we know why. Do you feel fortunate as a modern Black woman that you got to grow up in a family that was intact with two parents?

GN: I never thought about it one way or the other as being fortunate or unfortunate. This is the way it was. When I looked around at my grandparents, aunts, and uncles, that's basically how it was. You are right; it is indeed a stereotype that our history resulted in a fractured family. That has only come about in the last twenty to twenty-five years or so in the African community. We had traditional two-parent households, like my folks celebrating their thirty-ninth wedding anniversary. But anyway, we have traditionally had a man and a woman in a household, even during the times of slavery. People struggled to keep their homes together. We were so poor that we aspired to be working class, in an odd kind of way. But it was a different kind of poverty for them in the thirties and forties. You knew you were poor. You knew there were things you did not have. There was always hope that you could do better and your children could do better. And, indeed, that has been the case. My family's story is told hundreds of thousands of times over. But what stresses me, now you will get the poor who cannot visualize even being out of that kind of despondency. And, indeed, there was no place for them to go because there is this vicious cycle of young people having babies who are growing up without the needed socialization, without the grandmother's wisdom and the strength because their dad and their mom are so very young themselves. And, of course, there are no viable educational outlets in society. So there is a cycle of poverty that is doomed to repeat itself. That's quite different from the kind of poverty that we experienced. I guess, in short, what I'm saying, Kay, is that there was no impoverishment of the spirit when my parents were in Mississippi and when we stayed in Harlem. And that's what you have now. You have impoverished spirits along with the financial poverty.

KB: You still had your mirrors inside that Lester's grandmother told him about.

GN: Exactly. We all had the sense that you are somebody. It's as simple as that. You are worth something. And you can go out into the world and do whatever you wanted to do, which was a big leap for my dad who was very much a man's man and who was very up front with my mom that he wanted sons. And he didn't get any sons. That's how that went. After the third baby, he was doomed to be a sonless man. So, therefore, he went and instilled that in his daughters. So it made him something of a feminist, if you will, because he felt that we were his girls. No one going to treat his girls badly and I am going to equip them to go out in the world. And, of course, you were to be married. That was a given. You were to be married, but just in case, just in case he didn't do right or died or whatever, you must be able to stand up and do whatever you want in this world and take care of yourself and your kids, if that was to be. But my folks, you wouldn't necessarily call them nationalists; they were just people who taught each to have a sense of self-worth. And that is lacking, but it's not lacking because Black parents have changed or anything like that. It's lacking with the poor because they haven't been taught that they have a sense of self-worth. So that's how that vicious cycle in the inner-city goes.

KB: That mirror deep inside tells you when everything else can't get any worse, you can still go inside yourself and look at that mirror and recognize your reflection.

GN: You can recognize who you are. Get your values from there. Set your goals for yourself there. Have your own entrance. It sends up excellence, definitely, definitely. That's the comforting side of you. I can understand why they have that philosophy because they grew up in rural Mississippi. By God, if you look to the outside world, if you look around Robinsonville, Mississippi, what they said to you while you being poor and black is that there is nothing here for you to do. You're worth nothing, in a sense. There are no schools there for you. There are no libraries there for you. There is no art there for you. So, of course, you must turn in so that you can find a sense of self-worth. And you dream of having better for your children. For after all, there were radios in those days. There were magazines and newspapers. They knew that that was not America. Yes, so with that kind of training, it has helped me in an odd kind of way. Because as you go along and become successful and the paperwork on you piles up there's a tendency to say, "Yes, I find myself in reviews. I find myself in interviews." And that's not where you find you. Gloria finds Gloria in herself because that's where I must go in order to create my new set of characters, you know, and meet my new characters and meet my new challenges within myself, not on the pages of the review.

KB: And one of the things apparently in your world view as we see it in the three books that gives that mirror deep inside the self is memory. It is a memory of where you come from and that comes down from the land. And I find this very interesting in light of what you have been saying about this new cycle of poverty. It's also not a result of that thing that they wrote that happened on Willow Springs—commercial development that comes in. It's not just poverty that the people from your forbears from the South had to live with and mine, too, in the Middle West. It's not a land-based poverty anymore; it is a service-based economy and that really wrecks memory. That really leads to the loss of self.

GN: Not to have a center somewhere—I mean a geographical center somewhere in this country where there is a history for you, I think definitely wrecks memory. We have no surviving relatives in the South. That becomes my memory, my spiritual center, because of what we were speaking about before: the oral tradition, a passing on of culture. Yes, that's no longer true when you have people spread out all over the country and a child may have had three or four different homes, if their grandmother had three or four different homes. And that can go on ad infinitum. And there is no spiritual land. What stresses me is not so much our move as a nation from the land to the urban area, from a land-based setting to a service economy. What I am more worried about is the fact that we seem to have lost an emphasis upon ties—communal ties and spiritual ties. Those things can still be there. Those types of ties can be there regardless of where your spiritual land base might be. But we do indeed have to face the facts. We are no longer an agricultural country and will never be again. But I just hate the thought that we are a country that hasn't somehow lived up to the promise that we have of being one people. I don't mean one people in the fact that we would be of course all assimilated, but sort of all people—disparate people working as one people within a nation, caring about the most impoverished. That bothers me more than the move away from the land.

KB: But to continue this and make sure that we round this subject out, that is the thing in *Brewster Place*. Even though Brewster Place is a dead-end street for those people who come there, they pretty much have come to the end of their ropes. Mattie Michael loses her house that she paid for over thirty years because she wants to get her son, Basil, out of jail. Then he jumps bail. There are ties present, however. You find that Lucielia is the same little Ciel that grew up along with Basil. Do I have the name straight?

GN: It's Lucielia Louise Turner.

KB: That Ciel Turner is the Ciel that Mattie Michael had taken care of as a surrogate mother when her child was little. Anyway, there are family ties on this dead-end street in an urban area.

GN: Exactly. So that's what I was talking about. That to me is more important. Those different women on Brewster Place have very strong communal ties. And then, of course, there is the thing about memory in *Linden Hills*. What has happened to all the affluent people is they have lost their memory. Among other things, basically what I was trying to do with that novel, as my version of Dante and Virgil as they moved down to hell, my Lester and Willie encounter individuals who have given up those tenets that I have just listed. The first are ties with family, then ties with community, ties with their religious and spiritual values, then ties with their ethnocentric sense of self. And those are the worst cases, which are at the bottom of the hill because they are the ones who moved up the most in American Society. So, in *Linden Hills* I was trying to show that. So they have, in a sense, lost their memories. One by one residents have lost the memory of that which has kept us whole as a people.

KB: And that's what makes the Tilson family different sitting up at the top of that hill.

GN: And Kiswana is on the first circle. Her mom, Mrs. Browne, is on the first circle because I like Mrs. Browne so much after her appearance in *Brewster Place*. So I can't put her down too far down in hell. So they're sort of in the space that corresponds with Dante's circle of unbaptized pagans, you know—people whom he really loved, like Virgil. And he said the only thing that's wrong with them is that they died without the knowledge of Christ. So, they got the really good end of the stick in Dante's hell. So that's where I put my middle class Blacks who were savable.

KB: Like Lester.

GN: Like Lester, exactly!

KB: What is Braithwaite's role in the allegory?

GN: His role is that he has turned his back on true knowledge. He has allowed himself to be perverted. He has been brought over in this sense by the Nedeeds to write the history of Linden Hills. And he's the one besides Luther to warn the people. And he doesn't do that because of his own personal ambition. So he's just simply a recorder who does nothing with his knowledge. He just simply takes the knowledge in for the sake of knowledge. And it's never implemented for any good. He is the worse type of academic you could have: someone who could go through life sapping knowledge. And these people live in these ivory towers and do absolutely nothing else with it. And there are other academics doing the same kind of thing. But that's really what I was trying to grasp with him.

KB: It is Braithwaite that tells Willie that for someone like him, this probably will be the last place on earth. And, of course, the obvious question that readers raise about *Linden Hills* is: Is Gloria Naylor saying that the only real Black is the poor Black and that there is no hope for a Black person in this culture?
GN: Oh, no. Of course, not. First of all, people forget that the first Black people, the first Africans that came to this country did not come as slaves, but as indentured servants. Only after that there was a huge need for cheaper and cheaper labor. European Americans were unsuccessful in enslaving the Native American Indian or enslaving the poor that they had brought over from Europe because those indentured servants, when they tried to make them servants for life, would just run away and just disappear into the populace. So the Africans were also those indentured servants. In fact, they were much easier to enslave because of skin color. It would automatically stand out that you were indeed different. And a great book was written. Winthrop Jordan traces how the concept of blackness and whiteness developed in early America. If you were Black you could be indentured for life. And this could happen to your offspring. If you were white you could not be indentured. And it came from that. But yet there were the offspring of these indentured servants who come over and stayed free and stayed affluent. No, I'm not saying poor and Black; that's ludicrous. I'm not saying that at all. And I'm not saying that every Black person, every affluent Black would live in a Linden Hills. A special type of affluent Black lives in that community.

KB: Well, what is that special type?
GN: It's the type who is willing to give up anything in order to succeed; that's it. People who have lost those ties that I talked about before, because there are many successful Blacks who have not lost those ties, those who revel in ties of family and community and religion.

KB: And there is a difference, too. It seems to me that the implication is especially different for affluent Blacks in *Linden Hills*, with the exception of the minister whose job is in dealing with other Black people. It seems to me that the implication is that the assimilation is especially difficult for Blacks who move into what is thought of as white circles, as opposed to the older, as you say, multigenerational established Black affluent that often operated within a self-contained setting, like doctors who served other Black clients. Segregation, of course, perpetuated that. But there was a community. There was a Black middle-class and White people just don't know about it, that's all.

GN: Exactly. They just don't. Or they elect not to know.

KB: The undertakers who buried the Black dead in the Black cemetery.

GN: Oh, my God, insurance people are an example of that. You go to Chicago and Atlanta and meet the triple great grandchildren of these millionaires. It's amazing. No, some people elect not to know about that phenomenon. That has not been what the media puts forth as the image of blackness in America. And this is done for a specific reason, but those realities are there. And with my works, ultimately, when I can talk about having a whole canon of works, I would like to have examined various aspects of our experience in this country. So there are Brewster Places and there are Linden Hills and there are the Willow Springs and the Bailey's Cafes, or whatever. So just look because there is no end, absolutely no end to the richness that is there with my people, with my history.

KB: I have read that you felt at the time that you started writing that there was a need in contemporary Black literature to reflect a greater variety than there had been in the past.

GN: No, I know what you are saying. What I had said was that there was a need for traditional educational systems to reflect the contribution of Black artists in this country and then to reflect the diversity that makes up America. And that's what I had suffered from educationally when I was coming up, being a very avid reader. When I hit junior high school, thirteen or fourteen years old, the eyes of teachers would light up because they found a kid who loves to read. And then they would give me books. But I would never see literature from these people that reflected my reality either as a creator of it or a subject within it. And that is because of their own ignorance. These books existed. I know that these people weren't malicious people, but it was just not part of the standard school curriculum. So, when I began writing it was in response to this: my having been denied knowledge of the fact that I had foremothers and forefathers in the arts. I read the Brontës. I read Dickens. I read Thackery. I was reading Emerson when I was about thirteen or fourteen years old. I was that kind of kid. I read Emerson. I read Poe. I read Hawthorne, Fitzgerald, Faulkner, and Hemingway. They were all wonderful writers, very wonderful writers. Still, I never read anything that reflected me. And the irony of all ironies is that I was born in 1950. Nineteen fifty was the year that Gwendolyn Brooks won the Pulitzer Prize for *Annie Allen*. And I had never been taught of her existence. So as far as I was concerned, she did not exist. So I was twenty-seven years old when I learned that Black women wrote books. Can you imagine? And I am thirty-eight. To this day when I think about that kind of ignorance and the pain in which I lived, and it wasn't a conscious pain, but this disease of wondering why I was scribbling. Anyway, so that's when I began writing. So, I began to discover women writers and a whole Black culture that was there, and that happened in college as well. Now there was huge diversity because each of these writers within that tradition has been different. You're moving from someone as wild as an Ishmael Reed to someone as formal as a Ralph Ellison going on through Baldwin and Wright and those people. And if we look at the women, how vastly different they are. You know Alice Walker's vision from Paule Marshall's vision, from Ntozoke Shange's vision, from Morrison's vision, from Gwendolyn Brook's vision. So there is plenty of diversity.

KB: Was there a watershed book that you picked up and read that began the stream?
GN: Yes, *The Bluest Eye* was the first work by a black woman novelist that I read. When I think back, I was in high school when I read *A Raisin in the Sun* by Lorraine Hansberry. But somehow it did not sink in—I mean that she was Black, a Black woman who wrote this play about Black people in Chicago. But her play was not the first work of Black literature that I read. It was *The Bluest Eye* by Morrison. And then after that it was like a whole floodgate of them.

KB: And that is interesting too because of the parallels between Morrison and yourself. I think that *The Bluest Eye* evolved out of a period of great struggle in which Morrison felt that there was not a language that she could write in that was hers. You seem to have had a similar experience. So, I think that is deliciously ironic that Morrison's book is the one that you picked up and it opened up that wonderful stream of work. Going back to your background. I am very intrigued by your involvement with the Jehovah Witnesses. What was your attraction to that?

GN: Well, when I was thirteen my mother became a Jehovah's Witness. And my mom had that respect for religion, the Bible. She was a Methodist as a kid and she belonged to the Methodist Church. She then became a Baptist when I was about nine or ten years old. And she would talk to Seventh Day Adventist People. She talks to whoever would come to the door. If they were talking about God she would let them in. She would listen to Oral Roberts. He would come on television when I was a kid. And she would listen to all that stuff. So, then she liked the philosophy of the Jehovah's Witnesses. When I was thirteen, she joined that church. And I officially joined them when I was eighteen. I guess when I look back, it is probably a response to several things. Nineteen sixty-eight, that was the year I was to graduate from high school and go to Hunter College. And there had been an awful lot of turmoil at that time in our national history. They had assassinated Martin Luther King, Jr., in April of 1968. It was after that assassination that I just felt that there was no hope in this system, in this country, for any kind of real change. And up until that point, we had thought that there could indeed be change. And I said, "My God, if they kill a voice that is this moderate, where is the hope?" This is the messenger that must be slain. And that's a very mild message. Then there is absolutely no hope left. And so I decided to work for a better world. Some of my friends had gone off to become Black Panthers or become hippies. I said that through this organization, I would try to work for a better world because it wasn't just America; it was the whole planet I saw as diseased in an odd kind of way. And this religion offered a philosophy that talked about the opposite. There would be a real government ruled by God, you know. And that would alleviate all the inequities all over the entire planet. And that just sort of struck home for me at that time. Also, I think I was responding to my budding sexuality. They were fundamentalist and for them there are basically two ways to go: marriage or celibacy. I had no intentions of getting married. So, it was just marvelous to remain celibate. You know I could hide from the insecurities that would have gone about with beginning sexual activity. I think that was a part of it as well, to be honest, when I look back. It was a very safe way to move among men and to move through society. And it also gave me a cause. So I don't regret those years. Because one thing is that they brought me out of my shyness. You had to go up to people's doors and talk.

KB: But you didn't stay in it; you got out.

GN: When I was twenty-five I left that church.

KB: Can you say why?

GN: Well, Armageddon hadn't come. You know it had not come. The world had gotten worse. And I felt I could, perhaps, still make a difference in another arena.

KB: And it was then that you went back to school.

GN: That's right. That's when I went back to school.

KB: And eventually found your way into the vocation.

GN: I returned back to what I had done, exactly, as a child. I first started college to become a nurse, because it was a two-year program at Medgar Evers College. I said that in two years I could become a nurse, and just in case this paradise was coming, you know, the new world, I would have a vocation. But I found that I was spending much more time writing essays for my English courses than I was spending learning about the way that food got masticated and moved down through your body. The digestive system just did not interest me. So, I went on to become an English major. And I changed schools and went to Brooklyn College where I could take more electives.

KB: Now, have your parents been supporting your vocation of writing?

GN: My folks have this philosophy of no matter what we do they want it to be legal and moral and that we be happy. They're thrilled because I have, indeed, gone through these major phases in my life—that now I seem to be the happiest I have been in a while.

KB: What was the basis for your decision to go on to Yale and formally focus on Afro-American studies.

GN: It took me six years to get through undergraduate school because at that time I had my own place. I had to work, so I was working on the switchboards at hotels. By the time I finally got my undergraduate degree I was thirty-one years old. And I said I better not waste any time with this. I should go straight into graduate school. I always thought I wanted to teach. Now I had written the first novel, *The Women of Brewster Place*, while I was still an undergraduate there in Brooklyn College. That was completed the same month I graduated. So I said before that I had never started anything and completed it. So those were two things that I started and completed. I'd started college and completed it. I started that book and completed it. I had said I would go on and ultimately get the master's and then get the doctorate in American Studies. And then I could become a professor with this high-class union card, which is all I thought of a Ph.D. being. And I'd get tenure somewhere. And I could sit up somewhere very comfortably and take long vacations and have short work weeks. And I would write. That was the initial plan. So that's why I did that. I did not see one book making me a writer. It was never ever in my mind. This was what I was saying before about how I would separate what people say from how I feel. So even when the reviews were all really quite tremendous with *Brewster Place* and they were screaming, screaming, screaming about this bright new talent, I said they're out of their minds. One book doesn't make you a writer. All I had written was a book. That's all I had done. I had written a book. I was very pleased about that. But that was a long way from my calling myself a writer. So then my identity was a graduate student. And it was a full scholarship so they took care of me. All I needed to do was sit there and work. And I began *Linden Hills* during my third year.

KB: You went to school and wrote at the same time.
GN: When I went to Brooklyn College I was not only going to school, but writing and working. I didn't realize then that mine was an impossible schedule. I just didn't know.

KB: Well, how did you fit it in?
GN: I didn't do anything else. That's it. That was it. That's all I did.

KB: But which portion of those twenty-four hours everyday did you spend with the writing?
GN: It would be my days off from work. When I didn't have to go in to the hotel, I would take those two, sometimes three, days off, if I was working for a short week. And I would write then. And then I would take the manuscript in at night, because when I was just finishing school, I went on the midnight shift. And I was working alone because you know one operator can handle a hotel at night. And after about 2:30 or 3:00, I would sit there and edit what I had written during the day. I had to do it like that.

KB: Oh boy. You had such discipline.

GN: No, it wasn't bad, Kay. It really wasn't. I am not an overly disciplined person. It was something I wanted to do. It was something that was starting to flow out of me. It was helping me to achieve order because my personal life had been in total chaos. Yes, because I was going through a divorce and everything. So it helped me to order what was happening. So, I never thought of it. It was an odd kind of a thing, something that I just did.

KB: You have more time now, don't you, to write?

GN: Now I am a writer. I can say that's what I do as a profession. I'm a writer. I consciously elected not to go on and get my doctorate after I finished that master's up there. Because I was going to come back to New York, which was home, and try to make my living as a writer. That's the plunge I took in 1983 and 1984. I took that plunge. I happened to get a good job, which was nice in Washington, which was the Moore Fellowship. This was a writing fellowship. And I went down there for a year. And after that I went back to New York. So the whole process of at least beginning to define myself as a writer took about three years from the first novel. It took about three years before it finally came into my consciousness, the forefront of my consciousness, that I am now a writer. That is an identity that I now can claim. Before, like I said, there were other identities—switchboard operator who was going to school, then a graduate student who happened to be writing. But after *Linden Hills*, I became a writer to myself.

KB: Let's talk about the books in terms of where they came from. Where did *The Women of Brewster Place* come from?

GN: It came because I was twenty-seven years old and I had not read any books that reflected my experience. It took me that long to learn that there were such books. And I mean my experience as a black female. And so then I had said, well, if I just have one book in me, I want it to be all about what I haven't read a hell of a lot about. And that was all about me. And, therefore, the book sprang from that desire. The reason for the structure of the work was because I knew that one character, one female protagonist could not even attempt to represent the richness or diversity of the black female experience. So, the women in that work you find consciously differ, beginning with something as simple as their skin color, and they differ in their ages, their religious backgrounds, their personal backgrounds, their political affiliations, even their sexual preferences. And my whole thing with that work is to give a tiny microcosm of the black female experience. And there is a reason for the wall at the dead-end street: regardless of how diverse we might be and how diverse we may be, as black women we all share two thing in this country— and that is racism and sexism. And so that's what that wall represented for me, and in each of those stories that particular woman will somehow relate to that wall. In the case of Kiswana Browne, I make a point of saying that she could actually see over the wall because she is there by choice, unlike the others.

KB: Did you conceive of the books as being interrelated before the fact or did that just develop?
GN: It developed early on, from *Brewster Place*. I have a notebook from Brooklyn College where I was sketching out *Linden Hills*. And at first the idea was to make them concentric squares—people that lived in sort of these concentric squares that helped them through. But from the beginning, when I was midway through that, I had dreamed of a quartet, and in that notebook I have that quartet just vaguely, vaguely sketched out. And the first thing that came were titles. So I had, of course, that title which was initially called *The Women of Beekman Place*. But I had that title *Linden Hills, Mama Day*, and now, *Bailey's Cafe*.

KB: So, there's a fourth book to come?
GN: In the quartet, yes.

KB: And whose going to carry over?
GN: Well, that little restaurant which is mentioned briefly in *Mama Day*.

KB: Oh. So it is Willow Springs, then?
GN: No, No, No. That's in New York when George and Cocoa quarrel. You know, the scene where he slaps her and drags her to finally show her where he was born and what his mother was all about. Because she is always saying that he never tells her how he feels anything. He never tells her about his past. So then he shows her Bailey's Cafe. So the carryover character would be George, because George will be born in the next novel, since it goes back to 1948 and 1949.

KB: I see. So you're going to move back in time?

GN: Yes, there is a move back in time, so that is going to be very challenging. It would be the decade that I was conceived in, so I would have to rely a lot upon the unconsciousness memory for that one.

KB: From things that I have read about you and the way you work, you don't plot in advance. You're the kind of writer that gets characters, puts them in a situation, and then sees what happens.

GN: Yes, exactly. It would be totally futile to plot out too much. Because what I pray for is that these people will actually live and come into their own life. And if that happens, what's the point of my deciding if they're going to live on East 96th Street when they want to live on a 115th Street. It makes no sense. So, yes, you hope that those characters just start living. I have a general idea of what these characters might do because I have a vague idea of their personalities. But the particulars have to take place as they are born.

KB: Is there a particular section or piece in *The Women of Brewster Place* that serves as the origin of the novel?

GN: Oh, yes. It is the section that I read here for you. The work began with that rocking scene. And I had written that as sort of a catharsis for myself. I was going through what I considered as being a great deal of pain. And I imagined a woman who would be feeling pain that intensely but for other reasons. And I sat down and wrote that. And what I had hoped for was a kind of earth mother to just knock down this door and come sit here on this couch and just rock. I wanted to be rocked out of my pain. And that's how I invented Mattie Michael in that scene. And I put that away, had a good cry, and a year later, when I took the creative writing course at Brooklyn College, I pulled out that ending, changed the names, because the names were different then, and wrote a story around that scene. And, ultimately, a book came out of that story.

KB: What made you decide to structure the *Linden Hills* with the Dante's *Inferno*?

GN: Because of what I was attempting to do as far as trying to give a microcosm of the Black middle-class experience, the hyphenated American experience, and its worst possible scenario. And I had studied the *Inferno* at Brooklyn

College in a course that was called Great Works of Literature or something
like that. We did *The Canterbury Tales* and the *Inferno*. We just did the first
half of *The Divine Comedy*. And it fascinated me that Dante used the mirror
image of Florentine society that was fifteenth-century Florentine society.
So as you had sinned, so you would be punished. And as you went down his
microcosm of Florence, ancient Florence, you met people who had sinned
to greater and greater degrees, given his whole world view. So, therefore, it
would be sins of the flesh and sins of the countenance that were the least sins
in Dante's case. Then you move down and encounter those who have committed the grossest sins—treason against country and treason against God,
that kind of thing. And I said, my God. You know I can see how that sort of
thing can work as far as upward mobility is concerned. Because as you climb
up, you have, in my scenario, to relinquish ties or commit crimes against
these ties. That, for me, moves from the lesser to the greater ties to be relin-
quished. We were speaking before about this being this society in transition,
moving, indeed, from the agricultural land base to the technological service
industries. One of the first ties—and this has been happening now for the
last thirty five-forty years in American thought—one of the easiest, the
first ties to go, are indeed ties of family. Because you're raised in the mid west,
but the job calls for you to be in Los Angeles. The job calls for you to be in
Atlanta or to be in New York or wherever. So you find yourself going away
from a home base. And that became the upper part of hell for me. Ties of
family and friends can go easily, then there are communal ties. And these
are people who are no longer comfortable living in the old neighborhoods.
If you are Italian American, you don't want to live in the Italian part of
little Italy. You want to be on the upper west side where it's all happening.
And it was that kind of thing. And you don't want to live in Harlem. God
knows. No. You want to be on the east side. So it was communal ties. They're
the next that would go. Then, ties with religious and spiritual values. As
you move down in Linden Hills, meeting these people, then after you go
through Tupelo Drive and into the city of this Lower hell, you meet my
worse case scenario. You meet those people who wake up in the morning and
say to themselves that I have it all, but who in the hell am I. So that's why the
Inferno just intrigued me, and also because there were strong, vivid images in
there. I still remember to this day the guy who's holding his head and swing-
ing it by the hair.

KB: Some readers have noted a kinship with *The Tempest* in *Mama Day*. Was that intentional?

GN: Sure wasn't. No, *that* was not. I'd love to take credit for it because I read a really great analysis on *Mama Day* and *The Tempest*. Shakespeare is extremely important to me, and he has consciously played a part in each of my works. In *Mama Day*, where I consciously put Shakespeare was, of course, with *King Lear* and *Romeo and Juliet*. You know, George loves *King Lear* and I use that whole scene as their first seduction scene, whatever you might call it. And he and Cocoa are stark, gross lovers and there's an *allusion* made to that. Even though I have read *The Tempest* a couple of times, I did not consciously use it in my work. And someone said, but of course, Gloria, there's Miranda or there's the island, you know. And I assured them that I did not do that consciously.

KB: It is interesting that you can situate *Mama Day* within the larger context of the griot tradition emanating from ancient Africa. The role of the griot involves passing on aspects of culture.

GN: To perpetuate the culture, you mean. Yes. In the case of the griots that's quite true. Traditionally, in Afro-American societies and in early Afro-American society here where slavery played a huge part, there was only the oral, because that which was literate was denied to you. I always find it interesting. It's more than the fact that if you were Black and a slave you were denied literacy. It was actually illegal for you to obtain literacy, which was more ominous. So, therefore, you were a nonbeing, if you were a black who could read and write. And that, of course, had repercussions down to my parents' time, where my mother could not use the public libraries in Mississippi. And that's why she was adamant about going. But anyway, so, therefore, the oral tradition was vital; it became functional, if you will, because you had to pass on the culture and pass on knowledge, pass on training of children through word of mouth.

But now, once we obtained, as a people, literacy and then began to produce these words, I don't think that it becomes that much of a public function anymore or that art—in short, a book—becomes a comfort-sized verbal statement. It does not really have the same role that the oral expressions used to.

KB: To me, it is interesting in *Mama Day* because it is a reversal of that oral tradition. The book hinges entirely on things people don't say to each other using a different kind of knowledge.

GN: Yes, this is very true, very true. Well, as far as *Mama Day* itself is concerned, I had planned for it to be about the intangible. You know what is it that forms the basis for what we believe and why we believe it. So, therefore, it is vital that you be able to read, that the individuals can indeed read that which is not spoken because it's about belief. What do you believe is happening? How do you believe he feels? Do you really believe Cocoa has been rooted or hexed in some way? Do you believe something differently? Now, it is quite true in that opening section that I read where the young man who has come back from college is told to chew the mint. And if he'd known enough he would realize that no matter what he must pick up and chew the mint because that mint is a signal to the next sister that she can tell him certain things. The putting of the moss in the shoes signifies that he can enter an experience.

KB: And it's not said, not said.

GN: No. It's sort of through osmosis. Somehow it's known. Like Sapphira Wade's name is never literally said, but she is the guiding spirit for that island. And they know without quite knowing. So we're talking here about a historical memory, a racial memory, which, I believe, is perhaps as important as if not more important than a conscious memory. She doesn't live in the part of our memory that we can use to form words. Exactly. She goes beyond the conscious memory. Because you know we learn to read through memorizing. But she lived beyond that. So, therefore, there were no words for that which you cannot consciously conjure up.

KB: I'm very intrigued by those sea islands. Was this totally a mythical framework that you have set up here of an island that belonged to neither state? This, in fact, is not physically true?

GN: No, it's not physically true. With those islands they will fall within the territory of some state. Sure. They do. You know you just look at the state boundaries and wherever the island falls then they would belong to that state. No, but I needed, once again, a landscape to demonstrate a state of mind, if you will, or a metaphysical situation. So, I needed a place that was part of the United States but not quite part of it so there could be a bridge. And the bridge becomes very symbolic in *Mama Day* because it bridges reality from the world of magic. I needed that and the island was just perfect. I knew about those sea islands. And you could go across this bridge and you could sort of be there and not be there.

KB: Did you do a lot of research for this book?
GN: This was the most expansive book I have written to date. I did a lot of traveling because I went down to the islands. I went back to Robinsonville, Mississippi, because my grandmother is now passed on. All of my grandparents are gone. But my grandmother's best friend was still alive, a woman named Eva McKinney who had been the midwife and healer for that community when my folks were coming up. She was still there, quite lucid and chipper. And I went back to get from her the different remedies she used and bits about her life—put her on tape. I did that. I had to go to Mexico. I went to investigate certain herbs that were used. Then, I had to do research on herbal medicines, on diagnostic practices, because when Mama Day went to a patient I had to make sure that indeed that was what you would do. If you went to a woman complaining of a pain in her stomach and you thought it was something in her reproductive organs, what would the procedures be? I had to read about all of that. So, it took a lot. It was my most ambitious novel to date as far as research is concerned.

KB: Did you actually go down in the Charleston area?
GN: Sure did! I went and stayed with Jill Humphreys. And then I headed off on my own out to St. Helena Island, all out that way. And I stayed out on the islands for about three weeks or so. A woman who was working at the Penn Center which was there on St. Helena invited me to come home with her. I just called Miss Skinner last week because I am going back down there for vacation to let her know I was on my way. So, she invited me home. She had a trailer—one, two, three-bedroom trailer. So I stayed with her in her trailer and hung out with her.

KB: Is that where you got the idea for Miranda's trailer?
GN: I guess so. Maybe it is. Maybe it is, yes.

KB: But there is a great deal of information about the slave trade too, in Charleston. Isn't there?
GN: Sure is. There's the old slave mart that's there. There's a museum, which was literally a building where they would bring the slaves and keep them

chained up while the auction would go on. I went there to the slave art museum to get materials and also to imagine what it might have been like. And what's ironic is that the Charleston system was considered the most humane system in the South because they would not literally bring the person out there and have people touch them and look at their teeth and put their hands on their genitals and that sort of thing. They did it by number. It's ironic because now it's more chilling when you can now go buy the replicas of these sheets. And what they would have is you could bid by numbers. So it would be the auctioneer would go out to the balcony and it's all there and tagged. And he'd say number sixty-seven. And, say, it would be Mindy, age twenty. And if she was prime or half-prime or whatever it would be. And then you would bid on number sixty-seven. Of course, they presumed honesty on the part of the sellers, the people who traded there, that they would not sell them something that was not good.

KB: What does prime and half-prime mean?
GN: Prime would be an individual who was fit and able to work or to breed. It would depend. If it were a woman, she would be of her child-bearing years. And she'd be very fit and able to work. And if it were men, you have to be fit and able to work. Half-prime could be a physical disability or sort of what they called a moral disability. For example, if someone drank too much, that person would be considered half-prime.

KB: As in the case of Sapphira.
GN: Or tended to be sullen, exactly. Those are things that would be listed. You know, if they fought, a slave who would fight, they would be, then, half-prime. So, that document comes indeed from research that I had done, the actual documents. And what they would give would be warranties. By law, a warranty had to be given when you sold a person that you indeed sold a prime person. You know, therefore, if you bought a person and found that you had been deceived, that they were older—sometimes they would dye the hair of older slaves to make them look younger—if you bought someone, let's say prime property and you found out it was half-prime, the law gave you a warranty, just like with a toaster or microwave. You could then go and say, "I'm sorry there are vices or maladies here." The vices or maladies prescribed by law do not hold forth. So, Bascomb Wade bought her knowing that she was half-prime—that, in short, she refused to be a slave, you know. Basically, it boils down a lot of times to

your refusal to be an animal, that, of course, you were damaged goods. There is going to be a book about that anyway after *Bailey's Cafe*. I'm writing a book about Sapphira and Bascomb Wade and what actually happened between them.

KB: Oh, boy. I'm dying to find out what happens.
GN: I am, too. I really am because I don't know. I have no idea as yet as to what will happen.

KB: Because he died in 1823.
GN: And he was thirty-five years old.

KB: And thirty-five and so was George.
GN: That was intentional. That was intentional. Because George and John Paul—all three are in Bascomb Wade. John Paul and George were men who died of broken hearts. Of course, they would play on the broken heart.

KB: Another thing that comes up a lot in literature is the question of magical realism. And I wondered what your thoughts were.
GN: Well, I think that this last novel will be closest in that mode. And that would be on purpose. You know, I needed to find a way structurally to tell the story of George and Cocoa, so what I was doing was walking a thin line between that which is real and that what is not real, in an odd kind of way. So, I read Gabriel García Márquez ages ago. *One Hundred Years of Solitude* influenced just a tiny, tiny bit of the opening of *Linden Hills*. I wanted that whole sense of one man coming back and coming back and coming back. And there's really only one Luther Nedeed although there's five Luther Nedeeds. And that comes from Márquez. And so I don't have any problem with it. I enjoy reading some of the magical realists and I've even used them.

KB: Do you see in what's called magical realism an evolution, as it were, in the tradition of literature where the strands of realism and that extreme of romantic mentality are coming together?
GN: Yes, I do. And I think that's quite wholesome because we had moved from minimalism and the whole idea of what was just art for the sake of art, words for the sake of words. And we had a very limited view of what indeed language and indeed imagery could accomplish. You know what it was supposed to accomplish was just language, just supposed to accomplish

the imagery. To have writers now, and I call it broadening out to explore thematically what we do with the process itself, which is to deal with the intangible and to believe in ghosts. When you talk about characters rising up and talking to you, it is nothing short of the ghost of your own memory, the ghost of your psyche that comes forth.

KB: I believe you said before we started today that the hurricane scene you read today from *Mama Day* was a tribute to Zora Neale Hurston and I wanted to know if you would mind explaining that for us a little bit.
GN: Yes. I knew from the beginning that roughly a third of the novel would be carrying the collective, colloquial voice of the island. And I knew also that there would be a hurricane. I do give my characters a great deal of freedom, but some things they just have to do. And they just had to live through that hurricane for me. I'm sorry. They had to do that. I didn't care what they did when they got there afterwards, but you have to live through this hurricane. And it would be the island voice that would talk about the hurricane. And I was worried. I said, my God, I wonder if this voice would be capable of rendering that scene? And when I say, voice, I also mean the mentality behind the voice. It was that sort of arrogance in there, as well, an urban, educated arrogance. I wonder if the world view behind this voice could encompass something like a hurricane. And I also knew I wanted to write about the hurricane in such a way as to convey the central metaphor of the middle passage, because that's physically what happens as far as how those storms are born. They are born off the coast of Africa, hit the equator, and it is the force of the earth that sends the wind spinning.

Anyway, how could this voice do all that? And I thought about Zora Neale Hurston's *Their Eyes Were Watching God*. And I considered much more than just the work itself; I thought of Hurston's whole philosophy. At times during the Harlem Renaissance writers like Langston Hughes and Countee Cullen were glorifying the folk and attempting to raise the folk up to art. Zora Neale Hurston's very cultured, militant position was that you don't have to raise the black folk up to art; the black folk *are* art. That was her position, and she conveyed it through language—such as her use of the sermon. And I was real humbled when I remembered that.

And I remembered indeed that *Their Eyes Were Watching God* was a masterpiece told entirely in that colloquial speech. And she was right, you know. It is pure poetry. And I went back to *Their Eyes Were Watching God* and read her storm scene—you know, where the hurricane is coming to the flatlands out of Florida. And the lake breaks the dam. And it is just the most incredibly beautiful and moving thing. And I read that over and over until I was ready to sit down and have this voice, which was a different voice from her voice, do what it was going to do. And I was quite pleased with what it saw and how that worked out.

KB: One of the very rich qualities of your work is the wit.
GN: Well, I'm glad you noticed it. A lot of people just tend to notice the pain that's in my work. And I see life as being both extremely difficult sometimes suicidal and difficult for some. But at the same time I have seen a lot of joy, and there is a lot in my work that can be at times funny. You know—comical, if you will. And even the most ostensibly tragic situation can be humorous at some level. In *Linden Hills* I attempted to make a funeral quite humorous. You know, where the guy is bringing in a new wife.

KB: It is.
GN: He brings in the new wife before he buried the old wife.

KB: He's having the boys paint the rooms, too.
GN: Yes, exactly. They're going to do the room and there is to be a resurrection of sorts, because a minister is preaching this fiery sermon about Lazarus. Jesus raises Lazarus from the dead. And this minister is finally going to preach his last sermon. And this poor guy is thinking that maybe she will come back. So I thought that was funny. But all of the critics will say that this is such a depressing book. And I grant you that there is a great deal of Naylor that is somber. In the end the novel is definitely apocalyptic. But I feel it is vital that we not take ourselves too seriously. I know what that can lead to. You know, it can lead to poor mental health, if you don't learn to laugh.

KB: The interplay between Miranda Day and her sister Abigail is riotous. And I love the scene where George walks up and says, "I thought you'd be old." This gift of Miranda Day is as much as anything else the gift of laughter and joy.
GN: Definitely. It just keeps you whole and definitely whole as a people. That's how stereotypes come up that black people love to laugh, and that's not the case at all that you love to laugh. What you have had are people who

have retained sanity—communal sanity—by understanding the gift of humor. And so all of the Brer Rabbit tales and that kind of thing were situations that were extensively degrading transformed into humorous situations.

KB: I also wondered if you enjoyed putting private jokes in your novels.
GN: Sure do. With *Linden Hills* Wayne Avenue was named after a guy named Farmer Wayne. And Farmer Wayne was a shepherd. Well, I used to have a crush when I was much younger on a guy named Wayne Shepherd. So, I put that there. That is one of the subtle little silly things I will do. But there are, on the more serious side, things that I have embedded in those novels that people haven't ferreted out yet. And I wait, you know, sort of like a little kid who knows a lot more than people give her credit for knowing. My parents caught on very fast that I could spell well above my years. In my day, when people wanted to talk about things that children were not supposed to hear, they would spell out certain things. You know, there is a "divorce." I learned to spell, you know, very quickly. But I would sit there and not let them know that I knew words like "fornication," and "adultery," and "divorce," or "drunkard." So it's that little bit of the smart little girl in me that led me to embed things in the novel that I am waiting for the critics to detect, especially with the whole idea of place and colors in my work.

KB: If someone were to just ask you, as I'm going to ask you right now, Gloria Naylor, why do you write? What would you say?
GN: Because I have no choice.

KB: Thanks for taking time with us today.
GN: Oh, it was a pleasure!

Gloria Naylor

Pearl Cleage / 1988

From *Catalyst* (Summer 1988), 56–59. Reprinted with permission of Gloria Naylor and Pearl Cleage.

Catalyst: Tell me what response your new book, *Mama Day*, has gotten from readers and from critics.

Gloria Naylor: Basically the critical appraisals have been favorable. What I attempted to do in this work, which was new for me although it is not new in the tradition, was to deal with a Black love story. To have a man and woman attempt to work out some of the mundane problems and insecurities that we have to confront in just making a marriage go. That is not the reason for *Mama Day*, but that love story, my *Romeo and Juliet*, if you will, becomes essential to what has to happen dramatically in the work. A lot of readers and critics have responded to the love story quite favorably. The other important element is the issue of magic which I define as a sort of flowering of the human potential. In a sense all *Mama Day* does is get people to reach inside themselves and find the power that is there within them to create miracles.

C: It is interesting that you say that about the love story. I told a friend that I was going to be talking to you and she mentioned *The Women of Brewster Place* and the horrifying rape that occurs at the end of the book. When you sat down to write *Mama Day* were you trying consciously to show a different, less violent side of black female reality?

GN: No, not consciously. Each work has been about some part of the Black community. With *The Women of Brewster Place*, I was trying to celebrate the female spirit and the ability that we have to *transcend* and also to give a microcosm of Black women in America—Black women who are faced by a wall of racism and sexism that you have to come up against. In *Linden Hills*, there was another aspect of our reality dealing with upward mobility and what tensions are involved in that struggle to succeed and still retain what is yours. *Mama Day* is a celebration of love and magic.

C: Are the books connected in any linear way?

GN: When I began *Brewster Place*, I dreamed of writing four novels. *Mama Day* becomes the third in that quartet and the fourth will be *Bailey's Cafe*. Each book gives a little hint of the work that will come after. In *Mama Day* you get a little touch of *Bailey's Cafe*. With *Bailey's Cafe*, I look at female sexuality. So I knew a real general, hazy outline of each work and, of course, the closer you get to them, the clearer the images become. So far, I can knock on wood and say "thank God" because the books have grown beyond my original intentions.

C: When you conceived of the four books, did you consciously say to yourself, I have an idea and I think the best way to achieve this idea is by writing four books or did the idea come as four books?

GN: It came as four books and it was very ironic that they came in the order that they did, because my life has sort of kept pace in a way with what was happening with the books. *Brewster Place* was a reaction to the fact that most of what I had read did not reflect my reality. Ever since the third grade, I always wrote, and I always read voraciously and I had teachers who would throw books at me because they love a Black kid who can read! These were well meaning people and the books they gave me were works they considered good literature so I sort of cut my literary teeth on the English Classics and to this day that influence is still in my work.

C: When did all this reading lead to your own writing?

GN: I was always writing from twelve years old. My mother gave me my first diary because although you wouldn't know it now since I can go on and on for hours, I didn't talk much when I was younger. I was very shy, very repressed. My mother gave me a diary and told me that since I could not talk, get it out and write it down in there. So I've always written and I thought I was a freak for writing because after all I was reading nothing about Black women or that Black women wrote. The first novel I read written by a black woman was Toni Morrison's *The Bluest Eye* and I decided that I wanted to put my two cents into the pot, and that I wanted it to be all about *me*! And the *me* of course just couldn't be *me*. The *me* was Black women, the whole spectrum, from our physical appearance, to our religious backgrounds, political backgrounds, even our sexual preferences. So that work was trying to do justice to the whole spectrum, and it was a poor attempt at doing justice because in order to do that, I would have had to have eleven million chapters, which you can't do, so you try real hard to do what you can.

C: How old were you when you wrote *The Women of Brewster Place*?
GN: I started when I was about twenty-eight and I finished it when I was thirty-one.

C: Did the book help you define yourself as a writer?
GN: Not that book! It wasn't until, to be super honest with you, I was in the middle of *Mama Day*. I was twenty-five years old when I entered college as a freshman because between high school and college I went off to do other things with my life. And then I only went part-time because I had my own apartment, I had my own life, I had to work. So my primary identity in those years was as a switchboard operator who was going to school to get a degree and the writing which I was doing which happened to be *Brewster Place*, in my mind was no different than the writing I had done when I was twelve years old. I was trying to bring some sort of order to chaos. So it was natural that I'd be writing because I had always written, but then the book was published and that was quite energizing, because wow, here I had a book! I had always dreamed of being a writer but that's like saying "I'm going to marry Billy Dee Williams." It was that kind of deal. So I got a scholarship to Yale and I went on to graduate school and the book came out and that was fine, but a book in my mind didn't make you a writer. A book was just a book. It could be a fluke. You know all those crazy insecurities you have. Then I was a graduate student and I was writing and ultimately it worked out where I was allowed to present the first four chapters of *Linden Hills* as partial fulfillment of my masters degree and I finished *Linden Hills* when I was teaching at George Washington University. It was after that that I said, "Okay, I'm going to go back to New York and try to make my living being a writer." Now to other people that was sort of crazy because I won the book award in those years and had done the second novel and they considered me a writer, but that was their reality. I have always had to separate *their* reality from *my* reality. My reality was about hitting New York, which was home and trying to be a writer. And a lot of crazy things happened but I still kept going and that's when I knew midway this book that I was going to do this no matter what! So that's when I became a writer. And now I sit before you, a writer, because come Hell or high water I am going to do things, good

or bad. The point is to start it and complete it and make it the best you know how.

C: How much attention do you pay to reviews?
GN: Very little. You read them because you are human and you want to know what other people say about the work. I have friends who will read a bad review and go to bed for two weeks or cry, but I'm not that way. Once the work is done, and I know what I have given up to do it, and the effort that I've put into it, that's the real reward. So if it is a really bad review from someone who doesn't understand your work, it may sting. And if it is a great review even if they didn't understand the work, you kind of smile. But as far as getting totally upset, that doesn't happen because after all critics are outside of the reason why I am writing. If the review is good or bad, they don't understand. I told myself with *Brewster Place* that this must always be the case because with *Brewster Place* it was like unanimous screaming and applauding but I can't buy into that because if I do, I may think one day I'll *try* to write a book so that people will love it and to me that is the lull of death. So what was important to me was that I had written something and that was it. And I'm real glad that I figured that out because as you go along, the road gets rocky for different reasons and you can lose your perspective.

C: Do you feel like you are a part of a national community of Black writers?
GN: I know I am a part of a group of Black writers because I am grouped in with Black writers, but if you mean as far as any real exchange or a common agenda, no, that does not exist.

C: Would you like it to exist?
GN: I did when I first started writing. But I know that would be impossible because of different politics. When I was growing up, I thought it would sort of be like the Harlem Renaissance and I would go to these conferences and things and I realized that writers, especially the ones that were prominent, were coming to do a conference. After they did the conference, they would go their separate ways.

C: What do you see ahead for us? Are we in terrible shape, we Black women who are marooned in America?

GN: Yeah, we are. We are in terrible shape and the gap between women like you and I and women like my aunt is growing. It is because we are no longer living in the same places that at one time we did. But then I also see hope because we have indeed survived and slavery was meant to destroy us as a people. We were supposed to come here and work and do our thing and then die off the face of this earth. And the whole Black problem came about because we didn't die off. We really didn't. But to survive is one thing and the quality of your life is something else. I don't know. I'm not good about the solution. I'm better about the problem.

C: Do you feel a responsibility to propose solutions?

GN: One of my long term friends, at my first book party, gave me a book marker that said "Birds nest because they have an answer. They sing because they have a song." And I still have that book marker because what she was trying to say to me which I knew, intimately anyway was "yes, you can reflect a certain reality but you can't then go on with your work to solve that reality." That's sociology. That's getting out into the community. Living as a social worker, living as a political activist. No, my work is not about giving answers. In my own personal anguish, when we are talking I have often said and thought "what will the answer be" because it affects me. Because it affects my community. But my work is just the highlight, and I pray to God that it brings to life just a tiny little bit of the reality that I see through my vision. You know because there are a whole lot of other stars out there highlighting their little reality, but together perhaps it will form a whole picture.

Gloria Naylor

Mickey Pearlman and Katherine Usher
Henderson / 1990

From *Inter/view: Talks with America's Writing Women*, 23–29. Copyright ©
1990 University Press of Kentucky.

Gloria Naylor, who always has "to have a little bit of sky," lives in a sunny
cooperative apartment in upper Manhattan whose living room windows face
the Hudson River. She works at an oak rolltop desk (the one that most writers lust after), but only a foot or two away is the inevitable computer, and the
boxes of continuous white paper are piled up nearby. The plumbers were
there the day I arrived (Is it comforting to know that pipes break even at
Gloria Naylor's?), but we settled in to talk despite the bangs and the clanking.
     Naylor is a woman with a formidable intellect and a deeply ingrained
sense of personhood. She had recently returned from a fellowship at Cornell
where she had the space and the time to relax after the considerable accomplishment of *The Women of Brewster Place, Linden Hills*, and *Mama Day*. We
talked initially about a writer's use of memory and about identity. Naylor
said that when "you think about the process itself, within the artist, what you
are doing is trying to somehow give cohesion to the chaos that is all of you.
You are taking the memory of your personal self, your historical self, your
familial self [because] your writing filters through all of those things." For
most females, she said, your "identity comes through connecting yourself to
nurturing of some sort, to your body, and . . . when you write, the writing
flow[s] through that identity. That goes back to the nineteenth century. . . .
What has changed somewhat is *the way* women see themselves in relationship to the female *as body*, the female *as nurturer*, the female *as mother of the
family*." Now "you get literature that will sometimes rail against that" and
that tries "to broaden the horizons of what [being a female] means. As long
as we have woman defined [in the usual ways] in our society, as long as that
must be my identity," she explained, "I can either accept it or somehow define
myself against [it, because] . . . my art will indeed come through what it
means to be a woman. And, what it means to be a woman, unfortunately, is a
political definition, is a personal definition, and it ties me to my body and to

what society has told me is my fate, whether I choose to see it this way or not."

A writer, Naylor continued, uses what "has been your living reality, consciously or unconsciously, and you articulate through that reality." Naylor said, philosophically, that she doesn't "think this is a bad thing because male writers . . . had a certain identity that they had to live with, and they [have] articulate[d] through" that identity. The point is, "We get marvelous perspectives of the world, and now, at least, [we are] getting somewhat of a forum for the women's view." What is important is that "we used to look at women's writings, or at any writing that had not been involved in the traditional—i.e., white, upper middle-class, male canon—and we would look for [the influence of memory or identity]." But these influences "exist in everyone—they exist in James and in Faulkner and in Hawthorne and in Irving and in Mailer." It is only "when the politics of 'Is this included in the canon? Is this American literature? Is this literature, period?' " occurs that we "begin to say, 'Well, how are women doing it?' My argument," Naylor said, "is that all artists do 'it'—'it' being articulating through our concepts of self." The concept of self "depends on where you are placed within a society because of gender, because of race, because of class, and I think that's fine because great literatures come out of that."

That concept of self is closely related to women's perception of space, and we talked about the ways in which the physical and psychological spaces in *The Women of Brewster Place*, for instance, seemed to grow smaller and more confining as the novel progressed. In each case, it seems to me, the seven women on Brewster Place move from larger, more viable spaces to more limited ones. (The novel ends when the Black women on Brewster Place revolt against their environment and, with the help of their neighbors, tear down the walls of the dead-end street on which they are trapped.)

But Naylor said that closed spaces emanate from "a whole web of circumstances." A woman's sense of space grows out of "the society in which you are born, and the way in which you are socialized to move through that society," and that movement, or the lack of it "determines who you are, how you see the big *you* when you look into a mirror." That is why space was used "intentionally in *Linden Hills*. [It] was to be a metaphor for that middle-class woman's married existence [as] she was shoved into that basement." Naylor said she "saw women having been shoved, historically," and that this woman does "uncover our history, and she does it the way that women have made history, and that is in a confined place. . . . She is able to break out and to claim herself" after her husband locks her in the basement for giving birth to a light-skinned child. "Not the way I, Gloria Naylor the feminist, would have liked her to claim herself. But she did at least say, 'Yes, this is me, I can affirm myself, and I can celebrate me,' if you call that a celebration." Celebration, she said, "is not quite the right word, but yes, she claimed herself and the repercussions were whatever they were."

Space and memory also play a part in *Mama Day*, a novel about Miranda (Mama) Day, a descendant of Sapphira Wade, a slave, who is the matriarch of Willow Springs, a small sea island off the coasts of South Carolina and Georgia. The novel is "history concretized. My parents are from the south, from rural Mississippi, but what impressed me when I went down to Charleston [to do research was that] you walk around a city that has been contained architecturally and therefore you get a time warp. . . . I grew up around southerners and I know how provincial they are (and there's that old joke that southerners are still living through the Civil War)," but they "do indeed hold onto tradition, and all of that came together for me. . . . I said, 'My God, I'm walking on history, I'm talking to history, there is no separation in their minds often between one hundred years ago and yesterday.' " Willow Springs "was a living thing in their minds, and Mama Day was just sort of the most recent reincarnation, in a sense." Mama Day is an enchantress, but she is very much an earth-mother figure to her niece, Cocoa, a New Yorker; this novel is one more in a long list of books about mother-daughter combinations. I asked Naylor why this issue persistently recurs. Naylor said that in "finding out what it means to be a woman, you either accept or reject" what the mother represents. A mother's influence is "so strong, sometimes acknowledged, sometimes unacknowledged," that the mother-daughter conflict is "going to show up in books written by women. I don't see how it cannot. . . . I used to teach women fifteen to twenty years my junior, and the [issue is] still there. These women are going to go on and do things I never dreamed were possible for a female to do, and they are still struggling with what it means . . . to be a woman."

That gender-linked identity struggle is part of a larger struggle that is often linked to race. In Naylor's case, her identity as a Black woman "came at Brooklyn College, which was the place that formed me . . . I was twenty-five years old when I began college. I had gone off, hit the road . . . lived down south for a while, [been] a sort of street preacher . . . and at twenty-five

I wanted structure because I had had the freedom, and I realized that I had no marketable skills." Brooklyn College "made me conscious of what it meant to be me—and me in all of my richness and specificity" because it was where "I first ran into feminists. I had never thought about who I was—I had other identities: I was Roosevelt and Alberta's daughter, and then I was a Christian, and then I was a switchboard operator; but I never knew, really and truly, what it meant to be a Black woman. I did know what it meant to be Black." By the time she reached Yale for the M.A., she was thirty-one and had already written one novel, so she "went for security because I thought, 'Well, I cannot make a living out of being a writer.' I think that was a very wise thing to think because the odds were definitely against me. So I said, 'Fine, since I love books, I'll go and get my master's in Afro-American studies' because I wanted now to really deepen my knowledge about what had been awakened in me at Brooklyn. I'll do that," she thought, "and then I'll go on and get my doctorate in American studies. I'll get one of those high-class union cards, which is tenure, and I won't have to worry. What I was not prepared for was that the side [of me] that had started to grow while I was working on *Brewster Place*, the need to write, would really be that strong, and there was a clash. . . . I did not think I could do both [graduate work and writing] with the same amount of energy. . . . I found it difficult to always be thinking about how you take apart [a novel] and then having to shut all that out to just let the process evolve. Just the logistics of it! The work involved was tremendous. I'm one of those type-A personalities who like to do things well, and to do things well I read about 1,500 pages a week for those seminars. So . . . it was the clash between what I wanted to do with my [literary] output and what they required of me to be an academic. And that's why I left after I got the master's. I was ready to leave after the first semester and come back to New York and go back to the switchboard because I had written *Brewster Place* while I was working on the switchboard and it paid well, the hours were flexible, and I had started *Linden Hills* the summer before I went up to New Haven. But I was able to work out a deal (after my first year) with the department, where if I just did the course work, did the papers, my thesis could be . . . *Linden Hills*, and that freed me up. After that I decided to leave academia alone and to just try my wings as a writer." She supported herself through "teaching and fellowships."

Naylor said that at thirty-nine she now understands many of the ways in which she was formed by her childhood and "why my parents did what they did. They were trying to protect us from pain, and they took us up to

Queens . . . to put us into a good school system. They never talked much
about the racial problems that were going on in America, and I grew up in
the sixties, mind you. I would hear it at school and see it on television, but we
never got that sort of talk in our home: 'You should have pride in yourself
because you're Black, you should have pride in yourself because you're you,
and never let anyone put limits on you.' You were taught to treat people as
people and that sort of thing, which is all right, all very nice and good and
well, but you grow up terribly innocent and eventually you are going to get
hurt. So it is a matter of trying to ward off the moment when that would
happen." Naylor spoke of her "niece and nephew who do understand the
political ramifications of what it means to be who they are in America, so
they are getting their pain and the disappointments and the frustration
early. . . . They are talked to about why certain things happen, why people say
certain things to them." I asked Naylor if she thought racial consciousness
and pride brought with it an unhealthy separation of the races, but she said,
"They have to go to school with children of other cultures, their stepmother
is a woman of Italian-American [ancestry], the doctor who saved my
nephew's life and has been his only surgeon since he was twenty months old
is a Jewish man, so they have all their ambivalences," but "ultimately what we
learn in this society is that there must be coexistence, there has to be." Now,
she said, all people "face other cultures" on television and in magazines. "What
they do when they filter that information is something else again, but they are
aware of what this country is."

Gloria Naylor is now one of the six members of a committee that chooses
the books offered by the Book-of-the-Month Club. That job requires her to
have a sense of what literature has been and what it is now. I asked her, perhaps naively, whether a writer without the big agent or the powerful publisher had any chance of having her book chosen by the Book-of-the-Month
Club. She seemed genuinely to believe that "it depends totally on the composition of the jury" and the choices depend on "the individuals and the chemistry of that particular panel." Naylor expects them to be "open and fair
people who take their commitment seriously, and to look for . . . the best
books that we have read." The problem here is "what is best to begin with."
I was particularly interested in whether a woman without a powerful agent
or a contract from a New York publisher had any chance of being noticed.
Naylor replied, "Will you be disregarded matter of factly? Not today. Maybe
once when they had all men on those panels, it's possible that it could have

happened. Now, even some men who sit on these panels are sensitive enough to know that they may *not* know. Often a woman's voice will have *more* input because they want to do what's right and they are aware of their ignorance. But the bottom line is, good literature is good literature. I think that the people who make up these panels now are sensitive to gender, to race, to class, and to region. Region, believe it or not, is extremely important. I have heard that one time there was an eastern 'mafia' and if you were not an eastern writer, forget it. Now they will bring in panelists from the West or from the South to sit on these juries." I asked her if unknown writers had much chance of having manuscripts accepted by important publishers, and she said, "Publishers are out there looking for good writing. . . . The whole thing is what constitutes good."

Her most profound advice to writers is to "totally forget [about prizes] and to write their hearts out." They should write "with as much integrity as they can—to the story they want to tell, to the characters who entrust them with those stories. Try to use the language as beautifully as they can. When that's done [and here Naylor reminded me that "God said, after the seventh day, 'It is good' "], the writers will then be able to say 'It is good' [and] that is enough!" Naylor said that after she completed *The Women of Brewster Place*, she said to herself, "I did this!" She thought that "nothing would ever replace this feeling, and nothing has."

Naylor now plans to adopt two children. "I don't like the fact that I can live, totally gratifying myself, and live quite well, on all levels. My work nurtures me. My work gave me my sanity; it really did. But it cannot be enough. I think it is a matter of looking at the scope of my life and wondering how I can become a fuller human being."

There is much to be learned from Gloria Naylor. She is an extraordinarily talented writer, a woman of conscience and vigor who understands the writer's commitment to her work and to herself. She said, with passion in her voice, that when she writes, "I want to be good, and *each time* I want to be good."

"If I could have created myself," said Naylor, "what would I come here as? I would come here just the way I came by happenstance; I truly would. Because I celebrate myself. I see so many strengths in being a Black woman, so many strengths in being from a working-class family with a rural southern background, *so many negatives too*, for all of those things! But it gives me *Me*."

Gloria Naylor

Donna Perry / 1991

From *Backtalk: Women Writers Speak Out*, 217–44. Copyright © 1993 by Donna Perry. Reprinted by permission of Rutgers University Press.

When I met Gloria Naylor in December 1991, she was busy with several projects—adapting her recently completed novel, *Bailey's Cafe* (Harcourt Brace Jovanovich, 1992), for the stage; producing a film version of her earlier novel *Mama Day* (Ticknor and Fields, 1988); and raising her teenage nephew, Roger, who lives with her. However, sitting in the living room of her apartment in Manhattan's Washington Heights, her back to the Hudson River view, she seemed amazingly unharried. This daughter of former sharecroppers, who traveled the United States as a missionary, worked her way through college, and wrote four novels in just over ten years, knows all about juggling conflicting demands, I soon realized. And she knows that a writer must write, no matter what the distractions.

Naylor learned about ignoring distractions when her first novel—*The Women of Brewster Place* (Viking, 1982), written while she was a student at Brooklyn College—earned her international attention and the American Book Award for first fiction in 1983. Seven interconnected stories of strong women whose support for one another enables them to survive despite crushing poverty and personal tragedy, the novel established Naylor as a powerful new voice in fiction. Readers found the book's celebration of women's friendships convincing, and its depiction of violence and homophobia, including the rape of a character who is lesbian, chillingly believable. In her acceptance speech at the award ceremony, Naylor noted that the novel was only the beginning of a career that, she hoped, would be "as long and consistently excellent" as that of Alice Walker, who received the fiction award for *The Color Purple* (Harcourt Brace Jovanovich, 1982) that same year. She was determined to avoid the fate of so many novelists who never live up to the promise of that celebrated first book.

She needn't have worried. *Linden Hills* (Ticknor and Fields, 1985), Naylor's second, very different novel, confirmed her reputation. Using Dante's Inferno as a model for her hero Willie's journey into a black middle-class community,

Naylor exposes the hollowness of the American dream of success. She again explores the connections between women in a second plot: Willa, the abused wife of the novel's demonic antagonist, finds her own identity in the pictures, domestic objects, and diaries of her husband's female ancestors.

Love, tragedy, self-sacrifice, and the enduring strength of women remain as themes in Naylor's most recent novels: *Mama Day* and *Bailey's Cafe*. In the former, George and Cocoa, doomed lovers, learn the meaning and power of love from Cocoa's great-aunt, Mama Day, medicine woman and healer. In *Bailey's Cafe*, inspired by the improvisational quality of jazz, Naylor explores the painful lives of several women who end up living at Eve's Place, a brothel, and frequenting Bailey's a kind of last-chance café located "between the edge of the world and infinite possibility."

Since her days as a student at Brooklyn College, Naylor envisioned these four novels as forming the foundation on which she would build her career. The groundwork completed, she shows no signs of letting up, with plans for a play, a movie, and another novel. During our time together Naylor explained that she has made a conscious decision to make writing her first priority, that she considers herself a "filter" for stories that haunt her, that she hopes to have something to say to readers of the twenty-first century. With her determination, she certainly will.

Question: You describe yourself as a New Yorker, Gloria, but I know that you have deep Southern roots.
Answer: I was raised in New York, but I was conceived in Robinsonville, Mississippi. My parents were from sharecropper families, and they were young—nineteen and twenty-one—when they married. They left the South when my mom was eight months pregnant because she did not want to raise her children in Mississippi. They grew up in the Depression South and came North a month before I was born in January of 1950. So I am, technically, a native New Yorker. But even though people change their locations, they don't change who they are overnight. I'm the first of the three girls who came of that marriage, and we were raised in a very Southern home, with our foods and our language and a certain code of behavior. The way we were disciplined came from the South.

Q: So you got hit if you misbehaved?
A: They weren't always hitting us—we were not abused—but you knew you were the child and they were the adults. Southern children grow up to be

quite respectful of their parents and other people, older people. My parents are now very well off, but in the 1940s they were poor, and living in the deep South was like being in another country.

Q: Did they move North to give their children more opportunity?
A: Exactly. My mother couldn't use the public library in segregated Mississippi, and there were no schools for blacks in Tunica County beyond the ninth grade. So there was no access to books and no decent education if you were poor people. And she wanted those things for her children. She wanted music lessons—basically, what had been promised to every American, promises that were not forthcoming if you were a poor black in the South. My parents knew they would be poor people, working-class people, for most of their lives, and they weren't naive about what it meant to move North. It did not mean, in their minds, an end to discrimination. They encountered that full blast here. But it did mean that, at least as far as tax-supported facilities were concerned, their children would have equal access like any other taxpayer's child.

Q: When you won the National Book Award for *The Women of Brewster Place*, your first novel, you said that you accepted the award for your mother.
A: That's right.

Q: What is she like?
A: She's very much a part of my life—I just talked with her this morning. She was a very quiet woman and a little bit shy when I was growing up. My mother didn't have a lot of friends. She devoted herself to her family. My maternal grandmother, who died in 1977, and my mother's sisters and brothers ended up here [in New York] ultimately, so my mother was always very close to them. She was always very sensitive to our needs. People say to me that perhaps we were too sheltered as children—from my father's end for other reasons, because we were girls—but she was a woman of the fifties.

I think I kept writing as a child because I had my mother as a model. She always encouraged us to dream. Whatever you wanted to do, she would just be behind you. And she never made me feel odd. I was an odd child; I was extremely introverted, very quiet. And she would allow that because she was also an introvert; we were kindred spirits. She'd let me read a poem or a story to her sometimes, and she would encourage me to write. I think I kept going through her.

Q: So many women I've spoken with have credited their mothers with keeping their creative spark alive.
A: Yeah, these women who let you be a little different, as long as you weren't doing anything that was harmful to other people or to yourself.

My father worried much more than my mother did, as I said, I guess because he didn't get the sons that he thought he wanted. With three girls, he just wanted us to go out and be girls—be feminine and that sort of thing. My being so quiet and my scribbling away all the time and staying in my room so much bothered him, I think, more than her. My dad is not shy at all. Put him in a room of people and he works the room, but not my mother.

Q: Women's support for one another is a central theme in all your books—from the community of women in *Brewster Place* to Willa discovering the Nedeed women in *Linden Hills* to the sisters, Miranda and Abigail, in *Mama Day.* You must see a real power in women's love and support for one another.
A: I do, beyond a doubt. Historically, women have only had each other. It is only very recently that they have been given any exposure outside the home or even the ability to work outside the home and to live and make a living. Maybe because my mother had six sisters and two brothers, I saw this support of women for one another all my life. And my grandmother was like the matriarch there. I saw what women would do for each other. In my own life, when there's a problem of any nature, I turn to a woman. Your female friends are the ones you have the longest history with, for the most part, because they understand; they understand. The bonding of females will always come up in my work.

Q: Is there any of your mother in all these women you've created?
A: I'm sure there must be. I'm positive that if I ever had the inclination or the time to take them apart I would find things that would surprise me. Maybe she's there in a mother that worried excessively—Kiswana Brown's mother [in *Brewster Place*], for example. The kind of mother who would come visit you and check out your apartment.

Q: Does she ever give you suggestions for your books?
A: No, never. She definitely reads them, though.

Q: In doing research for this interview, I discovered that you spent a number of years as a Jehovah's Witness. Would you talk about that?

A: I did become a Jehovah's Witness after high school, basically out of disillusionment. Martin Luther King had been assassinated in my senior year, and I lived through the Vietnam War for all of my high school years. I had the mindset of a lot of people in that generation that there was nothing good that this system could offer me. So joining a fundamentalist group allowed me to preach about the coming of a theocratic government that would just tear everything up from the roots and build anew. I devoted seven years of my life to believing and preaching about the coming of that theocracy, the coming of a decent living for human beings. I saw no need to invest time and effort in a system that I believed was going to be destroyed and that I felt should be destroyed.

Q: Why did you eventually stop preaching?

A: Seeing that the theocracy had not arrived and that things were not really getting any better. I was twenty-five years old with a high school education and no marketable skills because I had been on a college track in high school. If I had been on a vocational track, I could have gone on to be a secretary or a printmaker or something. But liberal arts! What in the heck do you do with that at twenty-five? Not too much. So that's when I decided that I would try to make a difference inside of the system, as opposed to hoping that the whole thing would just somehow go away.

Q: That's when you went to Brooklyn College?

A: I went to Medgar Evers [College in Brooklyn] first for about a year and a half because initially I thought I would be a nursing student. That was a quick, two-year program. It was practical, and it pays well. But I found that I wasn't interested in medicine and in learning about digestion and all that stuff; I was spending more time with my English classes. That really had been my first love: books. And liberal arts. So that's when I transferred to Brooklyn College as an English major.

Q: When did you start writing?

A: I've written all my life. I started writing poems when I was seven, then I moved into *Twilight Zone*–type short stories. There were other popular shows at that time called *The Outer Limits* and *One Step Beyond.* I liked that kind of thing. When I was twelve, my mother gave me a diary, and I would write in that and then ultimately in notebooks and journals. What I do today is just a continuation of what I did then—putting feelings on paper, sorting out things.

Q: What got you to the point where you decided you'd try to publish your writing?
A: Well, I had been publishing in our high school literary magazine, the Andrew Jackson High School *Star,* and at Brooklyn College I would enter poetry contests and place maybe second or third. I really decided to venture out because of a creative writing course I took at Brooklyn College with [poet] Joan Larkin. Joan is a wonderful woman. She told us, "Well, grow up and join the real world. Send your things out and start learning what it's like to be rejected." And she also said, "Remember that when you write these query letters you always pretend that more is going on. Really build it up. Be assertive."

Q: So you would pretend this story was part of a larger piece?
A: Exactly. Don't say, "Please publish me." So I sent out a story to *Essence* magazine, and I told them in the query letter that this was a part of a larger collection. And the people wrote me back and said, "Well, this is wonderful; let's see the other stories" [she laughs]. I didn't have any other stories. I was doing a classroom assignment. So I hurried up and wrote another one.

In the back of my mind I did have a collection that I wanted to do, but I just hadn't done it. So after I wrote them this second story, that's when the editor said she'd like to have lunch with me and find out who I was. That was kind of heady and thrilling for an undergraduate—to sit with a real magazine editor. I've had many, many lunches since then, but the first is always thrilling. So those stories that became *Brewster Place* were written at Brooklyn College over the course of my last two years there.

Q: Which was your first story?
A: The one that dealt with Lucielia Louise Turner, the woman who had aborted one child and lost her baby girl when the infant stuck the fork into the electric outlet. Then Ciel's rocked back to health by Mattie. That story was written in a creative writing course. It began with the ending, the woman healing the other one by rocking her. I wrote that as a catharsis for myself, to get myself over a moment of pain. I projected my imagination out by thinking, Now, who could be feeling this kind of pain? It's not my story, not my specifics, but I tried to imagine what could hurt this badly. I had written this scene earlier and put it

away. Later, for the class, I took it out and re-created a beginning leading up to what I call "the rocking scene." So that's what they published.

Q: A lot of the women I've interviewed have talked about the fact that, when they started writing, no one had told their stories—I'm thinking particularly of Maxine Hong Kingston and Paula Gunn Allen. These women are a decade older than you, but was the situation different when you started writing?
A: Well, your standard high school English curriculum, even in the mid-to-late sixties, was basically classes in nineteenth-century male classics. That's what I cut my literary teeth on. If you go through these book-shelves, those books are still here. I learned about language and how to discriminate in my reading through the English classics. I was not taught any book by or about black Americans.

Q: So they weren't teaching black writers even in the sixties?
A: Not as a group, no. When I was in a senior dramatics course in high school, we did *A Raisin in the Sun* [1959]. I had very progressive Jewish teachers at Andrew Jackson. But somehow it never connected with me that Lorraine Hansberry was a black writer because, in our integrated school, whoever auditioned the best, that's the part that they took in the play. These teachers never said there was a whole body of work, this whole literary tradition of black writing in this country, no. It just wasn't taught. I did not find out about black writers until I hit Joan Larkin's class at Brooklyn College. Ultimately I took courses in the Africana studies department and discovered there was this whole discipline there. That's why, when I went to Yale for my master's degree, I majored in Afro-American studies—because I wanted to learn more.

Brewster Place really got written as a result of my discovering these writers. I realized all that I had been missing and the pain that I had gone through all those years in those journals and with the poetry and the stories, thinking that somehow I was freakish for doing this because, after all, black women didn't write books. How could I presume to do so? So it was liberating to find out not only that they had been writing, but also that they had been writing as well as they had. It was incredible when I discovered the kind of gorgeous language you get in writers like Toni Morrison and Alice Walker and Paule Marshall. That was when Ntozake Shange was extremely popular, too. It was quite something.

Q: When it was published in 1982, *Brewster Place* created a literary sensation. How did you deal with that?

A: Well, writing *Brewster Place* did for me what those journals did when I was a painfully shy, very troubled teenager. It got my life in order. Because I was now older, I had a messier life, okay? *Brewster Place* was one of the first things in my life that I ever finished. One of the very first things.

I was living in an eighty-eight-dollar-a-month apartment in Flatbush [in Brooklyn], taking the bus straight down Flatbush Avenue to the school on Flatbush and Nostrand. I will never forget the feeling when I had finished it. It was saying so many things that no one had ever said about me. It pulled me out of a year of horrendous depression, a time when I had had so many failures on many, many levels. Not with school or any of that, but in my personal life. It kept me sane. It was an affirmation of what I could do, my God-given gift. Nothing can surpass that, you see.

The writing did something for me that kept me going because I can be suicidal. That's why, in my work, I'm always looking at ways that people do these odd forms of suicide. My art saved me once again from that. So, you see, then there was nothing that the world could do to top it.

Q: So the writing itself was more important than the success.

A: Exactly. It was the fact that I did it as well as I possibly could. And since that point I have always striven for this internal sense of excellence. With this last novel, *Bailey's Cafe*, I have done the quartet that I had dreamed about [*The Women of Brewster Place, Linden Hills, Mama Day, Bailey's Cafe*]. As I look back, I wasn't keeping stock of time or anything, but this is 1991, and I finished *Brewster Place* in 1981, and now I have finished the quartet. This was to lay the basis or the foundation—I saw it like this little square foundation—for a career I was going to build. So I now believe that I will have the kind of career I want.

People have approved and sometimes disapproved of things I've done, and it hasn't mattered. Not in any great sense. We're human beings, so when you applaud me I am pleased; when you don't like me, I'm a little bit troubled. But it's never, ever central to what keeps me going. What does is that moment when I completed that manuscript and it was done well.

Q: How do you know when it's done well?

A: It just feels right. Nine times out of ten, I know that I hit whatever mark it was I was aiming for. I said what I wanted to say in the way I wanted to say it.

I didn't get sloppy and lazy and tired. As I went on in my career, I knew that often readers and editors would accept things that you knew you could do better. So sometimes, one time out of ten, you don't keep pushing for what you know could be "perfect" with that moment or that sentence. You say, "The heck with it" [she laughs]. But when I had hit the mark, when I believe that those characters are living for me and that the stories I have been entrusted with have been told to the best of my ability, then I think it's well done.

Q: You say "stories I've been entrusted with," which sounds like what writers like Leslie Marmon Silko, Paula Gunn Allen, and Maxine Hong Kingston say about their responsibility as writers. Do you see yourself almost as an intermediary?
A: I do. I've often said I'm like a filter for these stories.

Q: So you feel like you're telling a story that's been given to you in some way?
A: The process starts with images that I am haunted by and I will not know why. People will say, "How do you know that's to be a story or a book?" I say, "Because it won't go away." You just feel a disease until somehow you go into the whole, complicated, painful process of writing and find out what the image means. And often, when I've gotten into a work, I have been sorry to find out that that's what the image meant. But the dye is cast.

Q: Would you give me an example of one of those images?
A: I noticed after *Linden Hills*—I think of *Linden Hills* because I had stayed so long down in the basement with this dead child—that the children die in my books. I didn't even give it a second thought in the first book because it was in [only] one story, but with *Linden Hills* I began to wonder. Willa and her dead baby were half my life for three or four years or so.

One image that kept haunting me from even before I finished *Linden Hills*: a woman carrying a dead male baby through the woods to this old woman. I didn't know why she was carrying the dead baby, but I knew her name because the old lady said, "Go home, Bernice. Go home and bury your child." So years later I'm into *Mama Day* and the story is unfolding, and I realize what that image meant: Bernice, who went through all that trauma trying so hard to have this child, is going to lose him. And I said, "Oh, my God, he's going to die!"

Of course, I'm not a robot. I could have not had him die. But it never occurred to me because I was entrusted with that. I don't know why all of this happened. I don't worry about it. But I like to think that I did it justice.

Believe me, I didn't have much heart for it. When that baby died, I said, "Well, I really feel sorry for you, Bernice, but this was one of the early, early images."

Q: Do these images come in dreams?
A: Not sleeping dreams. They're just waking, psychic revelations that will happen.

Q: *The Women of Brewster Place* aroused strong feelings. Like Alice Walker and Ntozake Shange, who created equally powerful women characters, you've been criticized, particularly by black male critics, for what they call your "negative portraits" of black men.
A: From the very beginning.

Q: How do you respond to this?
A: I tell them to look at the title. If that is not self-evident enough, I will say to them, "I was not writing about men. This is a book about women."

But I've always thought that was not what they were really asking. I always thought what was under that was not, "Why haven't you written about men here?" but, "How dare you write about women? How dare you highlight or celebrate this which we have despised to the point that we weren't even taught that they existed or that they did such wonderful things for this country and the arts? How dare you be so militant about this happening?" But I never apologize, never ever. I will say, "I was not telling your story; I was telling your mother's story. Now please tell me what is wrong with that?" And then they'll say, "Well, but the men are all so negative." And then I have to explain to them the nature of creating art.

It goes back to Aristotle, who said there were three themes in all of drama: man against man, man against fate, man against God. Therefore, there has to be some obstacle that your protagonists climb over. You have to introduce conflict. Now, because of the kind of women they were—who weren't going out to General Motors or to Congress; they were staying on that street, on Brewster Place, in their homes—nine times out of ten my conflict bearers were the men in their lives.

Q: But the women have other conflicts going on, too.
A: Exactly. People tend to forget there are two stories in that collection where my conflict-bearers—the heavies, if you will—were not men. With Kiswana

Brown the conflict came with her mother and that whole clash of social classes. With my two lesbians the conflict-bearer was the stronger lover and the whole theme of power and struggle in relationships. But that criticism is all about the kind of society we live in. The underlying presumption has always been, until lately, that anything male should be central, and if males are not central, then it's jarring. And if something jars us we tend to think, Well, what is wrong with it? as opposed to, What is wrong with the way we have been programmed to think? I tended to explain all this in the beginning, but now I don't even bother. I'm getting old and cranky, and this country needs to grow up.

Q: Pat Barker said that she didn't feel that she had to create a sympathetic rapist just to appease critics, that sexism is a fact of life. Aren't you just saying that there's sexism among black males?
A: There's sexism in this country. Probably everywhere on the planet, but it's been concretized and institutionalized in the Western Hemisphere. And how on earth can someone escape that because of the color of their skin? How can women escape it? I also got that question [about the "negative portrait" of men] from women. I think it's important that that said. I've done a lot of rethinking about the socialization of females when, half of the time, a woman will stand up and say to me, "Where are the men in this book?"

Q: So women themselves are socialized to value men's stories over their own?
A: Sometimes, yes.

Q: Your books show that women are subjected to violence every day.
A: Violence is everywhere. We're all going to die, and some people inflict violence on themselves, by suicide and that sort of thing. A woman is raped in this country every six minutes. I don't think my books are any more violent than the reality of living, one, as a human being in this country, and, secondly, as a woman in this country. You know, every six pages I don't have a rape. What I do find in my work, and that comes back to how I cut my literary teeth on the English classics, is that I enjoy dramatic situations: the clash with nature and unfolding of human passion.

Q: I know that you've been in contact with Pat Barker, whose novel *Union Street* was made into a movie. What did you think of the made-for-television

movie of *The Women of Brewster Place* that Oprah Winfrey put together a few
years ago?
A: I saw it when it first came on television. I wasn't involved with that translation. I was not displeased with it, though. I felt that they kept the spirit of
the book.

I did not see the movie made from *Union Street* [*Stanley and Iris*], but I read
about it. At first I was so excited because Pat's a friend of mine, but I guess they
just took two of the characters and went off and did something else. I'm now
into producing because we are turning *Mama Day* into a feature film.

Q: How will this project differ from the adaptation of *The Women of Brewster
Place*?
A: I've started my own production company. It's funny because, from a producer's standpoint—and I'm now wearing that hat—you prefer not to have
the writer involved, because some writers don't understand that film is a different art form. From the writer's point of view, if you care at all about the initial thrust of your work or its message, then it's best that you leave it as a book.

Q: Other writers have talked about the risks involved in making movies out
of their books.
A: You can protect yourself if you have a contract where you have a final
script approval, but you don't usually get that. If you don't much care, if you
trust your producers, you hope they carry the spirit of your work to this new
art form.

Q: Were you pleased with the casting of *Brewster Place*?
A: What they [the producers] did do, which I thought was extremely sensitive, is that they tried to match the skin colors of the characters. Kiswana is
light. With Lorraine and Theresa: Lorraine is fair; Theresa is dark. Skin color
matters in the book, and they kept this in mind with the casting [of Robin
Givens, Lonette McKee, and Paula Kelly].

Q: You talked earlier about the influence of the classics. Where did the idea
for modeling *Linden Hills* on Dante's *Inferno* come from?
A: When I was a sophomore or junior at Brooklyn College I took a survey
course called Great Works of Western Literature. When we began to go
through the first part of *The Divine Comedy*, *The Inferno*, I said, "Yeah, that's

how this neighborhood could be structured." I have some early doodles from class when I had sort of concentric blocks, but that didn't work. I ultimately devised the idea that there be circular drives that would go down the side of this hill; so I guess the structure came from there.

Q: And you stayed with Dante throughout the book, didn't you?
A: That was conscious. I was with Dante until Second Crescent Drive. Winston and David, my two homosexual men, were Paolo and Francesca. Everything up to that point was transliteration with Dante: the green on First Circle Drive, Mrs. Tilson, and all that. I left Dante there because I had my own schema. Then I picked him up again at Sixth Crescent Drive when they enter into the lower regions of Hell for the Tower of Dis and are stopped by the demons. And then Beatrice sent the archangel Michael, I think, to cast out the demons. I went to Dante for that. I picked him up again at the very end with his image of Satan being a three-headed creature frozen in this lake and crying; that's what Willa and Nedeed and the baby are, coming out of that house, one body fused together with three heads. But that was perhaps my most formulated work. Some critics would say too formulated [she laughs].

Q: In this novel you made a conscious shift to the middle class.
A: Right. That's why Kiswana Brown is at Brewster Place: She's from Linden Hills. I knew that the next one would deal with the black middle class.

Q: You level quite a scathing indictment of the black middle class in the novel. Other than in Toni Morrison's *Song of Solomon* [Knopf, 1977], has there been another critical portrait?
A: I don't think so. During the Harlem Renaissance, in works by Zora Neale Hurston and Langston Hughes and Arna Bontemps and Claude McKay, the political thrust had been to emphasize the color and the vitality of the "black folk." But before that, black writers had basically dealt with the middle class—writers like Nella Larsen and Jessie Fauset—but in a very different way.

Q: Larsen and Fauset weren't commenting on the dangers of becoming middle class.
A: No, their books were taking black people and really just putting a black face on white middle-class jargon. Basically that's what it was about: the

bourgeois [she laughs]. In *Linden Hills* I'm looking at the whole phenomenon of hyphenated Americans and their ascension of the [so-called] ladder
of success.

Q: You certainly suggest that such a rise has too great a cost.
A: It was about the stripping away of your soul when you move toward some
sort of assimilation. That happens to any hyphenated American when you
lose that which makes you uniquely you. We've finally, thank God, stopped
that nonsense in this country where the ideal concept was a melting pot. Now
we're saying, "No, it's a patchwork quilt, not a melting pot." Because—guess
what?—nobody was melting. It wasn't happening. The novel was a sort of
cautionary tale about that, about attempting to do the impossible—especially
for the black American, because we're also a racist society. When you take on
the accoutrements of success, you go to all the right schools, you wear the
right clothes, you have all the right vocabulary, and you go as high as you
possibly can, you still get that ceiling. You come up close to the fact that you
are always going to be the Other; you will always be black.

Q: You split the perspective in the book between Willa and Willie, so there's a
double vision and dual center of interest.
A: For male and female.

Q: In terms of the story, there's more stress on Willie, the poet, though.
A: You think so? You don't think they got equal time?

Q: I think Willa is powerful when she's there, but there's just more space given
to Willie; and I wondered if that was an attempt to try something different
from *Brewster Place*. Why the decision to focus on a twenty-year-old man?
A: I wasn't at all thinking of *Brewster Place*. I basically followed *The Inferno*,
in that Dante sets out with Virgil on this trip.

Q: The character of Willa, Luther Nedeed's abused wife, down in the basement with her dead child is haunting. What's happening to her down there?
A: She's going from being a woman who was so faceless that she did not even
have a name—no one in the upstairs and throughout her neighborhood
knew who she was—to someone who reclaims herself.

Q: She's always described as "Luther's wife."

A: Exactly. But down in the basement of his house she is moving through history, reclaiming the other Nedeed women. That opening section of the book is sort of a chronicle of the Nedeed men and how they made history by procreating themselves. The wives were not important; they were shadows. Then, boom, you get to the last generation, and this woman produces this fair child, this white child. All those women had been light skinned. Willa produces something that, in Luther's mind, is illegitimate because it is evidence of the fact that there had been women in this historical dynasty.

Q: Even though the Nedeed men tried to efface them.

A: Exactly. When Willa is thrown into the basement with the evidence of the bastardization of their [the Nedeed women's] history, what she uncovers is the history of the women. She uncovers the way that women left their mark. No, they did not build huge real-estate empires and deal with political figures, like the men had done. But they left photographs; they left scribblings in their Bibles; they left recipe books. That's what she is doing. I'm taking her through the ways in which women have made history; and, through doing that, she ultimately claims for herself an identity. It was not the identity that I would have wanted her to claim; but now we get into the autonomy of your characters and when they start to live. What that woman finally came to, after that whole travail, was that she was a good wife and a good mother and that she could go upstairs and claim that identity. That is not what I thought Willa would do, but Willa was Willa.

Q: I wanted her to come out of that basement with an ax and kill Luther.

A: Yes, exactly. Me, Gloria Naylor, I would have said, "Go up there and kick his butt!" But no, it did not happen. You can't impose your will. Like we started talking about before—the writer is a kind of filter.

Q: It makes sense, though: She's reclaiming the house, too.

A: Yeah. I knew the Nedeed dynasty would be destroyed, but I was confused about how on earth that was going to happen if Willa wanted to go back up and be a housewife again. But then it all worked out. Personally, I think it worked out more powerfully than it would have if she had gone up there to try to push past him and get out the door and knock over the [Christmas] tree. There's something so eerie about the fact that this woman is cleaning up.

And her husband misunderstands. He thinks she's going to run out and tell the world [that she's been abused], and she's just getting some dust in a corner.

Q: Laurel Dumont, the character who kills herself when she has all these material things, is a tragic character. What is the significance of her death?
A: Laurel was very hard for me; it was very depressing. I don't know when I knew she had to die, but I knew she was going to be in that swimming pool. It was sad for me to know that with all that she had accomplished and how hard she worked she had indeed lost her sense of self.

Q: I kept hoping she would get back in contact with life, especially when her grandmother stayed with her.
A: It's too late by then. She was an empty shell. And because I think I identified more with Laurel than I did with Willa it was kind of hard for that to happen to her, for her not to be able to just pull it all together. But that can happen when you live so much in what you do [that] you forget about where home is.

Q: The idea of home brings us to *Mama Day,* where going home is a central theme. You said you're making a movie out of that?
A: Yeah. We have a second draft of the script, which I did, and now we're raising the money to do it. I would like to see a black love story in the mainstream film media.

Q: Other than Spike Lee?
A: Yeah. Spike did a good job, but we need another vision. I think more black women filmmakers need to be out there getting exposure. No one has said the things that *Mama Day* will say on screen yet about black community, about connections between family, between the black male and the black female. They haven't. And also about a part of this country few people know about: the Sea Islands. It's going to be a beautiful film for as much as I can control. That's one thing about making this transition: Film is a collaborative medium. So even though I know how hard I strive for excellence and how hard I work at something, you have to pray that you get the kind of people around you with the same mind-set that ultimately will be reflected in the product.

Q: Do you have a director you like?
A: A few people I would like, sure. Jenny Wilkes—she's a British director and also a friend of mine who has been really helpful to date; Rhonda Haynes,

who did *Children of a Lesser God* and *The Doctor*, with William Hurt; Joan Micklin Silver, who directed *Crossing Delancey.*

Q: You feel like you want a woman to do it?
A: For this book, sure. You need someone to handle this powerful older female and that relationship between the young man and the young woman sensitively. This is going to be a film that's going to pluck at the heartstrings of women, the same way the novel did, for various reasons and for women of all different ages.

Q: Where did you get the inspiration for *Mama Day*?
A: Maybe by listening to my parents talk about the South. Like I said, they're from a little rural hamlet where there were women who would work as lay healers. For the book I went back to interview one, a friend of my grandmother's who's still alive and who lives in Robinsonville.

Q: Was that Eva McKinney, the woman you interviewed for *People* magazine [11 March 1985]? She sounds extraordinary.
A: Oh, you read that. Yeah, I didn't see her when I was growing up, but she had come to New York once or twice to visit. I went back and actually put her on tape. Those are precious, precious tapes about the different herbs and things that she would use and about her life. Those women also dabbled in magic and the supernatural. So I grew up listening to my parents who would have these friendly give-and-takes about whether or not those things actually happened or not. I think the structure of *Mama Day* got born with letting you choose what side you're going to come down on. The story's told from three perspectives. You have to choose which to accept.

Q: What about the role of magic in that book? Are we supposed to believe the extraordinary events—like Ruby's spell—or not?
A: Well, you get a hint with the opening of the novel. I moved from the most universally accepted forms of magic into those things that we're more resistant to accepting. You're first made aware, in the first twelve or thirteen pages, that the act of reading, itself, is an act of magic. That's when the narrator turns to you and says, "Ain't nobody really talking to you." And yet, by that point you've laughed with these people; you've been moved by certain parts of their stories. And they say, "We're not real." And then the reader should go, "Oh, of course: the magic of the imagination!"

I move from that into having a man like George and a woman like Cocoa, who are totally incongruent, meet and fall in love. We all have in our circles two individuals who we don't know what in the hell they're doing with each other. We do accept that; we accept the magic of love. And then, from there, I take you to the last frontier. That's where there are indeed women who can work with nature and create things which have not been documented by institutions of science, but which still do happen. So the book's an exploration of magic.

Q: Cocoa and George *are* an unlikely pair. Why is she so afraid of George's love?
A: Because that's just the late-twentieth-century female dilemma. Living in an urban area like New York, women don't trust. There are so many bad experiences with men that if the right one came along, forget it, there's no way you could see it. She's a *Cosmo* girl.

Q: I found George one of your most interesting and sympathetic characters to date.
A: I really like George; I think he's a wonderful character. I cried for a whole year, knowing that George was going to die. I think that was a very believable love story [between George and Cocoa]. I'm very proud of that.

Q: He's really transformed when he goes into that chicken coop to save Cocoa's life.
A: His heart gives out on him. He was meant to find nothing there, to just bring back his hand to *Mama Day*. That was it. And she would have just held his hand, which would have been a physical holding as well as a metaphysical holding of hands with him and with all the other parts of Cocoa's history, the other men whose hands had worked and who had broken hearts. But George could not see that because he was a practical individual. There was nothing there for him. But he still saves Cocoa through the powers of his own will.

Q: That idea harkens back to the scene with Mattie and the rocking in *The Women of Brewster Place.*
A: The laying on of hands and the healing, yeah, a little bit, except there were two different dynamics going on. In that earlier scene, it had to be a woman doing the healing and the rocking. That was important to connect them up with other women throughout history who had their children torn away

because of the machinations of the patriarchy—that's the reference to the concentration camps and the sacrifices [mentioned in that chapter]. A man could not have done that. In *Mama Day* George's laying on of hands was possible.

Q: What is wrong with Cocoa? Is she really under a curse?
A: She's had a spell cast on her, and she's being eaten alive by those worms.

Q: So that was black magic?
A: Some people will say this; some people will agree with George, who never accepted that and who has a third of the book. He just sees her getting sick and dying; he does not accept that she has worms or that Ruby cast a spell. He has just determined that he will not let her die. I have seen people healed by the power of the human will, through love. So it didn't matter to George. Me, because I'm a believer in these things, I think she was being eaten up by worms [she laughs]. It doesn't really matter—just like my parents and their different perspectives. It's not the point whether Miss Eva dabbled in other things or not; it's whether or not you believe.

Q: Did Shakespeare's *The Tempest* influence *Mama Day*?
A: Consciously, no, although people have commented on that.

Q: The name Miranda, the idea of the island . . .
A: Exactly. Shakespeare has appeared in each of my works. For *Mama Day*, he was consciously there because of *King Lear* and with the star-crossed lovers idea from *Romeo and Juliet*. I read *The Tempest* ages ago, so even though I wasn't consciously doing that, who knows?

Q: Your novels have a certain theatricality.
A: I knew before I began *Bailey's Cafe* that ultimately it would be presented for the stage. It was the first time that material came to me three-dimensionally. But the first step was to get it down, literally. And that's what I did in August [1991]. Now I'll have a reading at the Roger Furman Theater [in Manhattan] in March [1992]. It will be open to the public and to backers. So the theater is something I'm going to go into. I find I like the headiness of it all because your gratification is more immediate with a play or a film than with a novel.

Q: Would you talk a bit about *Bailey's Cafe*?
A: *Bailey's Cafe* is going to come out in the late summer of 1992. It deals with female sexuality, and I've structured it around a set of jazz, in that you have the maestro come in—that's Bailey—and then you have a section called "The Vamp." This, as you know, in music is the introduction of all of the notes and all of the things that will be used. That happens; then there's a section called "The Jam," which has these different songs, if you will. There are no quotation marks in the book—this is all supposed to be in music. You'll have the different songs that will occur, all involving most of the women and also a man, Miss Maple, who happens to come to this café.

Q: Where is this café located?
A: On the margin between the edge of the world and infinite possibility. It is there as a situation that embodies a turning point in each of these characters' lives. The next step they take is that step into the café, where they will either redeem themselves enough to go back out into the world or they will exit the café into oblivion.

On that street is a brownstone owned by a woman named Eve. Women come to that café looking for a place to stay, and Bailey directs them to Eve's. It's about their stories and the story of this man, Miss Maple, who meets Eve there at the café and becomes her housekeeper.

If you take the stories apart, you are going to look at some aspect of human sexuality. I didn't go in doing that, but that's what came out: the ways in which women are victimized and men are victimized by our definitions of what it means to be a woman or a man. And, since there are these series of voices, it works out that, while it's not going to be easy to adapt to the stage, it's very adaptable for stage. It's my job to figure out how to do it.

Q: The themes of female sexuality and definitions of female and male have been in your work from the beginning.
A: Very much so, yes.

Q: In *The Women of Brewster Place*, you talk about C. C., the man who rapes Lorraine, as someone defined by his sexual prowess. And the lesbian couple, Lorraine and Theresa, are threatening to the young men because they are outside their control.
A: They're outside, exactly. Outside of C. C.'s definition of what they should be.

Q: Will the play have music?

A: Yes. I'm excited about it. I'm also going to write a play about the whole Anita Hill–Clarence Thomas case. I didn't know what I was going to do with all of that at first because I had to digest what it meant. After I got over the horror of discovering that we are leaderless in this country, I said, "Okay, it won't explode tomorrow, but, God knows, this society won't last if this is how we're being led."

Q: Will your play parallel the televised hearings?

A: What happened will be one issue in the play. There will be one woman on a stage and three male voices that you don't see. You don't see these men, these inquisitors, these judges. There will be voices and this one woman.

Q: How do you see your responsibility to your community, and does it have anything to do with your writing?

A: I believe that as I, Gloria Naylor, the real Gloria Naylor, the real person, live, I definitely do have responsibility to my family and my community. Personally. I do not feel that I have that responsibility in my work. I know that these stories do filter through who I am and what I think and believe. They ultimately reflect my sensibilities.

But I don't agree with this thing black middle-class people have about positive images. They say, "Well, you should try to portray positive images. This system is only too willing to show blacks negatively, and these negative images have destroyed many of our children. When we [these middle-class speakers] were growing up, it was just that we were invisible. But now, when we become visible, it is usually as someone doing something destructive." The idea these people have is that your writing should reflect the other side, what's good.

Q: You disagree.

A: Absolutely. I don't see that, I don't believe that. I think that my books are something separate and apart from how I live my life and try to help my community. What I write really are other people's stories and they come forth, I would hope, as complex as people are. Some of the characters are not great role models; some of them might be. But, ultimately, I think that human nature is dark; I really do. Whoever the human beings are. But that's just me. Other writers—take Eudora Welty, for example—have very different visions of human nature. That is my vision, and that vision comes through with all of my characters. But, no, I do not feel that my art should serve some political end. I can do that with my checkbook; I can do that with what I do with my private life. This is another world for me, and I don't want to tamper with it.

Q: What would constitute tampering?
A: I don't want to censor what my characters do. A case in point: I'm a feminist. And when I worked with Willie and Lester [in *Linden Hills*], they were twenty-year-old males who would sometimes say things and hold attitudes that would make me cringe. But that was them. I allowed them to live, to do what they had to do. Now, my plays might be a different story [she laughs].

Q: From your first book, you critique bourgeois, establishment values. Etta wants respectability and marriage to the preacher; he wants a good time, exposing the myth of romantic love. In *Linden Hills* you show us the evil, dark side of so-called "success." It's as if you are saying, "Respectability, middle-class life, house in the suburbs, good job, fancy car: it means nothing. It means not having a face." In *Mama Day* Cocoa and George must leave their rational, city selves back home. Is any of that turning of things on their heads going on for you when you write?
A: That's really interesting. Not consciously. I have always been a little odd. I think I started out saying that, being a little different. I remember how I believed in Santa Claus only one Christmas, just about one. I remember pretending for many Christmases. That was the case. I used to enjoy catching adults in lies because it gave me a sense of power and control as a child. I liked seeing behind the evident façade of things, or to pretend I believed in Santa Claus when I didn't—that kind of deal. You see me turning things on their head. I think you're probably right. It's not what I set out to do, but there's probably a reason for that.

Q: I was reading about Charles Johnson, who won the National Book Award for *Middle Passage* [Macmillan, 1990]. He said that he doesn't have any politics, and the author of the article quoted you as saying that "every writer has an ideology."
A: Every single writer from Homer. Every piece of art has an ideology. There's an ideology in my books. The problem has been that, depending upon whose ideology it was, it was considered a universal truth versus something that was

a particular truth. The great writers, the ones who last, are those who take the specific and somehow manage—a little bit through their talent but a lot through this intangible mixture of life being sparked into it—to make the specific spring into the universal. We all start from who we are and what we know—Henry James, et al.

My quibble is with people who construct literary canons and who construct book reviews and how we determine what is real writing and what is fringe writing. Those are all political decisions. I don't back away from saying that I'm a political being. I think, as a black American, I'm more political than others. My existence in this country was an act of politics. My continuing existence is such. And that's why I think it's more difficult.

Q: How different is the world for African American writers today than it was twenty or thirty years ago? Is it easier for them to publish now?
A: No, I really don't think so. The double standard still applies today. It's up to the whims of the publishing houses. The old myths are still there, that black consumers don't buy books. Publishers will often publish and tout that which makes them the most comfortable—e.g., why all this attention given to Shelby Steele's *The Content of Our Character* [St. Martin's, 1990] versus this book I'm reading now, *The Alchemy of Race and Rights* [Harvard University Press, 1990] by Patricia Williams? Because, right now, we're in a terribly conservative climate in this country.

We have not solved the problem of living together in America so, therefore, some kind of bomb that will come from a Shelby Steele takes the emphasis away from the fact that it's the society that's guilty. Not that his is a simplistic work; it's not that. But because he shifts the emphasis onto the people who are suffering, he makes the white system feel a little bit more comfortable. They can say, "I'm tired of being guilty; I'm tired of being uncomfortable. And these problems haven't been solved because it's *them!*" I think that controlling the means of production is the only way that a whole myriad of voices will be heard equally.

Q: What do you think about mainstream publishers, in terms of encouraging hyphenated Americans or anyone out of the white middle-class mainstream? Several of the writers I've interviewed have criticized the marketing of books.
A: Marketing is the word, if you're talking about commercial publishers. If you're talking about the health of American literature, I don't think that's a

problem because of the university presses and the smaller presses which are saving our literature for the twenty-first century. But commercial publishing, no. It is by accident that art will be perpetuated with commercial publishing. That's not their function [she laughs]. Their function is to make money. At one time publishing may have been about art, but that's no longer true.

Q: Literary criticism is certainly changing—it's exciting to see so much diversity in the field.
A: You are getting critics from diverse backgrounds looking at the literature that has really composed America: Asian critics, Native American critics, Latino critics, and, of course, a plethora of black critics. That is heartening. I think what should be done is a reexamination of the canon, but that's just academic politics. We know how the canon came about, but these critics are re-creating it. For the literature of hyphenated Americans to be discussed seriously is a big move from before, when it was just ignored.

Q: But your stories were published by Viking.
A: That's why I tell you I was extremely fortunate. It just happened.

Q: If, as you say, the publishers want books that will make their readers comfortable, yours certainly don't. You don't make anyone comfortable.
A: Donna, I would be writing this way if a publisher sold two copies or two hundred thousand copies, because I'm not writing for the publisher; I'm not writing for the reader. Bottom line: I'm not. It has just worked out that the publisher sells more than two copies. But if they didn't I would still be doing this stuff. When I wrote it initially, I wrote it for me, to resolve things within me. It has just been luck that people cared.

Q: Do you read all these articles and books and doctoral dissertations that deal with your works?
A: No, of course not. I think criticism is an art form in itself. They are creating, in that space between the text and themselves, an understanding of the text. Criticism works with its own rules, its own languages. You couldn't go through Yale and not be a structuralist; and I keep up because some of that stuff is just so wonderful. It's marvelous what writers like Northrop Frye and Jonathan Culler do with language. But it has not a damn thing to do

with the book. I don't believe it does. I will just read Derrida for Derrida's brilliance.

At Yale I realized that I was suspicious of playing the part of the critic because there was a part of me that was afraid of tampering with the creative process. At that time I thought it was like Hawthorne's "The Birthmark," where the scientist destroys everything, trying to find out the secret of his wife's beauty. I had already written a book before graduate school, so I knew that the creative process is mysterious.

Q: So you don't read criticism because, basically, you don't think it unlocks any mysteries?
A: Not really, no. But there's another reason I haven't read this stuff that's been written about my work: For years and years I was afraid of getting caught up in the one-book phenomenon, the whole idea of seeing yourself as a kind of celebrity, where you don't do your work. I didn't want that to happen. Now maybe I could read that, now that I'm more secure.

I only read an analysis of my books if I like the young person; otherwise, I give them [the critics] the space and respect to do their own thing.

Q: Do you get upset by reviews?
A: I read them when they come out, but I don't get upset. Some people do, but I don't. I would get upset if someone said that I couldn't write. For each book I have gotten bad reviews. I have only gotten one dishonest review and that was a political review of *Mama Day*. The reviews are there for the purpose of selling the book. My goals for my career go well beyond that. I want my art to be meaty enough or to say something important enough that there are doctoral dissertations on it, that it can be taken apart. I want to have something relevant to say in the twenty-first century.

Q: Is it hard to stay focused when there is so much hype in the publishing industry? Book tours, promotional interviews, that sort of thing.
A: Exactly. But you have to understand that this kind of celebrity is cyclical. I know this: that real artists create, no matter what. And since I am so diseased when I am not working, I make conscious choices throughout my life to put my work first. Some people might call them sacrifices. So be it. Right now I'm very fortunate because I don't have to do as much physical labor as I had to to support myself earlier. It's better-paid subsidiary work; I call it my secular work.

Q: What kind of job is it?
A: I'm on the executive board of the Book of the Month Club. You read manuscripts and meet once a month. But for years I taught—the whole idea
being that this work was a way to support the writing.

Q: Did you like teaching?
A: I enjoyed it tremendously. The only hope I have is for young people. If you
can get to them, not with an ideology, but just with the idea that they need to
examine assumptions, there's hope. I would try to teach my young people to
question everything. When I taught creative writing, I could never teach as a
sort of guru because I know that's not how the process is. The only thing that
separates me from them is that maybe I wrote a sentence that day and they
didn't.

Q: So it doesn't get easier?
A: I thought it would get easier. I thought it would reach a point where you
would pay your dues and it wouldn't be so demanding. But, no. You are into
new territory each time [she laughs].

Q: You just raised an important point about writing that is rarely discussed: the
need for money. Valerie Miner talked about how poorly paid writers are. Did
you have to begin teaching right after graduate school to support yourself?
A: I received a fellowship to George Washington University—the Jenny
McKean Moore Fellowship—after I got my master's degree. When I realized
I was not going to stay on at graduate school and get my doctorate, that
meant I would no longer be supported by scholarships. I knew I would have
to hustle. So I said, "Okay, I will get a teaching job." I moved to Washington
to teach at GW. They gave you time to write, so I finished *Linden Hills* there.

Q: So you had a light teaching load?
A: I taught an undergraduate literature course of my own design twice a
week and, one night a week, I taught a creative writing workshop for the
community. So I had basically three days. I gave those three to the university,
and I finished my novel. That was the idea—they made the teaching schedule
light because they brought writers in to give them a chance to write. After
that, it was another teaching gig, and I got a fellowship one year at NEA
[National Endowment for the Arts]. They gave me like twenty thousand

dollars and a whole year that I could work. And that's how I hustled for seven years. And after about the seventh year, it reached a point where I could make a living from just being me.

Q: So now you live on your writing, supplemented by these other jobs?
A: Yeah, but my needs are simple. Bottom line: I need a warm and quiet place to work. I have been more fortunate than some; I really have.

Q: What's your writing process like? Do you let people read your material as you are writing?
A: No. I have done public readings if I am not sure. I enjoy hearing the response to the stuff and seeing if I achieved what I wanted—like if people think it's funny.

Q: So you basically show the book only when it's done?
A: Usually. My editor, Cork Smith, is my friend. I've had only one editor since I started publishing, although we've changed [publishing] houses. I'll read something to him. With this last book, I read a section to another longtime friend. But I don't read for them to tell me if it's good. I've lived alone for so many years that I'm used to being independent in that regard.

Q: Do your books pretty much appear as you wrote them?
A: Exactly. All of my books.

Q: Your editor doesn't change much?
A: Not except editing for clarity. For example, in *Bailey's Cafe*, my editor suggested that I cut some of the opening chapter because he thought it was too long. Another longtime friend said the same thing, so I will, indeed, cut it. But I won't put up with ideological changes—no kind of nonsense like that. It's always on me, anyway. As my editor says, "Your name's on this, not mine. Not Mr. Viking or Mr. Harcourt or whatever—your name. So you have to be pleased with what's here."

Q: Do you revise a lot?
A: When I'm working on it; not after it's finished. I think what I did on *Bailey's Cafe* is the most I've ever done with a book after I called it finished. The way you see my books is basically the way they came out, except for copy editing.

Q: I see a computer in your work area. Is that how you compose?
A: The last two books; the first two were written longhand, and then I would type them. Now everything—letters, too—gets done on the computer.

Q: Do you ever have to do background research for your books?
A: Sometimes. When I found out that George was a football fan, I had to do catch-up with the character and learn about football. In the case of Laurel Dumont, I had this image of her listening to classical music with her grandmother. The grandmother says, "That's nice, but he ain't made peace with his pain, child." I was at Yale then, and there was this guy in my program who used to play the classical flute. I went to Gordon and told him my problem; I wasn't going to go through the whole canon of classical music. He said, "I think you should try to listen to Mahler because he will make you want to cut your throat on a rainy day" [she laughs]. He was right. It turns out that's what Laurel was listening to.

Also, from time to time, I have to go to a certain place. For *Mama Day* I went to the Sea Islands, a chain of islands running from the coast of North Carolina down to the tip of Florida. And for that book I also read loads of books on magic.

Q: What do you like to read when you have a chance?
A: Well, look around me. There are a whole slew of *Nation* magazines over there. I'm reading Jamaica Kincaid's new book now [*Lucy*]. I love Anne Rice dearly; now I'm into her erotica, but *Interview with the Vampire* [Knopf, 1976] hooked me on her. She did what Stephen King did for me. She made me believe that if I went down to New Orleans I would run into one of these jokers. It was all so plausible. Jo Humphreys and Robb Dew are friends; I read my friends. Louise Erdrich and Michael Dorris. I've already read all of the black women writers—I studied them in graduate school. Now it's nice because it's hard to keep up—you get galleys and books from new people all the time. I thought that John Irving's *Cider House Rules* [Morrow, 1985] was a really well done, sensitive book, although I couldn't get into him much before. That's who I read, but I don't have much time for it. I'll be reading more plays now. One year—maybe my fiftieth year—I'll take off and go back and reread all of the classics. I would like to do that, return to where I began.

Q: You've gone from being on your own to having responsibility for a teenager. What is it like having your nephew live with you?

A: Well, it's been different, incredibly different. Roger, my youngest sister's son, came when he was fifteen. I have learned things about myself since he moved in. I didn't think I could write with another human being sharing a space with me because I'd never had to, but I wrote *Bailey's Cafe* while he was here. Also, having to literally rear him, I could be sitting here typing and turn and give a lecture, and then go back to work. I found that was possible. Sometimes I'd be so into it [the writing] that I'd forget he was here, and then, aha! It would be a shock. It has shown me that you do what you have to do. It's taught me a lot about the human spirit and how it can expand and how it can love.

Q: Has his presence affected your writing habits?

A: I used to write in the early morning, but because I was mothering and working on the production company, I wrote *Bailey's Cafe* at night, from about 10:00 to 2:00. After Roger would come in from school and we'd have our time together, he and I would settle in to do our work.

Q: Are you a different writer now than you were when you started?

A: Oh, sure. I'm more confident than when I first started. I do think I'm more conscious of language. *Brewster Place* was just a gush of raw emotion. I haven't looked at the book in ages, but just thinking back, I know that I would just decapitate a writing student of mine if he did some of the things I did in that book [she laughs]—that's too hokey; that would never work.

Q: It's a good thing you aren't your own student.

A: It's a good thing I'm not. The book just drove itself in its own passion and innocence. But there is that point in your work where you don't control it and you don't want to because that determines whether or not life gets breathed into something. That's the magic.

A Conversation with Gloria Naylor

Matteo Bellinelli / 1992

Matteo Bellinelli: Gloria Naylor's writing, like her life, reflects the breadth of African American experience. Her family's roots lie in the rural South, but she grew up in the urban North and now sits among America's literary establishment.

Gloria Naylor: I was literally conceived in Robinsonville, Mississippi, and my parents made it to New York just a month before I was born. I was born in January 1950. They married in 1949 down in Mississippi, but the reason for that trip while my mother was pregnant was because my father was keeping a promise he had made to her. She made just about any boy who wanted to marry her agree that if they had children, those children would not be born in Mississippi.

MB: And so instead of being born in Mississippi, Naylor grew up in New York.

GN: We are talking about Harlem. That's where most blacks who migrated from the South usually ended up if they were headed to New York. My mother was drawn toward the North and the hope that her children could have things she could not have. I received my love of books, I believe, from my mother's genes. She was an avid reader as a child. But she was from a sharecropping family. There were nine of them—nine children plus my grandmother and grandfather. So to purchase books was a total luxury. It was just impossible. As a black, my mother was not permitted into the public library. She had to go to extreme means in order to get her reading material. She would work because at that time one had to work for the entire family. The family worked together for five days out of the week, and then on Sundays, they went to church. Because we're talking about the South now. This is Baptist and Methodist country. But then Saturdays would be your time to do laundry or go to town. My mother took her spare Saturdays and she would go hire herself out in someone's field. That was her way of earning pocket money, and she got a sum total of fifty cents a day for doing that. At the end of the month, she had two dollars. And she could take that two dollars and send away to book clubs. And that's how she was able to feed her love for reading.

During the 1930s and 1940s in Mississippi, my mother saw the North as the place where her children would have perhaps greater opportunity. What my folks found when they came to New York was that indeed there was as much segregation as in the South, but that division was more subtle. For example, they ended up living in Harlem, because that was where you lived if you were black. Even if you had the money, there were very few places in New York that would have accepted you. But what was important to her was that the schools were open and, above all, you could use the library. For her, access to public schools and facilities was the key to advancement.

MB: Gloria Naylor is one of the few African American authors whose work is set in the present. Her narrative project is to explore the diversity of African American life. Each of her books depicts a different class setting. *The Women of Brewster Place* is set on a crumbling street in the inner city. *Linden Hills* is located in a black middle-class suburb. And *Mama Day* takes place on an enchanted island in the South. Naylor herself moved as a young child from Harlem to the more middle-class burrow of Queens.

GN: That's when I first began to understand that I was different, and that difference meant something negative. And that's when my folks really began to work with us. I am the oldest of three girls. She ingrained in us that you don't look to the outside world for your validity. You must look within. You can do whatever you want. You set your own limits for yourself. I think those words of advice were wise. My parents had to instill that knowledge in us because we could not look to the outside world. The message the outside world conveyed was that as a black female you are nothing.

Well, as a female, you are to go and find a husband as quickly as you can, and he should be the best that he can be. Because that's your fate: to have children and be a housewife. And as a black female, you were literally to be invisible. So it was necessity that made them say that if they were to have healthy young women on our hands, we must turn them inward.

In my own life, it feels more comfortable to know who you are. I am a product of the 1960s. While the sixties brought a lot of upheaval, women were still indoctrinated into a traditional role. Yes, after the sixties people then said that you should go on to college. But you went on to college and *then* you got the man and had the kids. You could, in a sense, have it all. But part of the all included fulfilling your function as a woman. So to have that traditional role redefined was liberating.

It was important to understand why I had wanted certain things society suggested that all women should attain. I've always just wanted to be free, and I didn't know what that freedom meant. In those years it meant that you stay single. It also came to me that I wanted a way to express myself, which I found through the written word. But that's what feminism did. It gave me new definitions of self.

MB: In 1968, the year Olympian Tommy Smith and Lee Evans made their black power protest, Gloria Naylor graduated from high school. By the time she entered graduate school at Yale, the books of Zora Neale Hurston, Toni Morrison, and other black women were being taught for the first time in newly formed women's and black studies programs. Gloria Naylor thus became one of the first black women writers to have formally studied her literary predecessors.

GN: I have often said that I am a cultural nationalist. That means that I am very militant about who and what I am as an African American. I believe that you should celebrate voraciously that which is yours. That begins with something as basic as our skin color or our peculiar past. And we do have in this country as black Americans a peculiar past that sprung from that peculiar institution of slavery. We ought to celebrate the stress that happened there. We need to celebrate the survival of culture among the underclass. What is the most vibrant form of music right now in America? That music is rap. Where does it come from? You know that same group I had been talking about earlier who are lost in the ghetto? Even from there you see the art will spring. So that's what cultural nationalism means to me. To be militant about your being.

MB: Naylor's books argue that race remains the decisive factor rendering most black Americans powerless, even as she focuses on the black female experience and the afflictions of poverty.

GN: From the beginning of the twentieth century, Black activists were always split between self-determination or assimilation. The classic example of this phenomenon would be Dr. Martin Luther King, Jr., and Malcolm X. One of them said that the point is to move into this society and the other said no, we must hold and build our own. What we have found out since the Civil Rights Movement is that integration does not work. New York City, for instance, is a classic example of that. What we need to do is some backtracking and begin from the cradle to build self-esteem in our young. We should go grassroots in the community and build up our own organizations. So I believe assimilation can be extremely dangerous. It does not exist in fact in America and to buy into it is to hinder your own psychological health.

African Americans exist in two worlds. You never have full acceptance when you are on your own soil. But as soon as you leave America and, like many of us have done, go to Europe or even India, you are looked upon as being very much an American. And you realize how American you are when you are away. But when you come home and go through customs you become aware of being black.

So it is a schizophrenic existence that many blacks in America are forced to live. I think we have discovered that we are accepted only in ourselves.

MB: Naylor's own father Roosevelt worked as a New York subway motorman while her mother Alberta was a telephone operator.

GN: My parents believed that if they could educate their children, give them a sense of self worth, give them an American ideal with a work ethic, then those children escape a life on the streets. And indeed many of us did escape that kind of life. But what you see now are poor people without hope.

MB: Naylor's belief that racism makes the road to success a dead-end street for most African Americans is reflected in her book *The Women of Brewster Place*. Brewster Place is a dead-end street literally walled off from the rest of the city and now awaiting the bulldozer.

GN: As Africans, we have brought to this country our music, our form of dance, our love of colors, and our language. America has borrowed all of these things. We have taken from the European aspect of America our language, our clothes, for the most part, and our system of thought. When you converge together that which came from Africa, which would be our music, our words, and our values of family and combine that with the western train of thought, you have the essence of a dualistic reality. Our concept of time comes from the West. Our concept of family comes from Africa. One aspect of our African past has to do with the notion that a family need not be nuclear to be a family. A family can include the grandparents and the elders and adopted cousins. When you meld those two world views together, you get a sense of what the black reality in America is all about.

MB: While Naylor's books reflect the diversity of black life, they always return to a common African American experience—a uniqueness given expression in the black language.

GN: It is the language of bewilderment, it is the language of disenfranchisement, it is a language of incredible beauty and depth. This language stems from Africa, bringing with it the song and dance, and the color and the speech patterns. It brings the beauty of our skin. I think that is what African American language is. It is the language of the blues. It is saying, yes, I am here, but I hurt because I'm not quite here. But I'm here and look at how vibrant and strong I am. It is that kind of bitter-sweetness that is African American language, if there is that kind of thing. Or black language may be the appropriation of the English language applied to our own specific experience. Our experience is unique and calls for a creative use of the language. Langston Hughes comes to mind immediately when he plays with the blues and jazz in his poetry. Ntozake Shange has done the same thing in her writing. Writers such as these play with the English language and fracture it up in order to try to have the language represent what our reality is.

MB: Naylor's third novel *Mama Day* draws upon William Shakespeare's *The Tempest*. It is set on a magical island and its heroine is named Miranda. Naylor has said that for her, writing is gender-less and race-less. It is about dredging things up from the depths.

GN: To me, writing is a way to keep sane. I felt the same way when I was thirteen, and it is the same way now.

MB: Naylor has currently turned her hand to screenplays. She's writing one now on *Mama Day*.

GN: I'm trying to write into people's eyes with cinema. That's what I want to do. I believe I touch their hearts with my words. Now I want to touch their hearts with my images.

MB: Whether in screenplays or novels, Gloria Naylor updates the conundrum W. E. B. Du Bois articulates concerning two irreconcilable selves—one black, one American. Writing for her is a way of defining identity.

GN: For the black American, whatever the class, that person is writing about the need to struggle. We will never be fully assimilated into this society. An African American will never be considered as being equal to whites in this society, so the vibrant literature will always be there. The literature will continue to manifest the undertone of the blues because the racial duality remains a persistent fact.

An Interview with Gloria Naylor

Angels Carabi / 1992

From *Belles Lettres* 7 (Spring 1992), 36–42. Copyright © Gloria Naylor. Reprinted with permission.

Angels Carabi: Toni Morrison told me that, despite growing up in the North, she was surrounded by grandmothers and aunts who told stories from the South. Did you have a similar experience?

Gloria Naylor: Exactly. I listened to stories about fishing and going to the woods and picking berries. I heard about working in the cotton fields and about the different characters who were in Robinsonville: the women who worked with roots and herbs, the guy who ran the church, and the man who was always drunk. A whole microcosm lived in that little hamlet. I heard all the stories because I was a quiet, shy child. I was the kid in the corner listening when they were talking about themselves. And I loved books with a passion. So my mother was rewarded by her oldest daughter in that way.

AC: I understand that your parents migrated from Robinsonville, Mississippi.

GN: That's right. My mother was eight months pregnant when she moved with my father from Robinsonville, Mississippi, to New York City. She decided to travel before I was born because she was adamant that none of her children would be born in the South. My mother loved to read, but she was a sharecropper and could not afford to buy books. The only access to reading material was through the public libraries, the entrance to which was forbidden to black people. To buy books, my mother had to work extra hours. On Saturdays, she would go to somebody else's field and do day labor. At the end of the month, she would have about two dollars that she would send to book clubs. She was not formally educated, because schools went up to the ninth grade and children were supposed to start working afterwards. Yet she was a visionary in that she wanted her children to grow up in a place where they could read, if nothing else. She was so determined to accomplish her goal that she would say to anybody who wanted to date her: "If you marry me and if we have children, I want to leave the South." So when she married my father, she reminded him of the promise he had made to her. My grandparents

111

had left the South a few months before, so it was easier for her to make that move; she was going where her mother had already gone. They came to New York in 1949, and I was born in 1950.

AC: How did that move affect the family?

GN: Often people ask me why I write about the South when I was born in New York. The reason is that although we lived in the North, I grew up in a Southern home in terms of things like food and language. The grownups no longer worked in the fields but did other kinds of manual labor. My father started working in the garment district and ended as a frame finisher. My mother did not work full-time until the 1960s, when my sisters and I were older. We lived first in Harlem, then in a housing project in the Bronx, then in Harlem again. My parents wanted a nicer place for the children to grow up in and good schools to go to, but they discovered that, because of our race, we encountered the same racism that existed in the South, although it was subtler. Job discrimination was not openly stated in the newspapers, but the truth was, even educated black people could not find jobs or live in certain high-rent neighborhoods. Middle-class black people fought against this policy because they were educated and they had money, but even in the North they were not able to obtain what they wanted. My folks' priority was to work extremely hard so their children would not have to go through what they had experienced in the South.

AC: You received your Master's degree at Yale. Was it common among women of your generation to pursue higher education?

GN: I went to college later than most of the young women who were with me in high school. They entered professions; many soon married. But it was different for me because I was a bit of a rebel and chose to try my wings in the world. At that time I did not believe in higher education. But the women growing up in the 1960s had opportunities open up because of the Civil Rights and Women's Movements. The black woman profited from both, to a certain degree. Those who were talented and determined could push their way through; the assumption was no longer that your only goal in life was to find a "good man" and take care of the home and the kids. Women were being shown that they had a choice. Before the 1960s, it was very different. Whether or not you were talented, you encountered a stone wall in front of you.

AC: How did the 1960s affect you?

GN: I learned how deep the problems were, not only in my country but in the world. The problems were so widespread and serious that they could not be solved just by marching and demonstrating. I believed that I had to rebuild our whole social system. I could see no reason for the war in Southeast Asia, a war against children and women. . . . I could not understand the assassination of Martin Luther King. He was a man who had been preaching peace and love and brotherhood. I thought that there was not much hope. So I went around with a religious group for seven years that preached about a coming theocracy. I became a sort of radical, praying for the earth to be cleansed. In 1975 this new theocracy still had not taken place and I was twenty-five with no remarkable skills. I decided to go back to school.

AC: In the last two decades, there has been a explosion of Afro-American writers, especially of women writers. Can you talk about this phenomenon?

GN: The phenomenon lies in the exposure of what has been taking place for quite a while in this country. A writer will write, a singer will sing, a dancer will dance. You do that because you have no choice: Either you create or you explode. Black women have been writing in this country for over a hundred years. They began to proliferate in the 1930s during the Harlem Renaissance, and they continued to grow and build on each other. In the mid 1960s and the 1970s, we began to question definitions of "American literature." Is it just simply the literature produced by the white-upper-middle-class male? Or are there other realities that constitute this country? Look at those "invisible" black females making all that noise. Do they have a history? Do they have a reality? Yes, definitely, they do. Slowly, they began to enter the institutions. I had read Faulkner, Hemingway, the Brontës, Dickens, Thackeray, Emerson, Melville, Poe, and Hawthorne, and it had been wonderful and fine. I loved that kind of literature and it taught me about language, but it did not teach me about my reality. When black Americans and women found their way into the institutions, we realized that there was another history, other meanings. We started to change our vision of American literature. Then this trend infiltrated the publishing industry. So attention is now being paid to an effort that has always been made. I don't think that more black women are writing now, but I know there's a difference in perspective.

AC: Can you talk about some of the aspects of black women's vision that you consider uniquely rich?

GN: Oh my God! What the black woman is bringing is a whole hidden part of American history, of the female experience. What is so rich about it, I think, is that the black woman brings both her history as a black person and her living reality as a female. Black women writers make drama out of the so-called "small matters" of life. Their portrayal of the irony of what it has been like to have a dual existence in this country becomes a celebration of the self, of transcendence. The black woman brings to literature the merging of two hidden realities.

AC: From the beginning of your work, you create a sense of place, a sense of community where people interact.

GN: For various reasons, I am drawn to this sense of community. What makes a writer do what he or she does derives from so many rivulets of influences. I come from a very large, close-knit, and extended family. My parents were both from families of nine children each and I grew up with about twenty cousins on my mother's side. I also come from the black working class, and in my generation, they tended to converge class in communities. Besides, family and class community is my communal history as a black American. Our survival today has depended on our nurturing each other, finding resources within ourselves. The women in Robinsonville, Mississippi, who dealt with herbs, for instance, played a crucial role in our community. They weren't just magical women. They had a definite medical purpose, because you could not depend on the outside hospitals to take care of your needs. So people grew up within a community that birthed you and laid you away when you died. Community is what I know and what I feel most comfortable with.

AC: Brewster Place, in your novel *The Women of Brewster Place,* is an urban island where only black people live. It seems to me that, by isolating the place from white people, you are more able to concentrate your attention on the black community, instead of analyzing the effects of racism on black people.

GN: That is a trend you can find when you look at black women's literature in general. Men have a need to confront the world, to flex their muscles, if you will. The female confronts what is immediately around her.

I knew that there was richness to be found within the black community. I'm not concerned with the reaction of white Americans to me. That goes back to how I was raised. At home, we were told that no one can tell you who or what you are, whether or not you have value. You must tell that to yourself. I learned to look inward, to explore the problems "we" have and discover what the realities are.

AC: To talk about "the black experience" is to engage yourself in a vast field of inquiry. It seems that you provide a variety of characters who come from different backgrounds, with different problems that illustrate individual aspects of that experience.

GN: Exactly. By exploring the lives of different women in Brewster Place, I'm attempting to create a microcosm of the black female experience in America. This is why the book is structured the way it is, with the women on different levels in those apartment buildings. Where I placed them and how they lived meant something in relationship to the wall in Brewster Place.

People tend to talk about "the black experience," lumping it all as one mass searching but there is no one thing that can stand for that experience because it is indeed so rich and so varied. This agglomeration is done for the sake of expediency and also because race is something that people don't want to think about much, so they pick one or two examples and figure that they have thought about the whole problem. It's intellectual and moral laziness.

AC: Let's look at some of the distinct characters that you create in *The Women of Brewster Place*. For instance, when Mattie Michael arrives in Brewster Place, the smell of the herbs brings her memories of the South. Maybe it is the sense of the South that encourages her to live the ideal of community. It is Mattie who holds the place together.

GN: Yes, she does do that, which is why she is the first to arrive. The South has taught her that. Her personal experience is with her son. Mattie, for me, overcame one of the most painful things a woman can overcome, the loss of child. By coming to Brewster Place she creates a new home and a new family.

I have never been a mother and I was worried about how my story would develop. I always worry when my characters come to an experience that I have never had because I want to do them justice. I know I have the power of language and I know this can be abused, so I worried about whether I could write about a mother. So I talked to several friends, one of them being Amanda, a single parent who has two children. I could tell that the boy was her heart. It's not that she loved one child more than the other, but she had that attraction for her son. I never forgot what she told me: "I think the boy is so special to you because you know that's the one man that could never leave you." This is how Mattie's story got structured. She lost her father, and Butch, her lover, but she could keep this boy. I think there's a line in the story when she realizes that her son is empty and selfish and she says something like "she got what she prayed for, a little boy who would always need her, except that now he was a grown man."

AC: What is extraordinary about Mattie is that, in spite of having all these problems, she's generous and calm—almost magic yet very human. She allows people to feel free in her presence.
GN: Like an earth mother, I guess.

AC: Your characters are dreamers.
GN: Yes, every single one. And *Brewster Place* opens with Langston Hughes's poem "A Dream Deferred." I have always been a daydreamer. I come from a family of dreamers, and I'm from a nation of people who are dreamers, the black nation. I always dreamed that I would be a writer and now I know what it takes to have dreams come true. Now I'm dreaming to be a producer, and I will become one. But I know the work that goes into it. In *Brewster Place*, each of the women has a dream of her own.

AC: However, some of their dreams are unattainable. Etta, for instance, dreams of achieving respectability by marrying the Reverend; Ciel dreams that her husband will change; Kiswana is dreaming about becoming a revolutionary and changing the social situation of the black community.
GN: I guess they all have a dream they never quite realize. The idea was just to see them trying.

AC: Let's talk about Kiswana. She's from a bourgeois family, she's a poet activist, she's a social worker, and she dreams that she will be able to help poor people. However, at the beginning of the book, you associate with Kiswana the image of a bird that is sent to fly to the center of the universe. The bird, of course, cannot fly that high.
GN: That was intentional. And later, I think that there are bird droppings on the fire escape! You know, Kiswana was doing all the bad dreaming that wasn't going to be reality. But she's brought back to base, I think, in a softer

way and, ultimately, she begins to work with what she has. And the people show that to her. They tell her that it's not for her to tell them what to do, but that she should work with them.

AC: Kiswana changes her name from Melanie to Kiswana, an African name.
GN: Often in the 1960s people turned away from what they thought was oppression. Our names were associated with a past of slavery and people began looking at Africa for a sense of worth and pride. But actually, in the cotton fields and within the slavery system, many people found strategies that kept them mentally and physically strong. The dignity of the recent past has been restored, and I believe that you take from what is really yours. We are not Africans, we are Americans of African descent. Therefore, we have to root ourselves in this country and find pride in what happened here. There can be some pride in what happened in Africa, but there's so much glorious black history here.

Kiswana had every right to change her name, but Melanie was not a bad name. Considering the type of Melanie she was named after—a women that stood her ground—she should actually be very proud of having such a name. This is what her mother is trying to tell her.

AC: How about her mother's opinions, like telling Kiswana that the best way she can help the people in Brewster Place is by going to school and occupying a position of power?
GN: I think a woman from her background could say little else. I believe, though, that there are two ways of empowering people. You can be in a position where you can influence national policy or you can work at the grassroots level. You can open a social center, or teach people how to register and vote . . . both ways are equally meaningful.

AC: Even though your characters don't always fulfill their dreams, they are able to go on living with dignity. i'm thinking of Etta finding her way through Mattie's friendship, of Kiswana going to night school and helping the people, of Ciel cleansing herself with Mattie's help, of Cora Lee taking her children to a summer school. I think that the message that these women are not lost and that they take responsibility over their lives is very important.
GN: Yes, you are indeed able each day to decide how you will live that day. You can decide whether or not your dreams die. You can see these women

doing something that I saw women do all my life. The poor women that I grew up with knew it was Monday morning because they had to get up, get the kids bathed, get themselves dressed, and go out to the laundry and work for eight hours. And then they had to pick up a chicken on their way home and stretch it for six people. Then they had to sweep up, get homework done, go to bed that night, get up in the morning, and do it all again. And each day when they would bathe their kids they would be dreaming of the day that the children would go to college and they would not have to work so hard. And there was laughter in all that. They had good times. I saw more people depressed in graduate school than in Harlem! Only the privileged people have the luxury of feeling depressed. My mother did not know such a word. She started using it when we children grew up and spoke of being depressed.

AC: I think this attitude is reflected in your work, in the sense that your characters do not play the role of victims.

GN: You cripple yourself when you think of yourself as a victim. You can be victimized yet still go on with your life. When I walk the streets of Harlem, I think about the people with whom I grew up and about the people who are there now. They are very different. There were more men in the homes then; there were two parents who care for the future of their children. There was more community. I think that what is lacking is hope. Younger and younger women are having children, and those children are having other children and they stay in a vicious circle. They see no way out.

AC: How can the writer help to improve this situation?

GN: To be honest, I think that writing, like all of the arts, is an elite occupation. When *Brewster Place* came out I said to myself, how ironic for the women whom I am celebrating and writing about, because the majority of them would not read the book. However, I think that the writer as creator provides people with resources to help with literacy. So the value in writing books lies in telling people, "Learning to read will open your imagination. You will see a way out of no way." The writer can also show the discipline it takes to do something.

AC: In *Brewster Place* you solve problems through female friendship.

GN: Women only had each other in our history. Around the kitchen table or at the laundromat, they would go to other women with their problems about

children, about the men in their lives, about their jobs. And they would share
that in places that were unimportant to the outside world, gaining strength
from each other in quiet ways. Yes, I was celebrating this in my novel.

AC: Most of the men in *Brewster Place* are portrayed as immature, and they
try to solve their problems through violence against women.

GN: When I decided who was going to be the focus of this work, I had to
introduce conflicts into the heroines' lives so they could demonstrate what
we have been talking about: How their dreams had been interfered with and
how they achieved transcendence in spite of that. Well, with women of this
social group, nine times out of ten, the conflict bearers will be male. However, I had hoped the reader would see that there are two sides in most of my
male characters; for instance, even though Mattie's father rejects her, he loves
her. But for a man like that—an old man, a hard man who is demanding
obedience—it is not possible to accept disobedience. To him love equals obedience. So, when he beats Mattie, he's beating out the disobedience. Most of
my male characters are three dimensional. Eugene, Ciel's husband, is immature and can't take pressure, but I think he is the only one.

AC: Your chapter on the two lesbian women is impressive and very moving.
The fact that the community does not help them hurts the reader. Were they
being rejected because the community was not ready to accept the presence
of two lesbians?

GN: That was exactly what it was about. They could not reach over that difference. Just like the world had put a wall in Brewster Place, they had put a
wall between themselves and Lorraine and Theresa.

AC: So when Lorraine dies, the community's reaction is to have dreams.

GN: I must correct that. People often think that she has died. She doesn't. She
just remains insane. At the end she utters the word "please," which she will be
repeating for the rest of her life.

AC: Mattie's dream at the end of the book is a dream of bonding between
women. Is it a deferred dream?

GN: This is going to depend on the reader. When she wakes up, the party is
going to take place, but the clouds are coming and you know it's going to
rain. Is this going to be a deferred dream? Well, I decided to let each reader

decide. Will they tear down the wall? Or won't they? They are not quite ready yet. It's an open ending.

AC: Let's move to your second novel, *Linden Hills*. You begin, as you did in Brewster Place, by creating a sense of place; this time, however, the neighborhood is middle class and the novel revolves around a central metaphor associated with Dante's *Inferno*.

GN: In *Linden Hills* I wanted to look at what happens to black Americans when they move up in America's society. They first lose family ties, because if you work for a big corporation, you may have grown up in Detroit but may end up living in Houston. Then there are the community ties. You can create a whole different type of community around you—mostly of a mixture of other professional, middle-class people—but you lose the ties with your spiritual or religious values. And ultimately, the strongest and most difficult ties to let go of are your ties with your ethnocentric sense of self. You forget what it means to be an African American. Black Americans with a higher social status, often have to confront issues of racism without the things that have historically supported the working class, like the family, the community, the church, or just their own sense of self.

So that's what *Linden Hills* was about on one level. I thought Dante's *Inferno* was the perfect work for symbolizing when up is down. Dante presents an image of Florentine society and then slowly moves from the lesser sins to the greater sins. So that's what I did in *Linden Hills*. When you move down the hill, you encounter a greater alienation, the repercussions of upward mobility.

AC: Let's move now to your latest book *Mama Day*. Again, from the beginning there's a sense of place very carefully described.

GN: Yes, I think this is going to be my modus operandi until I die!

AC: Willow Springs is a nonurban island, away from civilization. In *Mama Day* you fuse the world of the supernatural and the realistic world of New York City. What inspired you to write it?

GN: It goes back to the stories I listened to when I sat in the corner of the kitchen, and to the different ideas that my parents had regarding the old women who not only worked as quasitraditional doctors, but who used roots and herbs and had supernatural kinds of powers. My mother believed that there were things that happened in life that you could not question but my father was very reluctant to accept "superstition." The structure of *Mama Day* emerged from this dual interpretation. I wanted as well to look at women in history, especially at women connected to the earth who could affect behavior. Until the Middle Ages, when the so-called "witches" were persecuted, women were the primary healers who knew how to abort or how to stop conception. They showed women how to have control of their process of creation. So these wise women were chastised and burnt for stepping over those bounds.

A writer, I think, begins to exorcise demons with her work when she writes about what she fears as well as about what she dreams. I had to get rid of some demons with *Brewster Place*. I had first to confront what it meant to be to be a black woman and to celebrate it. In *Linden Hills* I had to come to terms with what it meant to change class, which is actually what I did and what my parents had been working so hard for. But when a child from a poor class enters another class, there is tension. When I got to *Mama Day*, I wanted to rest and write about what I believed. And I believe in the power of love and the power of magic—sometimes I think that they are one and the same. *Mama* is about the fact that the real basic magic is the unfolding of the human potential and that if we reach inside ourselves we can create miracles.

AC: Beautiful. You're working on another book, *Bailey's Cafe*. What is it about and where do you locate it?

GN: *Bailey's Cafe* is going to deal with the various ways women respond to sex. It exists within the jazz and blues milieu of the 1940s, among the Duke Ellingtons, the Ella Fitzgeralds. Bailey has a juke box in his café. As you walk down 125th Street towards the Hudson River you head west, and if you don't happen to pick up a few spare notes coming out that juke box, you would simply walk into the river. So you pick up those notes and you enter Bailey's Cafe. My characters are the music and each has some sort of song.

AC: In what direction is black American literature moving?

GN: I think it's moving towards reflecting a middle-class experience. The people that are now writing don't share my experience or that of Alice Walker or Toni Morrison. They may be second- or third-generation urban blacks and they speak about other aspects of life. Surreal novels and novels of the absurd are coming out that deal with how to confront America, and what it means to be young, black, professional women.

AC: When you write, do you address your writing primarily to black people?
GN: I address it to myself. I talk to myself and to my characters—and I let them speak to me. I feel that they have chosen me, for whatever reason, to convey their stories to the world. I try really hard to listen internally. I often do things with my own life to make myself a more fitting vessel to communicate their stories. I always worry if I am saying the right thing, because I have the words and they have the story, which I am recording. The best writing comes out when you just are quiet and you let happen what must happen.

A Conversation with Gloria Naylor
Virginia Fowler / 1993

From *Gloria Naylor: In Search of Sanctuary*, 143–57. Copyright © 1996 Twayne Publishers. Reprinted by permission of The Gale Group.

The following interview took place between Gloria Naylor and Virginia Fowler in Virginia Fowler's home on 6 September 1993.

Virginia Fowler: Gloria, to what extent do you see yourself as being a political writer?
Gloria Naylor: I don't. I used to call myself a cultural nationalist. People have commented that for some reason racism doesn't really exist in my work, that I seem so very centered on the black community itself. That's simply because the white world is not important to me. I know how it shapes me, how it shapes my family and my community, but it is never uppermost in my mind because self-determination is the most important thing for a community. And taking two steps backward, that is a sort of political statement. Now, had I been of age to be involved in the politics of the sixties, I would not have been an integrationist, I realize that now. I would have been a separatist, although neither of those is the answer. But sitting next to you or going to your school is not what will "better" me as a human being, or even solve my problems. The other way wouldn't have either. So I think my work probably evidences *that*. That's not political writing in the sense that I was taught political writing, you know, the protest novel. If you want to call my work political, I'm willing to live with that definition of its being political. It is just very ethnocentric. And that springs from my own politics.

VF: Do you see yourself as having some sort of prophetic role as an artist?
GN: I see myself more as a filter than I do as a prophet. I see myself—I call myself within my own head a wordsmith. I'm a storyteller, I really am.

123

VF: That's an interesting shift, then, that I guess has been made possible for you as a black writer by the people who have come before you.

GN: You have to be aware that there is even a problem before you can say to yourself, I will use another strategy at addressing the problem. The problem has to be evoked. When I was in the beginning stages of becoming a feminist, I had to first be made aware that there was a separate entity called *woman.* Period. Then, *black woman.* And then how do I place myself in that whole ideological range. If the women had not come before me to say, hey, you have a different experience, a different history than men, then I could not have even thought of being a feminist. The same thing was true of my coming into consciousness as a black American: people had to have come before to say, there is a voice here. There are things that need to be said. So I could indeed read something like "Ego Tripping" [Nikki Giovanni, 1970] and say, yes, so this is being said.

VF: I asked you whether your writing is political, and it seems to me that it does have very strong feminist impulses.

GN: Yes, it's very female-centered, has been from day one. I've been real clear about that.

VF: Female-centered and feminist? Do you see a difference?

GN: Well, now comes the inevitable question, Ginney, what is my definition of feminism? It is inevitable, because they are not one thing.

VF: There are so many feminisms.

GN: Exactly. Feminism is for me the simple belief that all human beings, regardless of gender, are equal. I believe that there is nothing that should be denied me on this planet that isn't denied any other human being. And I am not determined by an accident of my biology. Feminism to me is political, social, economic equality for all human beings. That's part one. Part two, I must as a feminist celebrate that which is female and love that which is female.

VF: It seems that in a lot of women's texts, biology becomes the determinant.

GN: Because you're writing about women, yes. You're writing about the situation as is. There is an ideal and there is reality. What I would like to believe is that you take two steps back from the work, then perhaps there is a "statement" being made about what I feel about women, although I have just told their stories. But let's face it, it's being told my way. It is.

VF: And they are your women.
GN: And they're filtered through me and everything I do, everything I ate that morning—that whole thing.

VF: Do you think you see women as victims primarily?
GN: Interesting. No. I do see them as powerless to a degree. I see them as more reactive than active. I would hope I don't see them as victims. I personally see them as capable of self-determination and perhaps not always utilizing that capability. Margaret Atwood said that people without hope do not write books. So, therefore . . . no, there's always for me at least some sort of redemption involved. When I think of *Brewster Place*, which is probably where the best argument could be made for the idea that my women are victims, even there I saw a little tiny victory in each of those lives. And to me a victim is someone who is stomped on, who stays stomped on, who believes she should have been stomped on. Victims don't fight back. There's no resistance. And I've always seen my characters—even if they're driven, like the woman in the basement in *Linden Hills*, to insanity—as somehow resisting in some way, if the resistance is only then to resort to insanity. I couldn't write otherwise, I couldn't just leave it like that. It would be too depressing. It's depressing enough.

VF: Yes, you have a lot of horrifying stories to tell about women.
GN: I think we live a lot of horrifying lives.

VF: In your work, do women have a certain moral superiority—they are not equal to men, but better?
GN: I don't know. I would have to think about that. In every book, I've always had a few women who are heavies. Who are bigots. Or just cruel. There are a couple in *Brewster Place*—that woman Sophie—who victimize, literally victimize Lorraine and Theresa. And there was Ben's wife. And those were women who were doing things to women. With *Bailey's Cafe*, if you want to talk about changes in my perspective, I will grant you this: it is quite true that in the early days of my coming into feminism, I fell into that school that thought, if we only had a chance we would do it better because we have

known what it's like to be oppressed. Slowly, with maturity, I have changed; I have seen that when women have assumed positions of power, they have not handled it better. If anything, they often have attempted to prove that they are better than men at being hard-nosed and pragmatic.

VF: They become honorary men.

GN: Yes, and that disillusioned me somewhat. And I have been further disillusioned by observing the various ways that children can be abused and by understanding that often older women are accomplices to that. *Bailey's Cafe* became the work for me where I began to see that women are probably the handmaidens of the oppression. And I think if I were critiquing that book I would see in each of those cases that it is not a man at all—they are not involved at all. It all culminates in that story with "No man has ever touched me." So at one point I did think women were morally superior. I no longer feel that.

VF: Women have certainly participated in the socialization into gender roles of their daughters, their granddaughters, the children around them.

GN: And they have often benefited, you know, from that. When I was looking at the whole concept of "whore," I realized that most women benefit from the fact that we have a delineation for "whore." And sometimes they are conscious that this is going on and they play into it, perpetuate it for their own ends. They are not unknowing accomplices.

VF: To some extent, isn't it about survival? Not only their survival but the survival of the child?

GN: But I feel this way: unless someone has a knife to your throat and your life is at stake, then it's not about survival. And I think there are payoffs, for wives, and women who regard others as whores. That's all. So I'm still a feminist, but I'm a more realistic one now—about the limitations. It's probably more akin to my whole philosophy that all human beings are equal, which means that women are just as capable of being venal as anyone else [*laughter*]. But as a matter of fact, I'm just watching the different ethnic groups in the city in which I live, and you would think that the history of one ethnic group going through oppression would somehow make them more sensitive, and it does not, because that is human nature.

VF: That's something you make so clear in the very first book, with Lorraine and Theresa and the community's response. So suffering does not necessarily give you greater sensitivity to other people who are being abused. You talked about celebrating women, and to me there's a great celebration of woman, of women, of the female, in *Mama Day*, but not so in the other novels.

GN: I don't know. *Bailey's Cafe* is another ball game. But I think in the first one, that was what I set out to do in the first one . . .

VF: . . . to celebrate them?

GN: . . . yes, to celebrate their spirit. You know, I didn't want to paint a fairy tale, but I did want to show them with a spark of hope. Remember [Langston Hughes's] *Montage of a Dream Deferred?* Well, each of the stories in *The Women of Brewster Place* is about a dream deferred in some way, which means that it gets pretty brutal. However, the women still continue to dream. You know, that's why I end the book the way I do, with the dream and then the little codicil of "Dusk," where the street is still waiting to die. You know, it wasn't to be about anything spectacular. I was trying to celebrate common lives and common love, and the way most women live. For me at that point, the philosophy was, if you do manage to survive, you have committed a victory. So that was all I was trying to do with *Brewster Place* in that regard.

VF: I'm interested in what you see as being religious impulses in your work. Does a religious vision inform your work?

GN: Because religion played such a huge part in my life in my formative years, it would be impossible, I think, for that not to be there, so if people found that there, I would not quibble with it; it does not offend me that it's there. I know there are times when I consciously will use biblical allusions, from *Brewster Place* on—that business about the rain for forty days is a biblical allusion. This last book [*Bailey's Cafe*], I did nothing but rewrite biblical women, rewrite their lives. I've used it because I think it's a part of me. I find the Bible interesting.

VF: But using the Bible, I mean . . .

GN: That's different from religion?

VF: From having a kind of . . .

GN: But that goes back to a question, I think, Ginney, of do I see myself as some sort of prophet? And I don't. I don't think that I am on a mission.

VF: Do you have a moral vision? Don't you see your fiction as very moral?
GN: Other critics have said that, too. That I ask certain questions in my work, and that they are moral questions. I'm a moral woman, I think.

VF: Do you believe that human nature is essentially corrupt?
GN: No, I believe that within human nature, side by side and intertwined, are the potential for incredible corruption and the potential for incredible heights. But I don't believe that the essential material of human nature is corruption and evil and that we always strive away from that. I don't believe that. I believe that human nature is a mixed suit, that both are there, and that it just simply depends on how you dip into it. That's what I think. I think that I am capable right now of the most degrading, the most heinous acts that have ever been perpetrated on this earth. I, Gloria Naylor, am capable of doing what Hitler did, of doing what Idi Amin did, I am capable of that.

VF: You, Gloria Naylor?
GN: I, Gloria Naylor, am capable of that, because that is part and parcel of being a human being. That's what I believe. And I believe that I, Gloria Naylor, am capable of what Mother Theresa has done, and what Martin Luther King has done, that that's part and parcel of being a human being. And what we all do, those of us who are not either those demons or those gods, is something that's a mixture in between. But I think it is all there. And why we don't do it, ah. . . . That's what I think is essential human nature. Pure evil and pure good. Truly. I am fascinated by serial killers—people they call the voids, the ones who run around just simply approximating human emotion because they have none. I think those people are the closest to having perhaps 99 percent of their nature being made up of evil. It just fascinates me, that's all. Purity fascinates me. Of whatever sort.

VF: You've talked a lot about the impact that Toni Morrison's *The Bluest Eye* had on you. Are there other writers who have been an influence on your writing?
GN: I aspire to do what James Baldwin did with his career, when all is said and done. Which is to leave behind a moral vision, right or wrong, and a very long and prolific career, and a courageous one. I aspire to do that. It'll be a different set of politics, because indeed it's a different era.

VF: Not to mention the fact that you're a woman and he was a man.
GN: Yes, that too as well. But I wasn't really thinking of that, but that's true. Among writers who affected my work, yes, definitely, direct influences where I have even written against them in my work, would be Faulkner, his whole depiction of the Dilsey character, and the fact that she's based on Caroline Norton. Caroline Norton, he said, was under five feet tall and wouldn't be ninety-nine pounds soaking wet. And he loved this woman, he really did. She was his mother. And the process, the whole social process that turned her into a Dilsey. I wrote against that with Mattie Michael in *Brewster Place*. He has affected me.

Zora Neale Hurston—I have used her spirit for things and her politics about the celebration of the speech of the folk. I did that in *Mama Day*. I have used writers sometimes when I've had a problem, a creative problem, I have gone to them. When I was becoming a feminist, Ntozake Shange and Nikki Giovanni were very important to me, because I started out as a poet. But the very strong black women—these women may not call themselves feminists, but I conceived of them as being so in those years. I identified those as black feminist voices in those years. Now that helped me just with establishing a separate entity in my mind as the black woman. Because remember I told you I built from nothing in the late seventies, I literally built from nothing. So those writers have been important.

VF: What would make a writer decide consciously to rewrite a Dante? Or why do you continue to invoke Shakespeare, and what does he mean to you?
GN: With Dante, it was simply because when I was a sophomore and I read *The Inferno*, there was something about the grotesqueness of those lives that just simply called to me. They were some of the most vivid images that I had read in literature to that date, and I think even to this date. And I think also because it was a whole new spin on hell, and I had dealt with different concepts of hell, and here was a new spin on it that called to me for some reason. Just intellectually, I saw that it would be a perfect fit for what I wanted to say about the black middle class, and to say about life in America for the black middle class. Here was the quintessential mirror image—for some odd reason, mirrors are always important in my work. So when I take it apart I think those are probably the reasons why.

Shakespeare? I had to be thirteen, because I remember it was the house in Queens and I'd memorize sections of *Romeo and Juliet* and I would be at the bottom to be Romeo and I'd run up the steps to be Juliet. And it was the first play I'd seen, which was before I was thirteen, because they used to bring "Shakespeare in the Park" to New York. My mom took us over because we lived at 119th Street, and Morningside Park was just two blocks up. My mom took us over to see "Shakespeare in the Park" and the play was *A Midsummer Night's Dream*. Then once in junior high school I saw *Macbeth* performed, and just something about the way in which Shakespeare used language resonated within me. I loved tragedies. I loved the idea that everybody died. And now, in later years, I simply look at that career and I admire it. I've always hoped to be prolific, I never wanted to be just a one-novel person, or even a writer of one type of work. So I admire the span of his career, the things he attempted—not always successfully—and the courage of his vision. He got beyond his little world. Now I grant you, his Romans are like Elizabethans and his Caribbeans are like Elizabethans and his Norwegians are like Elizabethans and everybody's like Elizabethans—however, he had the courage to dream different worlds. And like I said, with this new book, for some reason Bascombe Wade possesses those original folios. So he's probably about as close as I will get to the source of whatever it is that resonates in Shakespeare.

VF: Perhaps that's a tie-in too to the scenic quality of your work.
GN: Well, the Victorian novels were also important; I read the Brontës at a formative age. I loved the size of those triple-deckers, and also the whole sweep and passion of the stories. I'm always dealing with cataclysmic events, and I walk a thin line. And one day I know I'm going to fall on my face with that—I walk a thin line between drama and melodrama. And often it's just skill that has kept it from tipping over to the edge. My last book is a more mature work; I have learned to evoke emotion quietly. And I see that happening—well, at least *I* see it happening—in *Bailey's Cafe*, where there are quiet moments that are still powerful moments. I'm an old-fashioned writer in that I think novels should tell a story first and foremost.

VF: Why do you give Miss Maple such an important placement in *Bailey's Cafe?*
GN: Because he and Bailey are bookends to a story that I'm telling about sexuality and sexual identity. The core of the work is indeed the way in which the word *whore* has been used against women or to manipulate female sexual

identity. That's the core of the work. However, in order to talk about what is female sexuality and female sexual identity necessitates talking about what is male sexuality and male sexual identity, because you cannot have one without the other. The same way we could not have white people without black people here in America. So that's what Bailey and Miss Maple will do, and Bailey and Miss Maple—if you take them apart, experience by experience— they are antithetical to each other. You know, Bailey went to war, Miss Maple didn't. Bailey was the typical—what would you call him?—man about town, preyer on women. Miss Maple was not. Their classes were different. Their take on history was very different. That's why Miss Maple served what he served to do. He was to say, all right now, hopefully you've subliminally gone through women who would be classified as whores, and the writer's taken you into that word, all around the edges of that word, and even, if I did my job right, in the case of Sadie made that word sing for you, sing beauty for you. Now you will look at what's been going on: what she's been attempting to do all the way through is to upset your assumptions about what is male or female, what is purity, what is whoredom.

VF: Is Bascombe at all related to a Miss Maple kind of character?
GN: Don't know yet, Ginney. It's too early. I don't know yet how to analyze him because he's being born. I know that I'm fascinated with him, I know that I feel for him. I think it's very sad to be such a gentle, gentle soul in the world in which he must move. That's all I know yet about Bascombe. We have to get to know each other more. I have to show him that I mean him no harm.

VF: He's your first major white character.
GN: He will be the white character that I will give the most space to, yes, to date. That's true. Except that "white" wasn't around then, so he is a Norwegian. See, we had not yet invented white in America.

VF: What kind of audience do you write for?
GN: I don't (and to this date I still haven't, although with each book it gets more difficult) think about who is going to be reading my books. I think that you cannot control popularity. Just from being inside of publishing proper, part of my job is to attempt to predict what people are going to buy, and we spend time arguing about what will people buy and why. It's a crapshoot with

any book. The tastes of the public are indeed fickle. So from a commercial standpoint, I think it would be foolish. For a writer—and there are writers who write to sell, and there are writers who write because they feel they are fulfilling something—if I talk about the latter group, I think it would be suicide a little bit to try to write for popular success. But if you want to know what I'm working for, about my ambitions—I have wanted to last. You want to know where my ego is? Yes. I have wanted and desired and prayed and fantasized about being here a hundred years after I am gone. I have wanted my work to last. And I know that that's something I can't control. Politics and publishing, I can't control those. Only time will tell.

VF: And the politics of the people who make canons. I don't think that the best necessarily survives. I don't think that merit alone does it.
GN: I kind of started saying that that's my ambition. To write work that will resonate for many years to come. If I have an ambition, it is that. And my ambition is to be excellent. It truly is. I'm driven that way.

VF: How do you achieve excellence?
GN: By keeping myself as uncorrupted as possible. And maybe that's what I—if I fear anything, I fear that as, indeed, prominence grows. And that's why I kept one editor and followed this editor, because he is an honest man. And because he also cares about my work, he would not let me embarrass myself. I keep this man. Because I was afraid, because success came early, and people will not tell you the truth, and sometimes they don't know the truth themselves, they're blinded by certain things. I will always try to have someone who cares about me, cares about the quality of the work I produce, and will be honest enough to look me in the face.

VF: Let's shift gears for a moment. What kind of narrative structure will "Sapphira Wade" have?
GN: I think the next novel is going to be from two different perspectives, if not three, you know, because there will be Miss Ophelia. I know that their voices will emerge through the elements to her because there are no written documents. I know I will have two distinct voices, if not three, because Sapphira—you know Sapphira is Scheherazade, you've probably already figured that out. I see somewhat that there will be different voices in "Sapphira Wade," but for different reasons than *Mama Day*. *Mama Day* had

to have those voices because I was making a commentary about reality and truth, among other things. When this interview lives in our minds, it will live in two totally different worlds, two totally different perspectives, and what is the truth? None of it and all of it. And that's what I was attempting to do with that. One of the things I was attempting to do—I was doing a lot of stuff. Faulkner was in that, in the structure of that. *As I Lay Dying*.

VF: Yes, I remember you've said that.
GN: It's true, it's literally what I had to read to get over the hump. Because I was trying to write that book in third-person past tense. Trying to do it. And it was not coming. But I could have, I know how to write third-person past tense. I could have pushed out this story third-person past tense.

VF: But it wouldn't have been the same book.
GN: There you go, there you go! It was a living resistance, and I had to say, there's something here greater than me, there's something I am not doing. I'm not doing it. What's wrong? And so you stop, you stop and say, well, I don't know what's wrong. I was in Guadalajara visiting my girlfriend Andrea. I was depressed, and so I went walking. I knew that each embassy has a library, I knew that from being stranded in places all over the world. And I went shuffling through books to get something to read. And I said, oh, I've never read *As I Lay Dying*, and I'd heard that that was sort of his six-week wonder. And then it was like, *aha*.

VF: Gloria, could you talk about One Way Productions and the projects you're trying to do there?
GN: One Way Productions is basically about self-determination and being able to control the production of images to a larger audience. The intent is to reach as many people as possible with these images. I realized that so often we are just the producers of things and we rarely control our own talents. So now I do. I just legally control anything that happens to my own personal work beyond its being in book form, because it belongs to my company. I want to present positive images of the black community to as many people in America and the world as possible. That's the goal. It is an extension of what I do when I write except that it's a public business so you get as many people as possible involved.

VF: So that's where your political activism comes in.

GN: Maybe in a way—it's cultural activism. But with my novels, that's a whole other area—maybe it *is* sacred. If you want to know about religion, my novel-writing is sacred territory. It's another place, you see, because I know how my sanity was saved that way. And I'm going to protect that. I know how I remain sane, and no one touches that. I do what I can to preserve that. But yes, with One Way Productions, it's to reach people. And make lots of money! [laughter]

VF: I wanted to ask a question about *Brewster Place.* You seem to suggest, with your treatment of Mattie and her relationship to Basil, that somehow the mothers have to answer for the punks that we're getting. And does Basil have a relation to Eugene or C. C. Baker?

GN: I think that Eugene and Basil might be closer to each other in my mind than they are to C. C. Baker, because they perpetuated a certain violence against people who loved them, who had made them, in a sense, what they were. I'm not saying that single mothers are responsible for crime in the streets. But I do believe this: that they are responsible for how their sons perceive women. And perceive of themselves as men. Mattie, I held her accountable for the monster that she had created. There were warnings that she was given.

VF: Yes, Eva tries to tell her.

GN: Yes. Even the child's father in a dream—the whole business of the sugar cane was about that—he's saying, let go, you can't get all that sweetness. I was making a comment about, in a sense, bad mothering, but that was part of what I told you about writing against Faulkner and Dilsey. I created an Earth Mother, and I wanted an anti–Earth Mother in that regard, so by the time Mattie serves her Dilsey function on Brewster Place, she's been given the things Faulkner never gave his Dilsey. She's been given a sexuality, she's been given a sort of ulterior motive for mothering, and it's selfishness on her part. She wanted to *keep* him.

C. C. Baker was a different case. I remember deliberately taking the narrative risk with that rape to stop the action (now that's Victorian), to stop the action—it's two paragraphs long—and to explain why that young man is raping her and to point the finger toward society and their definition of manhood. It was real clear to me. Because today I would not do that. If I were writing that scene today, I would just write it. But I remember consciously

saying—now here's where I undercut my own statement—because that's a
place where I remember consciously saying, I don't want anyone to read this
and think—because, see, I had a problem with Susan Brownmiller's book
Against Our Wills (that was the sort of hot book at that point), a real problem
with how she treated black men in that work. And I said, I don't want anyone
to read this and think that black men rape, that they just rape because of
whatever. I wanted them to see that what's raping this woman, among other
things, is society's conception of manhood, and their low evaluation of
women. And no, I don't connect that at all to mothering, to how C. C. Baker
was mothered. It was how he was taught he could be a man by society.

VF: Yes, you make that very clear.
GN: Yes, and outside of that novel, in my own politics, I don't think that single
mothers are the reason why we have so much crime. But I *do* think that mothers, either single or married, are part of the reason why women are not thought
of better by young men, I really do. And I'm not going to back off from that.

VF: You're right that you do give it a very clear social causal analysis. And
yet—and maybe it's just my failure as a reader—when I meet C. C. Baker, to
me he is a more extreme form of Eugene and of Basil, and so maybe I'm
making the mistake of seeing those three as having similarities.
GN: I would not see them as the same because Mattie's son, and I knew him
fairly well, he could not rape. He was just selfish, he was spoiled. He didn't hate
women. Rape is an act of hatred. He loved his mother. Basil loved his mother.
He loved her in the way he had been taught to love her, to love her as a
provider of his needs. To love her as a something that would empty itself to his
ends. She was loved for the function that she provided, and that was his total
cushioning and gratification. He did love her. He would not have raped a
woman. I don't know what C. C. Baker's parents were like. The life of a
C. C. Baker—he could not have had Mattie for a mother. Those people trouble
me. Eugene—I don't know about Eugene. Eugene was not a well-drawn character. That was my first, my very first story. I could have given him, I think,
with perhaps more skill and more empathy a bit more depth than he has.

VF: Were you too hard on the men in *The Women of Brewster Place?*
GN: That's an early work. I think if you want to know how I feel about that
subject, the last work is probably more telling of my present feelings on the

whole subject. There the men, if they do fail, they are well meaning in their failures. Bailey, even though you call him a sexist, he's the only one who will not judge what's going on at Eve's.

VF: I like Bailey.
GN: I think my attitude toward men would probably be closer to what I did in *Bailey's Cafe*, as well as my attitude toward women.

VF: Do you believe that readers get from your work what you hope they will?
GN: Well, what surprised me with *Linden Hills* is that no one quite got it. I don't think most people did. But then again, I haven't been analyzed that much. But as far as I'm concerned, that was my masterwork.

VF: *Linden Hills?*
GN: Yes. It really was. And I'm really waiting for people to go to *The Inferno* and go to my work and see what I did as far as images and the terza rima. No one has gotten it yet. Granted, I bobble the terza rima just a tiny bit toward the end of the book, but for a good seven-eighths of it, I have re-created through images what he did through rhyme schemes. And no one has seen it. And the colors, and how I play with colors, no one has gotten it yet.

I'll tell you the kind of kid I was. Before my parents discovered that I was as bright as I was, I used to love to watch adults play out their lives, and I would know more than I let on that I knew and then proceed into their fantasy of what was actually going on, and I would like that feeling of going "ahh." That's why I love irony. A feeling of superiority. Or a feeling even that you don't control me. I've hated always to be controlled. You don't control me, and childhood is by definition a helpless position. Anyway. So a little bit of my watching what's happened with *Linden Hills* and hasn't happened with *Linden Hills* has been that kind of thing, like, "You don't know what I really did with that work." I think that maybe in time—if I'm still around—in time someone will figure out what happened with that book and Dante's *Inferno*. Besides what's really obvious. In general, people have never gotten it, as far as what I do with colors. And I don't think that they're so obscure—you know, some symbols can be self-serving—but that they are actually an integral part. I was on tour with *Mama Day*, I think, and this woman said, "I read *Linden Hills*, and you didn't have a lot of editorial help, did you?" [*laughter*]. But just for the record, I've never rewritten a book, or an ending, or whatever, because of editorial intrusion. What readers have from me is truly my own vision.

VF: Do you show the manuscript in process?

GN: I wait until I'm through. I did that once. I took a contract on *Linden Hills* mid-book because of my insecurity. I said, I wonder if this is any good. And then my editor left Viking Press, and the contract was with Viking Press. *Linden Hills* was finally published by Ticknor & Fields, but I had to go through all kinds of permutations—got rid of an agent because of that whole mess—to have this book with this man at the new house, which was Ticknor & Fields. So after that I said, unless I am literally starving and cannot get another switchboard job, they're never seeing anything from me until I'm ready to have it published. I'll *read* from a work in progress, I enjoy doing that, because you never know. I think it's funny—do they think it's funny? I think this is riveting—do they think it's riveting? That I will share. That comes from the old habit when I was in college of reading your poetry and stuff to people. The times I enjoy the most reading my work is when it's in progress. For example, with *Bailey's Cafe*, because it is now in paperback, I'll have to do a little small mini-tour again with it. That will be the least pleasurable reading of the work—after it's old. What I'm eager now to do is to read new work to people.

VF: What do you read from *Bailey's Cafe?*

GN: I will read Esther's story and then go on to read Jesse's story. Because one is so intense, and one is kind of funny and revealing.

The Human Spirit Is a Kick-Ass Thing

Sharon Felton and Michelle C. Loris / 1996

From *The Critical Response to Gloria Naylor* (Greenwood 1997), 253–64. Copyright © 1996 by Greenwood Publishing Group, Inc. Reproduced with permission of Greenwood Publishing Group, Inc., Westport, Connecticut.

This exclusive interview with Gloria Naylor and Michelle C. Loris was conducted in New York City on 29 May 1996. Questions for the interview and editing of the material was done by both co-editors, Sharon Felton and Michelle C. Loris. Original material printed with permission of Gloria Naylor.

Michelle Loris: Do you think your work is political?

Gloria Naylor: I don't think that it is overtly political, but I think that literature is politics; I think that life is politics. And I take political positions all the time but when it comes to my fiction, I don't take political positions because I believe after all is said and done that what I am doing with each book is trying very hard to capture a story . . . to tell a story and to elucidate a life as strongly and as truthfully as I can. But, hopefully, there will be a body politic in what I am doing with each book.

ML: Your work seems to focus on the politics of gender.

GN: I think that you may garner that out of my work. Women's literature in general began to explore the caverns and internal workings of women's lives. I have tried throughout my career to give voice to the voiceless and this hasn't been a conscious decision on my part—that I, Gloria Naylor, will now speak for gay women, will now speak for poor women on dead-end streets, will now speak for the middle class women hidden in basements, the basements of life. No, I believe that I am a transcriber of these lives that have always been swirling around in my unconscious, and I have been chosen, in a sense, to give voice to this. What I do is to make myself as ready as I can to do whatever prep work is necessary in order to tell these stories. Now when you see what this has meant for the last fifteen years, what you see is a whole array of stories.

ML: You do present a complex array of women in your stories.

GN: Yes, I thought about that when, as *Bailey's Cafe* began to form that in *The Women of Brewster Place* I was romanticizing the female condition a bit. In *Bailey's Cafe* you see women who are victimizers; in *Brewster Place* the women are mostly victims who are trying to transcend a situation. In *Bailey's Cafe* you see females participating in the acculturation of younger women in ways that I think could be considered oppressive. I think that there was a newness about my feminism when I was writing *Brewster Place*. I was just discovering feminism at Brooklyn College and thinking that if women held the reins, the world would be different. With *Bailey's Cafe* you come through ten or twelve years of seeing women in power often making the same foolish mistakes, making the same expedient choices as men who have been in power have made. And so I say to myself maybe this isn't a gender thing, maybe it's a human thing.

ML: You said in an interview that your work is female-centered. Would you distinguish that from feminist?

GN: Yes, I do. I define feminism as believing in social, economic, and political equality for all human beings. So a man has the same rights as I have. But to be female centered, I think, is to see the world "gynecologically," to see the world through the eyes of a woman. Women have to operate differently because of the way the power structure is. I think that feminism is a political term and to be female centered is more of a cultural term, a humanist term.

ML: How is the gynecological view different from the phallic view?

GN: Well, the gynecological view is one that is more reflective than active; it's more inner than outer; it's one that doesn't roam as much. I could not envision, for example, with *Linden Hills* two young women doing what those two young men did. Besides the fact that it is a refashioning of Dante's *Inferno* and that I have to have a Dante and a Virgil, when I thought of motion and travel and of adventure, I did not think female.

ML: What do you think accounts for that perception?

GN: The way I was raised, the society in which I came up, the literature I read. . . . For example, the Brontës, you know, the furthest that those heroines went was onto the heath. But Melville had his men cross the planet. So there—it's about how we have been bred as far as our literatures, as far as our societies go.

ML: You don't see women as going on adventures or being in motion. Do you see yourself as a woman in motion?

GN: Yes, I've always been in motion from the time I got my driver's license. I was nineteen and I bought an old Dodge Dart and I took that thing on the interstates back in my twenties, you know, when you could go ten hours and not get tired. I always liked the idea of moving, of movement, to me that was a sort of freedom.

ML: That was a departure from the typical idea of female.

GN: Yes, and I don't know why. It wasn't a conscious thing; I just knew that I was restless. When my friends all started to get married, I knew that I didn't want to get married. I didn't know why I didn't want to get married, and I didn't know what I was looking for running up and down those interstates. But I was just searching and I knew the motion, the freedom of it all, would give me an answer. I just knew I didn't want to be still. And I think with the movement and the looking, the looking physically, the looking metaphysically, I came back to what I had been doing when I was eleven or twelve years old . . . and that was writing.

ML: So you write because . . .

GN: I write because I have no choice. I began writing in a sense to save my sanity because I could not in my early years articulate as I can today. So scribbling away in a little diary, writing little snatches of poems and that kind of thing became my way to be human because it meant that I was communicating. Once you cease to communicate, you cease to exist. So writing is my way of living. It's kind of a mission. It's a life's mission to continue to tell the stories.

ML: Can you talk some about your creative process? How you work and write?

GN: Each book has required more and more research. *Bailey's Cafe* was the most recent work until I began *Sapphira Wade. Brewster Place* was just an outpouring, a spontaneous kind of outpouring; in a sense my very personal novel. I've had to do intensive research beginning with *Mama Day*. Well, you know, the quartet was there from *Brewster Place*. From this work I had the quartet in my head and it was around *Mama Day* that the realization came that there would be a Sapphira Wade, and that actually this woman had been guiding me. I started out with just very broad sketches with the first novel, a general outline and then I began to fill it in. I heard E. L. Doctorow once give a metaphor for what writing was like and I always liked that metaphor: "writing is like driving from New York to California totally in the night. Your headlights let you see about three hundred feet in front of you, but, three hundred feet at a time, you make the whole distance." Writing is like that: a journey of discovery. I always begin with the title and the first line and the last line. And then I have my notes. But if you are very fortunate you do not end up with what you thought you would end up with. The work takes on its own internal life and grows. That's what I meant before when I said I was a transcriber of stories. You hope that in the process it catches fire and you have to run and catch up. You never even use half of your notes; they are just like little anchors and then you start to free fall. This book (*Sapphira Wade*) will be a little scary because I am free falling into the mind of a woman who is a little bit insane. The characters become real; they are definitely real, more real than real life.

ML: Since you bring it up, can we talk a little about your next book?
GN: Just a little. In the book I am writing now, Cocoa comes back as an old woman. It's 2023. This book will be the cornerstone. Always in my head Sapphira Wade would be the cornerstone because she has been the guiding spirit for now close to twenty years, and now it's time to grapple with her. Even when I was back working the switchboard—I was maybe twenty-six years old—she came to me, this woman. You know how a realization will sometimes bubble up to you. Well, I have someplace on a yellow pad a sketch of her picture. I was just sitting sketching and little snatches of what will go into this novel came to me then twenty years ago. This is the creative force. Sapphira Wade has been with me since way back then, although she was never mentioned until *Mama Day*. And now it is time that I bring her forth. I have had to do intensive research. I've been to Norway and to Africa for this novel. I actually had to physically go to the place in order to walk the terra firma . . . to breathe the air with this novel. I had to end up in Norway and on the western shores of Senegal. I'm going back to 1817–1823 in this book and I had to gather the material for that time period. And I am writing about two cultures neither of which I've had, and I am writing about a gender I've never had. So I have been gathering these materials for the last six or seven years.

ML: You are writing about Bascombe Wade as well. This is your first white man that you have written about, isn't it?

GN: He was Norwegian. White men weren't invented yet. White was starting to be invented in this country at that time but when he comes he will be Norwegian.

ML: So you are writing about him as a Norwegian rather than a white man?

GN: Well, to be a white male or female is to be a political definition. You know it is a definition of power . . . of privilege and of not being a slave. That is how the term evolved; it evolved out of the condition of the Africans who had come and of the need to politicize an economic situation. So Black emerged meaning what Black means today out of that economic situation of slavery. White emerged because you had to define something against not being Black. So you are Norwegians, or you are Scots, or Poles, or Irishmen, Englishmen, or Italian or Armenian and you became white. So I am writing about the meeting of a Norwegian man and a Fulani woman and a Choctaw male on the shores of Savannah. They're going off to create Willow Springs.

ML: You write about the South. Would you distinguish that from being a Southern writer?

GN: Oh yes, I think so, because the whole school of Southern writing means that there is a certain style to the writing that I don't think my work falls into. I have used the South often as subject matter, but I don't think that there is the element of the grotesque or of community, or of the land as a metaphor. But I have been raised by southerners so I am touched very much by that region and I have my second home in Beaufort, South Carolina.

ML: I'm shifting gears a little here. I was wondering how you would describe the moral vision that your four works exhibit now to date.

GN: People have told me recently that I am a moral writer, that I take moral positions in my work. I believe that my work is saying that the African American community is a diverse people. But there has been this objectification of our identity and objectification is often a denigration of those qualities that compose your culture, be it your skin color, or the way you dance, or raise your children, or whatever. So I think that my work presents to you, the reader, a community of people who are both saints and sinners, who have beauty and blemishes. I don't glorify the African American and say we're all perfect. We are all human beings and that means complexity, that means light and shadow. I would hope that my moral vision has been to present human beings in light and shadow.

ML: You know some of your works have been described as mystical, allegorical, religious. And you were a Jehovah's Witness. How would you describe your religious views now and how might your religious vision show itself in your work?

GN: I consider myself more spiritual than religious, because I don't have an organized religion from which to channel my beliefs in the intangible and in higher powers. But I do know that my religious background shows up in my work. For example, in *Bailey's Cafe* I am retelling classical Biblical figures; I am retelling their stories. And Mariam gives birth to a character whose name is George. And in *Mama Day* George is a Christ figure. He sacrifices himself for love and he dies at thirty-three years old.

ML: So your Christ figure is born in *Bailey's Cafe*?

GN: Yes, because *Bailey's Cafe* predates *Mama Day*. George saved Cocoa and in that way he saved the whole line of the Days, all the women.

ML: You said that you are more spiritual than religious?

GN: Well, yes. In my life that means that there is a belief in something beyond the machinations of flesh and blood and that there is a belief in the intangible, be it love, or be it the creative process, or be it hope.

ML: You once said that people don't write novels unless they have hope.

GN: I used to quote Margaret Atwood as having said that. Then someone told me that it was Flannery O'Connor. In any case, the quote is: "people without hope do not write books." But what I was saying about my spiritual vision as it shapes my work is that I think the transcendence of the human spirit, the power of the human spirit, moves throughout these books, and my hope is that which is transcendent within us will outweigh that which is bestial. We have laws, the government, organized religion all playing a part in helping us balance that tension between the bestial and the transcendent. We also have the arts.

ML: How do you see that relationship between art and morality?

GN: I think that the execution of the artistic in us is a way of sublimating that which is bestial. What was that quote of Shakespeare's—that music calms the savage beast? Everything can be thought of as artistic: the nurturing of life, be it children or plants or animals.

ML: Do you have hope for race relations in this country?

GN: Not within our lifetime. I used to—academically. I don't know if you've read my introduction in *Children of the Night* where I speak about that subject. That was an academic exercise. When I tried to think and to look back over the last thirty years of race relations in America, I realized, it's just thirty years. And that is nothing compared to the time that has gone into creating inequality. To think that thirty years will undo this kind of tangled morass. No, not within our lifetime are we going to see this big thing called race relations ever resolved. What we will continue to have, what we always have had are one-on-ones, and if there are enough of those one-on-ones of people attempting to understand, then maybe we will get a block that lives together, or we'll get a neighborhood that might live together, or a section of the country that might live together, but no, I do not have too much hope for race. Our lifetime is just too short.

ML: I'd like to broach a historical question as it relates to race and *Bailey's Cafe*. Bailey is a World War II veteran and Hiroshima figures prominently. In what ways was the Holocaust in your mind with regard to your fourth novel? Mariam is Jewish. … Are you bringing together two cultures?

GN: She has to be a Jew because she's giving birth to Christ. The book ends with those two events because those are two of the defining events of World War II and also of the modern age. That these events were two conscious governmental acts changed how we think, how we think of ourselves and our government. In contrast, slavery is a whole different ballgame; slavery is universal. Even talking about African slavery, that was filtered over many centuries. But with the government-sponsored genocide in Japan and Europe, in a very small and concentrated period of time—that's something very different. We've had genocide before; we have genocide right here in this country with the Native American, but that horror took place over a series of decades and with different types of policies. In the World War II era, however, we see man's inhumanity to man that was organized—Hiroshima was organized, and the extermination policies of Nazi Germany were organized and methodically executed.

ML: What about relations between the sexes; do you have hope for that?
GN: No, even less (laughter). No, let me stop. I think that the definition of gender is slowly changing. And this is where young people could, might carry a part, but you know, I think that the big snakes are creating little snakes. I used to look at the exceptions, you know, like when you see fathers with their children and their baby carriages and they're taking them off to daycare—but those are truly the exceptions to the rule. I think probably what's going on is the status quo where younger people are coming up, young men are coming up to expect young women to assume certain roles. That's what I mean by big snakes creating the little snakes.

ML: That would suggest that you don't foresee change between the genders.
GN: Well, we have had change. Will there be massive change? I don't think there will be within our lifetime; I don't. I used to believe that once women would—sort of—be the vanguard of that happening, that once women got into positions where they could make decisions they could make a difference. But when they've gotten into positions where they *could* make a difference, there were so many other forces that held, that made them conform, either made them conform or they wanted to conform and they have just perpetuated the way things have always been.

ML: Do you think that the way we "mother" our children has changed?
GN: Motherhood? That's changing, I think, to a degree. It has been changing since the post–World War II era. It took a while for the ideology to begin to creep up to the reality. Single mothers began in the workforce in the 1950s and after World War II. Parenting is now changing to include men. I mean, men have always changed diapers and helped with the kids, but now the ideology is catching up with the reality of the fact that our dads did a bit of cooking. Like when one's mother had to be in the hospital to give birth to another child. You know, in those days, they kept women in the hospital for seven days or so. Husbands caved in and did things. I see motherhood expanding in the sense that extended families are important now. And that extended family might not always be a grandparent or an aunt or uncle; extended families could be so many single women with children—a friendship network, a childcare network. Children are being raised now by tribes more so than by a nuclear family. And as an African American, we do not have a matriarchal society. It is definitely a matrilocal society, where women and the idea of mothering is almost central to our community. I can see why mothers would

play a part. Also, my own mother—who is here in the house with us today; she's been here for about six months—my own mother was a very strong person throughout my life. As well as my father, but because one's father went off to work in the 1950s, my mother has always been kind of a dominant presence in my life.

ML: In your work would you say that you are equally concerned with race and gender, or are you more concerned with one or the other?

GN: I have never thought about it that way. The two in my mind are interwoven. Like how do you separate being a black woman? I think that when I am in certain situations that it is not my gender that will govern the interactions, it is definitely my race. I think that my race has a more powerful effect upon influencing an environment or shaping a perception of me than my gender. I think the gender is the subtext to text for me as a black woman. In my work, though, it's interesting because these characters don't get made up with formulas like that. If they come out like Lorraine and Theresa in *Brewster Place*, it wasn't a formula, "Black female Lesbians." You start out with the picture of that face with that body in motion and then you go in search of her story.

ML: You know, I was wondering. *The Women of Brewster Place* has been made into a television film, and I think when we met a while back [at Sacred Heart University], you said that *Mama Day* might be made into a film?

GN: You're sitting in One Way Productions and this was designed, this began to film *Mama Day*. Well, now, One Way Productions is doing programming for children which is very nice.

ML: Well, why don't we talk about One Way Productions?

GN: One Way Productions got started as a legal entity in order to bring *Mama Day* to the screen. Where we stand now is here. I finished a draft in December of '95 and that was going to be my last involvement with that work because it's now in the hands of two producer agents who are taking that draft as well as whatever wherewithal they have with packaging to try to make that happen. It moves me into the seventh year of attempting to bring that novel to film, and so I had to then move on. I have to say I have learned the screenwriting process by working by the seat of my pants. But '96 was the year of the novel, and in a way '96 has been the year of the novel in many levels. I've had novel experiences this year.

ML: In the translation from the novel into the screenplay, what do you see happening to your work as it gets transformed from one form to another? Is there anything lost or gained?

GN: Oh, God, yes. You lose a lot because you cannot translate a book to the screen. What you can do is take the basic elements from a book, take the spirit of the book, and then proceed to create a whole new animal because a screenplay calls upon you, the creator, to do different things. One, you're not even dealing with language. For a script, you're dealing with pictures. It is a singular art when one is writing a novel, and a very collaborative art when one is making a film. All these talented people come together. We've done what we had to do and a hell of a lot of praying, because once again, even all of these disparate figures with disparate talents cannot necessarily make the magic happen. It's one of those crazy mystical things; I learned that doing theater. The screenplay's only got the bare bones, the blueprint, of the process. I learned that what will come out of that process will be a film that will reflect the spirit of the novel. You lose an awful lot of characters, you have to invent new situations, disregard other situations altogether. Unless you are going to do voiceovers, you cannot even retain the language that might have enthralled you with a book. But what you want to make is a good film about an old woman on an island somewhere who can work magic with the human soul—and that's what you do. But I'm real comfortable with the cast of characters around me now who are pushing to try to make this happen. We'll see.

ML: So that's how One Way Productions got started. What kind of work does it do now?

GN: Well, now what it does is design work for children. It got shaped into its own mission and our first One Way Production project will be a one-act children's play for the Lincoln Center Institute. We were due to go into production this year, then we had director's problems, so we'll be doing it for the next school year. It's called "Candy." What the Institute does is to bring dance or drama or art or music to the school systems after they have first brought in the teachers during the summer, so that the teachers have a way of integrating whatever the Institute will bring into the school into their curriculum. So that's it's not just a one-shot deal; here we are, kids, goodbye. The teachers have been prepared and the students have been prepared throughout that whole semester for this event, and then it just becomes a part of the whole learning process. So "Candy" is a one-act play that they commissioned us to do.

ML: Can you talk about what some of the personal, the more dominant personal experiences have generated themselves into your art work? For example, *Brewster Place* . . .

GN: I think in those days what that was about was the fact that I was searching for a sense of self, you know, a sense of my female self, and just a sense of personal self with *Brewster Place.* I had always been a great beginner and never finished much of anything, so that I began a ministry that I didn't finish, I had begun a marriage, I didn't finish that, and I had begun school at a late age—at twenty-five, twenty-six years old, and I wasn't sure if I was going to finish that, you know, given my track record. . . . So writing *Brewster Place* became number one, one of the first things that I began that I finished . . . finished it simultaneously with getting my undergraduate degree. So that was kind of neat. It also became a way of putting myself into reality, because you know I read voraciously. I just hadn't read books that reflected . . . things that were worthy of my person, my history. So writing it did that for me. I wanted to celebrate what had been invisible.

ML: How about *Mama Day?* What was inside of you that translated out into *Mama Day?*

GN: Oh, my belief in love and magic. That's what that book is about. I saw with my nephew, because he was very ill—terminally ill when he was young— and I saw the power of love literally save his life. And so . . . I know that it can be tangible, that you can cut it and dish it out, you truly can. It has a texture and a weight to it. I know that love can do that, I know that love can heal . . .

ML: An interviewer once asked Albert Camus if there was something in his work that had been overlooked by the critics—a theme or a symbol—something that was really important that had been overlooked. He said humor. Do you think that there is anything that has been omitted or overlooked by the critics or the reviewers in your work?

GN: Well, reviewers and critics are two different things, but I would say with the critics that I would like someday for someone to look at the importance of naming, the whole act of naming, names themselves within my work because that's real conscious when I play certain games with that. I think the naming of characters and what place names play and how they play out. That would interest me to read about my work. And especially I think because I get names first and when you asked me about the creative process the first thing I did were names. Named the book, named the characters, then the other stuff gets filled in later.

ML: Is there anything else you think critics have overlooked?
GN: Well, I am hoping that someday a critic will look at the rhyme scheme in the *Inferno* and then look at the narrative structure of *Linden Hills*. What I did with images, and how I mimicked the rhyme scheme of the original poem with images in my book. That was a conscious design feature. I did it almost all the way through; I think it did fall down a little at the end. The *Inferno* has a *terza rima* rhyme scheme—of A, B, A / B, C, B—and I do that with *Linden Hills*.

ML: How do you imagine literature might change as we reach the twenty-first century?
GN: It already has. I mean, it's not going to be in the form as we know it as far as ink on paper. Literature has gone electronic and I think we'll go even more so. I imagine books being read in virtual reality, where you experience *Moby Dick*, as opposed to actually reading it. I think because the writers of the future will have been born in the electronic age that's going to affect how they think of words on paper. I believe that books will get shorter. I think that images will probably be kinetic and sharper, because of how these children come of age thinking of reality.

ML: Do you think it will affect your work personally?
GN: I'm too old. I'm forty-six and I'm just at the beginning of the television age. I know that working with word processors, I think, has probably affected my work. I'm more verbose than I used to be. But I think I'm too old to be affected by this new wave of technology that other writers will be.

ML: What would you say you would want your achievement to be as a writer? What legacy or influence will you want to leave? You mentioned that at the very beginning of our conversation that "my works are going to be here beyond me" . . .
GN: [long pause] A couple of things. I would like for people to see how I played with structure and how often the form of the work has been either influenced by the content, or either the content demanded the form of the work. I would like for people to say, well, you know, that she was a little bit of a cutting edge of dealing within a very conventional narrative with some structural avant-garde elements. And so I would like that to be left. Also,

I would like it to be said that after all is said and done, that she gave us a world of people . . . that's what I'd like.

ML: Can you tell me about your garden in South Carolina?
GN: I designed it from scratch. I had the stones delivered. Put them in the ground myself. So it's several little raised beds as you move throughout this path and in the middle is a little statuette of a little child leaning over a book and reading. And he's surrounded with strawberries and lilac and thyme, and I call him Sweet Charlie. So you walk into the garden and on either side are these squares and then two long squares and in the middle there's Sweet Charlie, and there are more squares on the other side. And as you move through it with your lettuce and tomatoes and asparagus bed and water-melon bed and . . . 'cause you know you gotta have watermelon growing. All that good stuff like the peas and the sunflowers in the back. Charlie's in the middle with the strawberry bed because the strawberry beds are perennial and my asparagus bed would be perennial. This was my retirement home, so I figured what's done might as well keep going . . .

ML: What does the garden do for you? What does it mean to you?
GN: It reaffirms my belief in creativity and in life. Despite the weeds, the obstacles, those turnips came up. It's about what I do for work. You take a tiny little seed . . . and I have giant marigolds that I grew from seeds. Those seeds came up. And now there are these absolutely gorgeous marigolds. And so what a garden does for me is to say the human spirit is a kick-ass thing. That's what that garden does.

Note: On 11 December 1996, several months after this interview took place, Gloria Naylor informed me that it was not yet time for *Sapphira Wade*, the novel. Ms. Naylor explained that her vision of the meeting of an African woman with a European man to be used as the founding of a country would certainly become a future project, but at this time, Ms. Naylor has begun working on a project entitled *The Men of Brewster Place*. She explained that this new work would be written from the perspective of the men who were on Brewster Place but whose stories could not be written until now.

Michelle C. Loris

An Interview with Gloria Naylor

Charles H. Rowell / 1997

From *Callaloo* 20:1 (1997), 179–92. Copyright © Charles H. Rowell. Reprinted with permission of the Johns Hopkins University Press.

This interview was conducted by telephone on Monday, 3 February 1997, between Charlottesville, Virginia, and New York City.

Charles Rowell: In your conversation with Toni Morrison published in *The Southern Review* (Vol. 21.3, July 1985), you said that, in your early years writing, you felt most complete when you expressed yourself through the written word.

Gloria Naylor: I was shy as an adolescent. There was a lot I wanted to articulate that just never made its way up out of my mouth, because I found it difficult to say what I was really thinking. And that went back to the time when I was seven or eight years old. I would begin to write little poems, you know, with the *aa bb cc* rhyme, the kind of verse you would expect from a seven or eight year old. And even as an adolescent it was still difficult for me to speak my mind. I have no problem doing that now. I'm forty-seven years old. But when I was twelve or thirteen it was a problem. I was more of a brooder. And so the things that most troubled me in my home life or at school, I would write those things out. And indeed that made me feel complete for the simple reason that it is unnatural for one to just tramp down feelings. And that's what I was doing a great deal.

CR: When did you first realize that you wanted to be and could be a writer?

GN: Those are two separate things for me: wanting to be a writer and then believing that I could be a writer. I had wanted to be a writer from the time I was twelve or thirteen years old. But whether that was going to be a probable goal for me didn't come up as an issue for me until my college years. It was in my college years that I began to learn about writers like Toni Morrison and Zora Neale Hurston. Ntozake Shange was extremely popular at that point, both for the feminist critics as well as for the public at large, because *For*

Colored Girls was playing on Broadway when I was still in college. So having those role models around me helped when I began to feel that I could be a writer. Being a writer, then, was not an unrealizable dream; it was a very plausible goal, because these women were there. They had done it, and I could perhaps add my voice to that whole stream of consciousness that I was ignorant of before, because of the way the school systems were.

I was a gifted child, and I read voraciously. But very little that I read had anything to do with my specific experience. As a reader I can make believe, as all readers do with good literature. So when I read *Wuthering Heights* or *Jane Eyre*, I could make that leap from those personal pains to my pains. But there was a distinct difference in learning that right within my own home, "my home" meaning of course my home as a community, the African American community. Within my own home there were books being written that were directed towards me, books that were especially about my experiences. So I didn't have to take that sort of second step to get to the goal of understanding a work. It was just one step, one step to what was my reality, and from that going on to doing my own work, as opposed to taking that leap that I had to take before reading good literature. I still have a fondness for the Victorian novels, and just long, messy stories with loads of drama in them and different sorts of natural holocausts going on. I think that early cutting of my literary teeth with nineteenth-century literature is something that still lives with me, because it had such a profound impression upon me when I was younger.

CR: What do you mean by "a profound impression"? What kind of impression?

GN: It took me into the world of those characters, and you know they were always very messy and traumatic worlds in nineteenth-century British novels. Or there were moral viewpoints with the likes of Thackeray or Dickens. I had not read literature like that before, and I think it just hit something within me, because I, too, am a moral writer whether I want to think about it or not; I do have a point of view. And I write dramatic novels. It's important for me that there be drama. It's not always external drama, but internal drama that is going on. You know I just don't subscribe to that art for art's sake; I don't believe that a text is written in beautiful language for its own sake—lovely language that is in itself enough. But I don't dismiss the people who love that sort of writing. That kind of writing has just never been my cup of tea. And it's certainly not how I write. I think I have a strong narrative drive, and I have a moral point of view. I think, for example, of John Irving whom I have enjoyed reading since *The Cider House* Rules. With that novel, I believe he, for the first time in his career, began to make an overt moral stand. Of course, I picked up on the other nice things he was doing with his work. It's like when you walk into a crowded room and there is instant chemistry, let's say, with someone far across at the other corner; you pick up the chemistry of that one person, and you know you're going to click in some way. Literature worked that way for me. When I read Edgar Allan Poe, something clicked. When I read Charles Dickens, something clicked. And what was clicking, if you will, was just, I think, my own birthing. I was waiting to be able to deliver. That would not have been possible if I had not gone on to discover, as I told you, writers who reflected me and my own life.

CR: When do you think you became conscious of the formal practice of the novel—that is, the novel as a particular form, as a genre, a convention? And the innovative techniques associated with it?
GN: Are you referring to me as reader or to me as writer?

CR: I like how you make the distinction. Will you speak of both—as reader and as writer?
GN: I definitely see the difference between my connecting with what I've read or my connecting with something in order to write. My consciousness of the novel as a form for myself as a writer—believe it or not—did not occur until I worked on my third novel, *Mama Day*. My first novel, *The Women of Brewster Place*, was interconnected short stories. I told myself, well, I may not be able to write a whole book, but I can write one story. And then, well, I can write another story. The idea of sitting down and writing a novel was too intimidating for me in my early years. And then I look at what I did with *Linden Hills*, the next book; it feels more like a book. If you go into the form and take it apart, there's nothing but interconnected lives that those two young boys encounter as they move throughout that neighborhood. But with *Mama Day* I truly felt that I was writing a novel in, at least, the traditional sense. Beginning, middle and end. And they were not connected stories, although they were connected voices. So it was as a writer that I began to tackle the form of the novel, as a novel. As a reader, twelve years old, thirteen years old, you know, I was reading those things from cover to cover. And to me they spoke novelistically.

CR: What do you mean when you say "novelistically"?

GN: They spoke to me as creating a whole world, creating within the context of a narrative that went throughout a universe which you stepped into. With a poem you step into a moment. With a short story you'll step into the day in the life of, or the year in the life of. But with a novel you've got whole universes swirling. And you're attempting to make sense out of that.

CR: In a *Paris Review* interview, Milan Kundera spoke of "novelistic thinking" as opposed to philosophical thinking.

GN: To think novelistically is to understand that you're in a fictive universe. And you understand that it is a mirror to reality, that it's not reality itself. But, to be very honest with you, biography I think of as being novelistic—and even some essays because you are creating a persona for yourself. You are creating a forum for that picture of one's self. So to me history is just recreating what had gone before, the past, from one person's point of view. A biography is the recreation of a life through another person's point of view. With fiction the rules are slightly different; it is impossible to get a mirror true to life in fiction. Like they say, fact is stranger than fiction. There is so much you could not write that's truly happening if you say you are writing fiction. To get away with the bizarre things that go on within this world, you have to come out with an essay about it. You are limited by fiction; you are limited by the convention that it be probable.

CR: Prose fiction always has a direct or an implied narrative action. I have heard general readers complaining that a certain novel didn't have a plot, didn't have a storyline—that a particular short story was not a narrative.

GN: I guess that depends upon how you're defining "narrative." I define it as anything which drives the story forward. That might be language or characters' internal dialogue with themselves. Lack of a plot does not necessarily mean a piece of work is missing a narrative. Nor does lack of storyline. But to me plot and storyline are really the same thing: the meat of the short story. But one must look at a plot or storyline in an expanded way to understand that a stream-of-consciousness, where you're totally inside a character's head, can also be narrative if it's driving the story forward.

CR: When I speak to fiction writers, they talk a lot about character and characters, the agents of the action. Character seems all.

GN: Your work must be character driven, because what you're doing, as I said, is entering a universe. Okay, then what is going on in that universe? People are running around being themselves. Your job, as a fiction writer, is to try to figure out what those actions themselves mean for each individual character. And for me specifically, before a book begins, I have to see images and pictures of things that are going on. And then I go in search of what those folk are doing. When I started work on *Bailey's Cafe*, I saw—literally I saw—an older woman and an older man dancing on a pier, whenever I turned on Duke Ellington's *Mood Indigo*. Now I don't know at that stage what that meant. I knew it made me want to cry for some reason. And so what I do is then go in search of those characters and in search of that movement that night on that pier. And then it becomes a chapter in that book, called *Mood Indigo*. You know, character is all for someone like me. I live with those people. I dream about them.

CR: Will you say more about the genealogy of *Bailey's Cafe*—more about how that novel came into being? What was the writing process like for you as you created *Bailey's Cafe*?

GN: Well, it started with that image. It started with the image which turned out to be Sadie and the Ice-man who were in a situation that was hopeless. In a sense, he loved her, but she had grown to believe in a dream. She could no longer believe in reality. I had that image, and I had the music. Because the only thing I knew at that point about this novel is that it was going to be shaped by jazz. And then I first had to go to the music to pull from the music the people who I knew were there and waiting. I think of everything that I do as my being a transcriber for these lives. And I go in search of what they were doing, why they were doing it, trying to keep my ego out of it as much as possible.

Let's go back to *Mood Indigo* and *Bailey's Cafe*. . . . There was Sadie, after all that she had gone through, being homeless, selling her body in order to get her wine, because her wine brought her the dream of a house that she had already lost. I would have loved for her to look into the Ice-man's eyes and see salvation. That she could get off the streets. That she had someone who wasn't going to beat her, who understood her history, who would cherish her. I would give anything for an ending like that. But my books are character driven, and that was not going to be the ending. You know, so that's one example of my respecting what happens with my character. Another one is in

Linden Hills, where a character turned on me; and I was working on *Linden Hills* for two years. There was a woman who was in a basement with a dead child, and for two years I thought what that woman was going to do at the end of that book was to barge up those steps and to say to her crazy husband, Luther Nedeed, "You do what you want but I'm out of here." When the time came for me to do that scene, that character turned on me: she said she was happy to have been a wife. That's how she got her identity. She loved cleaning that house. She loved making a way for her husband. What she was going to do was climb up those steps and not tell him "get out of my way," as in some great feminist dream. She was going to climb those steps and start cleaning house. It floored me. It absolutely floored me. And, I asked, where did this come from? Well, when I look back on the two years of work, she had been telling me that all along. She is meant to discover women's history. Down in that basement with her was an old Bible, photographs, and recipe books. She encountered the other generations of women. Each time Wilma resisted. I was not seeing her do that until we came to the grand moment, and she said to me, "That's what I am. I'm happy to be a wife." That was rough. I even stopped writing for about two weeks because I was so angry. I had already chosen the metaphor for her to barge up those steps with. I had taken everything into account, except the woman herself. My being a feminist or not being a feminist, my righteous indignation for her—none of that mattered, because she was who she was. Thank God I had enough sense to go back to the book and let her do what she wanted to do.

CR: Is there a connection between *Linden Hills* and *The Women of Brewster Place*? One deals with the middle class and one with the poor. I am very happy to see our fiction writers deal with the black middle class. African American fiction writers, earlier on, seemed almost to have idealized or romanticized the life of the poor as metaphor of authenticity in their novels. And all these earlier writers did not come from the underclass; many were middle- and upper middle-class themselves. Thanks for taking the step beyond the class issues that became a kind of intra-racial stereotype. Perhaps it is you and other recent women writers who have been allowing the whole spectrum of socio-economic classes to appear in African American literature. African Americans are not a monolith—and of course we have heard that over and over.

GN: Is there a connection between *Linden Hills* and *The Women of Brewster Place*? Definitely. And you addressed the issue at the end of your question: we are not a monolithic people. I demonstrated this dramatically by having a character in Brewster Place, Kiswana Browne, move from Linden Hills into the poorer section of town. I used that character to foreshadow the next novel in which I deal with the black middle class. I am myself from a working-class family, and so my perspective is always going to include characters from that class. My family came out of the Mississippi Delta where they were tenant farmers. And in one generation they saw me graduate from Yale University with a masters degree. But for young writers, who may not have had my history, their stories are going to be rooted in what they know—the middle class. And I see that happening with the spate of new novelists who are coming along now.

CR: Wonderful.

GN: And I think, too, what is going to happen increasingly as we move into the twenty-first century is that we're going to see a lot of young writers who have never had a connection, no direct connection, to their Southern roots. These writers are coming out full blown and middle-class. And it's fascinating to see some of the things they will hold on to. I just read a couple of interesting books, called *Only Twice I've Wished for Heaven* by Dawn Trice. Her book deals with class. I have also read Edwidge Danticat's work; she brings a Haitian-American view of things, which is also middle-class. We can only pull from what we know. Octavia Butler is writing science fiction, but it's really about the world we live in now. She is pulling from what she knows about this world. That's what those young writers are going to be doing. Maybe I am sort of the foremother of that happening, because I'm old enough to be their mother. That's for sure. Looking at all of our experiences, we discover that it is not all about the South. It's not all about cotton. That's sort of been made into the classic black experience. These kids don't know about that; some of them don't want to know about that, but they are still giving us viewpoints about how we as a people live.

CR: And all black people in the rural South are not sharecroppers or tenant farmers. Some of them own their own farms. Some of them are professionals. Some of them are middle- and upper-middle class. Neither do all black Southerners have an intimate relationship to the growing or harvesting of cotton, sugar cane, rice, tobacco, etc.; some black Southerners are urban people.

GN: Exactly. There is (and was) also a black middle class in the South.

CR: But we seldom see these people in our literature. I am not speaking of the brilliant South-centered work of Ernest Gaines or Alice Walker; they are descendants, they have told us, of economically poor people that white plantation owners in Louisiana and in Georgia, respectively, exploited. What about the writers who come from middle-class backgrounds? Why don't they write about that middle-class dimension of black life in the South?

GN: It is said that you deal with your demons first. And maybe it's that demon that hung over a lot of their heads. As a writer, I'm going to tell you that it's more interesting to write about people who have struggled. Then, too, my novel *Linden Hills* proved that even the middle class can have struggles. There is something very seductive, though, about our roots in the South. That South is the closest we'll ever come to Africa. You know, I recall, when I went over to Senegal and I was researching a historical novel I'm going to write, I had my hair braided there. The woman, the beautician in the beauty shop, had a little low stool; they sit you on that little low stool, between their knees, and they braid your hair. A lump came into my throat, because it brought back memories of how my mother did my hair. She'd sit you between her knees.

CR: Yes, I remember seeing my mother and my sisters braiding hair.

GN: So I think that perhaps for some writers the South might be the closest thing we have to our connection to the Motherland. Perhaps that's the reason. And we may have recently fallen into that trap that it's only the poor folk who are colorful enough, you know, to give you enough drama. No, not necessarily. Drama can be internal.

CR: Why did you study at Yale University? What attracted you there?

GN: It was a free scholarship. They gave me a scholarship, plus a stipend to live on. It was also "Yale," but then Cornell had accepted me, too. Finally, I went up to Cornell to teach; they never forgave me for that—they said, you see, we wanted you way back when, before any of this happened, we wanted you. That was quite funny. But I chose Yale also because New Haven was close to New York, and I didn't want to be too far from my family at that point. Sometimes when the going got rough there, I'd just hop on the train and take it to Grand Central, walk around Grand Central, get a cup of coffee and go back, because sometimes I would just feel suffocated in that whole campus setting.

CR: Will you talk about *The Women of Brewster Place*? Was that your first novel—the first you wrote and the first you published?
GN: The book is a novel in seven stories. Yes, it was. It was the first one I wrote. But when I was sixteen years old, I used to go up into the attic of our home (I used to pull a sheet across part of the attic and call it Gloria's Gallery). I began a novel at sixteen, but, as far as serious work, *The Women of Brewster Place* is the first novel I wrote.

CR: How did it come into being? What is its genealogy?
GN: Well, *The Women of Brewster Place* came into being when I finally hit Brooklyn College and I looked back on all that reading I had done and been directed to do by teachers who really cared about me. I realized that we were all working with this benign ignorance of what was out there in Black America and had been out there, since the eighteenth century, beginning with Lucy Terry's "Bars Fight," a poem about the 1746 Indian raid on Deerfield, Massachusetts. And I realized that I had been deprived through benign ignorance of knowing about this literary history. I decided that, if I had one book in me, I wanted it to be all about me, and the me in this case was a multi-faceted me. So that's how *Brewster Place* began, and the structure of it, as I said, came about because of my being a novice at that time. My thinking was this: well I don't know if I can write a whole novel, but I can write a story. And then I can write another story. That's sort of how it happened. Now what's going to be interesting for me is to see how *The Men of Brewster Place* finally comes to being. I'm pretty sure it's going to be looking at relationships between men and their families. When you do get writing about black men, normally it's directed at men struggling with the white world for something—for dignity, for self-respect, for some gains, financial or psychological. Their opponent is always the white world. I would love to look at black men in relationship to their families. Don't take them anywhere out there to meet what's going on past Brewster Place, but right there—right there where they're standing. It's going to be interesting to see what comes out this time. Add that to the fact that I'm a very different woman from the woman who wrote *The Women of Brewster Place*. We'll see.

CR: I'd like to go back to the time when you were an undergraduate student in creative writing classes. I am very happy to see the great number of black students now entering creative writing classes. It's a very interesting phenomenon. I am not certain one could cite a real cause and effect relationship here—that is, to the rise in the large numbers of excellent young black writers. The numbers are high—so many very good ones that I, even as editor of *Callaloo*, can't keep up with them all. There are a lot of very good young black writers, too.

GN: I've taught in several creative writing programs. But I have been a little ambivalent about whether these kids need an MFA or not. I tell my writing students, Okay, what we can give you is a forum. I can add a pair of very intelligent ears to what you have to say, and your peers can add something to what you have to say because you're bouncing off of readers. But I cannot teach you to write. I cannot put into you what God left out. I am not a guru. I struggle each day like you do with the blank page or now it's the blank screen or whatever. If I can approach it that way with the class, if they can really buy that perception of what we're doing together, then I get nurtured when I'm teaching creative writing and the students get nurtured. But to look to me to answer. The Question for them of how do you make it happen is like asking someone to dissect the spirit within our body. How are we made to live? No one knows that. You know they've been writing about the mystery of life from the beginning with Hawthorne and his cautionary tales about leaving alone that which is the kernel of one's existence. If we can go along together for a semester like that, then I will have wonderful experiences, and I hope my students will also. Should these kids just take such courses, or should they get out there and pump gas, wait tables, do whatever, to live? I think a little bit of both—to have the academic structure with which they can write if they have the right writing teacher as well as having life experience. But I tell you if it were a toss up and I had to choose only one, it would be life experience.

CR: What is it that a creative writing program offers or gives students in the classroom? What do you do there together?

GN: What we do together is to give them an audience for what they're going to produce. That's all we're doing. The young writer says to me I want to move Ms. Naylor, from A to G. I don't want to go to H or I; I just want to move my story from A to G. My job and the job of the other students in that workshop with us is to show that student how best to move from A to G. Our job is not to show him that he should really move from A to F. I am not to ask him why he is dealing with the alphabet at all. No. I respect whatever vision students bring to the class, because I demand that they respect my vision. What we try to do together is to get each individual student to the place—and to discover the best way how—that he or she wants to go. That's how I was taught, and that's how I proceeded over the years to teach—to say to the student, "You map out the journey, kid." I can't map out the journey; I can't map out the mode in which you will travel, but I sure as heck have read enough to tell you if you get there.

CR: I want to go back to "the written word" and how it served you in your youth. You spoke of that earlier in this interview. How does the written word serve you now?
GN: That's quite a question, Charles, because now it gets so tangled up—doesn't it? —with commercialism; and it also gets tangled up with ego and one's sense of one's self, which has changed. It does more than pay my rent now; it also keeps me a little bit stable, because I think most creative writers, whatever their venue, are a little bit nutty. I really do.

CR: Another way of asking that question is this: Why do you keep writing prose fiction? Writing is one of the most difficult of activities. Why do you keep doing this to yourself; why do you keep writing?
GN: Because—and I know it sounds trite—but because I have no choice, Charles.

CR: But what does that mean?
GN: Some things you can choose to do, and I have no choice, meaning that if I didn't write I would have a very flat life. It is so entwined now with my sense of myself that it was almost impossible to answer that question. Why do I do it now? I could survive, sure, if I just taught or if I just lectured. I could survive, but what kind of survival would it be? I have had the privilege of being shown a richer way in which to lead my life and that is to grapple with these words and these forms and these characters. I'm not ready to stop that now. Maybe at some point in my future it's going to cease being prose fiction; it's going to get turned into drama, because I've been writing plays lately. I love working with the theater. So one day it might be that. But, I'm telling you, until I kick out of here I'm going to be communicating in some way, shape or form. To deconstruct *why*, I'm not sure. I just know that I'm not happy when I'm not working. Life takes on a different texture when I'm not working.

CR: How much of your private self, your interior life, your identity as a black woman, do you think is bound up in your writing prose fiction?

GN: A lot of it. Most of it; it goes back to how I perceive myself in the process: if I'm a transcriber or a filter, then everything I've ever lived or wanted to live as a black woman comes out in my work. The very act of writing is a statement about how you see yourself in the world. It's quite arrogant to think that anybody would care about what you have to say. Unless you have that within you, to know that someone's going to care—if no one but yourself—then you aren't going to write. You've got to believe that someone needs to hear this. In the beginning I needed to hear it for myself. As you go along and the process gets all entangled in a career, then you might choose other audiences. Or it just needs to be said. All of that is arrogant. All of that means that one has a good strong sense of self.

CR: What is "a good strong sense of self"?

GN: Meaning that there is an ego. Here's the irony of it, one of the many ironies of life: in order to be a writer you need a tremendous ego—you really do. As I said, just to feel that someone wants to hear what you have to say is a great deal of ego. But in order to write memorably you have to suppress your ego. That's just like *The Handmaid's Tale*—I love that book—in which one becomes a filter for those other lives that pass through. So how is that tied up with being a black woman? They're passing through a sieve that contains Gloria Naylor, the black woman who came from parents, who migrated to New York City; and they came from parents who were tenant farmers and myriad things which make me. All of this goes into that filter, and I can't tear it apart or snip it apart and ask: how much of this is a black woman, how much of this is a personal history, how much of this is a racial history? There is no way to know that—there isn't. That's why you have a job, and that's why other critics have jobs: to simply take apart that which I think can never truly be taken apart and explained.

CR: In your *Southern Review* (July 1985) conversation with Toni Morrison, both of you—at the beginning of the exchange—talked a lot about male culture and its self-willed authority. I'll call it self-willed power. You said that the "whole sense of adventure and authority tied into maleness has a lot to do with how books are created and who's created them—and in what numbers."

GN: I had told you before about how you influenced me and how *The Bluest Eye* . . . gave me a validity to do something which I had thought was really male terrain. And all my education had subconsciously told me that it wasn't the place for me. Okay, I'm forty-seven years old. I'm coming of age in the 1960s or so, right? I am a participant in a school system taught by people who were born in the 1920s and 1930s. They were relatively young teachers when they taught me. What on earth were we given to read to be well read? You had to read Dickens, you had to read Thackeray, you had to read Emerson and Poe and Hawthorne. The bow that they gave to Emily Brontë or Charlotte Brontë was about the only one they gave to a woman writer. Maybe you were going to read *Wuthering Heights*. Ninety-nine percent of everything you were given or told to read was written by men. Now, of course, you grow older, and you understand that that's just a political choice made and that the literary canon itself is a political construct. But of course that's what you would think. Huck Finn, Tom Sawyer—they were all doing marvelous things. Jules Verne is traveling with people around the world and under the sea and this sort of thing. Women weren't doing that. Finally you are able to say, I can send myself on an adventure. I think that's why the film *Thelma and Louise* hit so many chords. If we're going to talk about popular culture for a quick minute, *Thelma and Louise* hit so many chords in people because there were women doing things that men normally do, which is to travel. You know Jack Kerouac—you know men were movers and shakers, and they were the adventurers. They were the adventurers from the inception of the novel, a form which, they say, begins with Cervantes. There he was out there conquering things, and where was poor Dulcinea? Stuck in an inn. You came of age implicitly being told it is a white male world, and everything that's been given to us of substance, everything that has lasted, has been just that because their buddies kept them in the canon. I hope that answers your question. But that's probably all the things that were going on in my mind when I made that statement talking to Toni Morrison. I think it is slightly different today for the students in academia, but it's not as pervasive as it used to be. What has contributed to Western literature has been a lot more than just white males. And there would be no Western literature, I believe, without the black woman. I really don't think so. We really would have been much deprived in this country if those voices which were always there hadn't started being realized and being put into the pot to enrich us all. And although today white men are still the power base for the literary establishment and academia, things are slowly beginning to change. You have white women who have a say in the creation of the canon and selecting the curriculum for universities. There are also a few black men and women who are entering the power structure and making those literary decisions as well. I don't feel, as I once did, that I lack authority to pick up the pen because: 1) I do write now, and 2) my work is being taught. And the decision to teach my work or validate it in academia does not depend totally upon white males anymore. You, yourself, are an example of that. You made the decision to print this interview with me. And you make other decisions each month with your journal, *Callaloo*, that affect the lives of countless black writers.

CR: You said "if there had been no black woman" there would be no American literature. What do you mean?

GN: I don't think there'd be American literature without black women. What is America? What is America now that we're moving into the twenty-first century? It is said that the majority of Americans in six years will be nonwhite. Now can you keep feeding people that anemic soup of Hawthorne and Emerson and Poe? When you're not eating properly, you feel weak, don't you? You feel there's something missing somewhere. And one of the things that we were missing the most was creations from the pens of black women. When I went to Brooklyn College during the late 1970s, there was an Africana studies department, and there was not a single course on black women writers. But it was there that I learned about James Baldwin and Richard Wright and Jean Toomer. Their books were wonderful, wonderful things for me to have read. But at the same point I had to ask, What about me again? And then literally across the quad there is the Women's Studies Program. It wasn't even a department. It was a program, and I got in there and they taught me Simone Weil, they taught me Georgia O'Keeffe and what she had done. Except for this one lone teacher, this one teacher in creative writing named Joan Larkin, no one was teaching black women. No one. All of this happened when I was in college. So I had to piece together what I knew. But things have changed slightly now. I think that it's almost impossible to get through a black literature course without doing Alice Walker or Toni Morrison. But James Baldwin and Richard Wright are also in there. Unless it's just a very foolish teacher. Ellison probably helped to redefine the novel in America. It was a black male that he sent on this quest. I hadn't read anything like that before in American literature. As a matter of fact, I know nobody else had read anything like that because nothing had been written until he did that. This country is definitely a patchwork quilt. This country's not a melting pot. We as a people are still resisting that. I don't want to say multi-cultural; I'm trying to shy away from that word. We have resisted the hodgepodge that we are. And that's been boiled down to issues of black and white. Where on earth are the Asians? Where are the Latinos?

CR: And where are the Native Americans?
GN: Yes, and the Native Americans. There is this resistance, and some black people are very happy to have it that way. But it's just lying about the complexity—that was probably the word I was looking for—the complexity of American life and American literature. So were you talking to Maxine Hong Kingston this morning or talking to the likes of Julia Alverez or Sandra Cisneros, I would hope that they would say the same thing to you: that without us there would be no American literature.

CR: What is it specifically? What is it that comes from the pens of black women and other women of color?
GN: It's a real simple answer: themselves, their lives, the announcement that "I am here" and "I am to be reckoned with," and that even "The things that you write, I enrich those, even though you may or may not know it." I live here in New York City with over a hundred nationalities in this city. How can one just walk down the street, see the people who are on it, and come away with a piece of work that would be about New York, and yet write only about a white male or a white female? You would have to have blinders on. Writers hardly do that; we go through our world very perceptively. We see practically everything or we see a lot more than most people see. You can't do it, Charles. You can't hear music, and you can't go to the cinema without being exposed to the multiplicity that is New York—and that is America—and then you're going to turn your back and deny that? Well, you can turn your back and try to deny that if you want to, but the work that you produce is going to be lacking in a lot of things.

CR: Gloria, where are you in relation to other American writers? That is, how do you view yourself in relation to other writers in this country?
GN: To be very honest, I don't think about that a lot, and I'll tell you why. It tends to make me too self-conscious. And as the years go by and I'm writing

more and more and I'm building a reputation (you know people tell me a quite awesome reputation), it is too easy to get caught into *what* you are because your writing is through *who* you are, and that may mean that you're a lot of things that aren't pretty and you're a lot of things that may not serve as role models. Then, too, your basic personality may not be the most pleasant one going, but writing through who you are means keeping a running tab on how you are developing as a person, how you are changing as a human being. I am always doing introspection in that regard. You know, how am I different from five years ago, ten years ago? And that to me, Charles, is safer than, well, how many awards have I gotten, who's thinking about my work, or why are they thinking about my work? It's hard enough just to write, or at least for me it is. I want to be remembered, I want my work to outlive me, and those are things that I cannot control at all. If I get into where do I stand in relationship to John Irving, where do I stand in relationship to Joyce Carol Oates, where do I stand in relationship to Julia Alverez—what in the hell does any of that have to do with the fact that I've got seven men now waiting for me to tell their stories? That's how I look at it. I think now that we're creeping into the twenty-first century that my work will still be taught and be studied, and that gives me a great deal of pride. I'll no longer back down from saying that. People teaching your work and people writing about your work—these acts help you to stay around, to be remembered. And that's what I've always wanted: that my work will outlive me.

CR: Let me ask the question another way. How do you stand in relationship to the next blank sheet of paper and the typewriter or the computer?
GN: Oh, God. Scared. So scared I can't breathe.

CR: Which is how you are standing now as you face the composition of *The Men of Brewster Place*?
GN: Where am I standing, now? I have written the introduction. You published it in the last issue of *Callaloo*. Scared. That's what I tell my writing students, you know. I am right now no different from some kid whose right down there with you at the University of Virginia. I'm no different from a student who's in Rita Dove's class. That blank sheet is a humbler. Death, they say, is the equalizer, the ultimate equalizer. That blank sheet of paper or that blank screen can be a mother, I tell you.

Where I stand in relationship to my men of Brewster Place? I'm going to write their stories. I have to write them a letter or something first; I've done that. Time to time, I write my characters letters, letting them know that this or that is what I want to do and that I need their help to do it—that kind of thing. Or that I'm very excited about this or that—very, very excited. A friend sent me a quote—I think it's from Dorothy Allison—which said "two or three things in this life I know for sure, and one of them is that telling a story to its utmost completion is an act of love." This book was crying to be done, and I was going to do it a little bit later, but it turns out that I'm going to do it now. Something will come full circle at that point, and then I can worry about the big book that's going to lay the cornerstone. But I'm happy now, Charles. I love having a goal, and this is going to be quite a tough goal to achieve. But I'm going to do it the way I've done everything: I'm going to do it slowly, do it with pride, and do it honestly. And not honestly to the people who are going to be reading it, but to the characters who have allowed me to come into their lives. I've never wanted to rough-shod a character. Never. Even though the question of how I treated men used to just come up all the time with *The Women of Brewster Place*, people just didn't understand, and I didn't bother to enlighten them but so much. I knew what I was going to be doing with my life, God willing. So I didn't spend a lot of time answering those critics back in those years, but it's a different country now from the 1980s, at least academically it's different and critically it's different in terms of what people expect to be reading about women. At that point, that was sort of an avant garde thing to do: just to name a book the women of anything. But anyway, where I stand with my guys? I hope in good stead. I hope they forgive me my past sins or whatever and just come on into my life like they need to.

CR: Listening to you in this interview this morning, I am convinced more than ever before that the writing life is not anybody's ordinary life.
GN: To some extent I believe that's true. It can't be anybody's life, but to do it well you have to be aware of the sacrifices. And you sacrifice a good deal of your life to be with these characters. Writing is a solitary existence. You need a lot of quiet around you and within you. That's how you get the opportunity to listen to those voices that want to break through. If you're quiet inside yourself, and listen, those characters are going to talk. There are many things I could have chosen to do with my talents and my intelligence, but I find writing the most fulfilling. The writing life, all these years, is indistinguishable from my own life. And when I look back, I wouldn't have it any other way.

Conversation

Gloria Naylor and Nikki Giovanni / 1997

From *Callaloo* 23:4 (2000), 1395–409. Copyright © Charles H. Rowell. Reprinted with permission of the Johns Hopkins University Press.

Wintergreen Women Writers Retreat, Wintergreen, Virginia, 17 May 1997

Gloria Naylor: You did a conversation with James Baldwin, didn't you?
Nikki Giovanni: I did.

GN: That was twenty years ago or so?
NG: Maybe a little bit more than that. Because Thomas was not in school, and we did it in London, because Jimmy lived in France. And London was like the half-way point, because he didn't want to come to the United States, and I can't say as I blame him. And so, it was probably more like twenty-two, twenty-three years ago. And I did one with Margaret Walker.

GN: That one I don't know.
NG: You don't? I'll give you a copy. Before Margaret began writing *Demonic Genius*, she was having trouble organizing it. And I said to her editor, "Why don't you just sit down and talk to her, and let her talk it through." And she said, "Oh, that's an idea, isn't it?" And I said, "Well, that would be the best way to do it because once writers start to talk about things it organizes in their minds." And so, about four hours later, she came and said, "Why don't you do it?" So we went down because of Margaret's age—I mean, she is senior to me—so we went down to Jackson [Mississippi], where we did two days worth of talking in her den. Then after we transcribed it, we did the rest of it in D.C. Jill Krementz—you know Jill—the photographer, she did the pictures. I like Jill's work and I like the fact that she has devoted herself to writers. But that is a question, Gloria. Does it help you to talk ideas out?

GN: To a degree. To a limited degree. Because I feel that if I say too much about the book—you talk the book, you've written the book. And so I do take

168

that under advisement. But I will in very broad outlines. I stopped doing that because, one, the ending will change on you, because it takes its own organic growth. And it spins off and you're there with your computer trying to take down what all these crazy folks have done. So, in that regard, that's why I do keep it to a minimum. But I love to read a work that I feel is quasi-complete. Like, if I'd known people were going to read here, I would have brought something of my new book. It's very new and I'm not reading it much, you know? I wrote it so quickly that it hasn't really digested in my head. This last baby— and I call them all babies—was the strangest one to date in what it took for me to get it delivered. I was going through a lot of harassment, a lot of stupid stuff that was going on. I left my home in St. Helena, where I had gone to write a historical novel. But under all the mess they were doing to me I couldn't write. So I said, there's another book that's been in the back of my head to do. I was just going to call it "The Men . . ."with an ellipsis, but then I said I may as well go ahead and call it *The Men of Brewster Place*. Because there was no way when the publishers got through with it that they would let me call it just "The Men." But it was always in the back of my mind to do this book. So I brought it to the forefront of my mind, and I began to work on it. And it took no real research, whereas "Sapphira Wade" took a lot. But I watched some guys play one-on-one basketball, I did do that. And I did a little reading on idiot savants. There's a character named Brother Jerome who is really the embodiment of the blues, and he's really playing out all these different men, playing their textures and their songs. But beyond this kind of minimal research, this book could just come. And it was something that I wanted to do for my dad, a long time ago, so, here it is.

NG: Are we going to pick up, for example, Basil?

GN: Definitely. Basil has a big story in there. And Eugene Turner, who's the husband who didn't show up at the baby's funeral. So now you'll know why he didn't show up at the funeral. See, *Women* left a lot of unanswered questions, and there are also a lot of issues I've thought about since the Million Man March. I don't know, I was very moved by what I saw, as were many people. And maybe it was just a little bit different for me because we had just lost my father. That would have been his idea of the impossible, you know. Having a kid who went to Yale was for him the equivalent of the fact that men could walk on the moon. And he had lived long enough to see both happen. And the Million Man March would have been his third miracle, to have watched that many men come together. Because he followed Malcolm X for many years, and then Louis Farrakhan. And there's a lot of sane talk coming from those guys. And we're asked to emphasize the insane stuff they do, but for me nine-tenths of the weight is on the prescription they have for my people, and I think it's a darn good one. I believe we should try self-determination. We tried integration, and that didn't work. And at some point people have got to start realizing that. It has not worked. Integration hasn't worked. So, where do we go from here? But we never get into that conversation. We just get into the conversation, how many more of us can we squeeze into this opportunity? How high can some few of us go? And just totally missing what's going on in the whole community. We do not have a true backbone, that I believe. Maybe it's the church, to some small degree, and maybe some businesses, but to me every nation marches on the shoulders of its merchants, and Black Americans have gotten into a service economy, you know. They will be the new drones, to replace the scriveners of Dickens's time. Well, that was a long way of answering a short question, Nikki.

NG: I'm not going to argue with you about what you're saying about integration—you have a point.

GN: You think it works?

NG: I believe it's insignificant on a certain level whether it works or doesn't. What we have to do that I think is important is raise our tolerance for each other. And that's black people and white people; everybody needs to raise their tolerance. And I have a lot of faith in the ability of black people to raise their tolerance—

GN: —sure, because that's what we've had a history of doing, so-called endurance.

NG: But it's important that we raise it. And what the Million Man March showed a lot of black men—and we're in agreement here—is that they could in fact tolerate being close to each other. At the point of the Million Man March we did not have crime, we did not have them beating each other. Usually black men pick up newspapers and magazines or they watch TV and what they see is that any time there are two black men, they will be fighting. And what Louis Farrakhan and the March showed was that, no, this is somebody else's image. TV could be a teaching tool. But nobody wants to use it that way; they want to use it as a commercial tool.

GN: The same old stereotypes are there.
NG: They want to use the same old stereotypes.

GN: Yes, you have the black people in black face. You've got your Butterfly McQueens. Do you watch television?
NG: A lot.

GN: Do you? You see I stopped watching television, I did. For a while I was watching stuff and just comparing what their spin on my reality was and what reality really was. But it just got so disheartening to me, Nikki. I felt, you've got to find something and try to make a difference somewhere in this world, Gloria. That's part of the reason for the work I've done with my niece and my nephew, beyond the fact that I also love them very much. Because I would say, how does one person, or let's say a hundred thousand people, who turn that thing on, know what it's about; you can see the substructure, and you go from news channel to news channel and they all have the same story. It is spooky as hell to me. So, to keep my sanity, I think, I had to leave that puppy alone. What I will do is watch old movies; I like those. Not the old John Wayne films, but those old Bette Davis and Joan Crawford films, some of those classic, kick-ass films. That I'll do. I'll deal with, like, American Movie Channel, but the news, the McNeil-Lehrer—no. If something has happened, then I'll go to the McNeil-Lehrer for it, or sometimes CNN, if you can endure CNN for like two hours. And they'll give you a little bit of in-depth coverage of the news. But what I'm looking for now is some kind of political niche to put my toes into and begin working for. Because I have time now on my hands, since I've finished my major work. I'm not one of those people who can just put down one and do another; see, you can do that, but I can't do that.
NG: No, no.

GN: I thought you could.
NG: No.

GN: Well, you can almost do that. I know Joyce Carol Oates, she can do that.
NG: Joyce writes with two hands.

GN: She can turn in one novel in the morning and start a new one in the afternoon. Wild, wild, wild. She never sees the sunlight. But . . . I forgot how I got into all that stuff . . . oh, time on my hands. So, now that I've done that, it's sort of like, what else do I do with my day until it's time to start teaching or whatever, you know. And there is this boredom. I've become more aware of time and what I'm doing and not doing since 1996 [and my experience in St. Helena]. We will just for shorthand call all that happened my 1996 experience. After that, I do look at time differently. And I look at my life differently. Not the way they had hoped, because those folk are out to destroy you. So they didn't get that done. But there is a change that you do go through. Because I was trying to remember, Nikki, all right, when I finished the book before, did I feel this way, did I feel like I have all this time on my hands? And the answer is "no," but then my nephew was with me when I finished *Mama Day*. So with a teenager in the house that's why I didn't feel like there was nothing to do, because he was a bad-behind kid, there was always something you had to do with him, so I don't know. What do you think of time? But you teach, though, so . . . the time that you have at home is precious time for you.

NG: Yes, I teach, and I enjoy that. I like to think that even if I hit a lottery I would continue to teach. I like it because I teach undergrads. And so my classes are not restricted. So I'm not just teaching what is called "the writers" because I don't believe in "the writers." If that was the case, I would have never been taught. Because nobody thought I was a writer. And so I think it's important to reach that kid. Going back to our earlier conversation about opera divas—Jesse Norman and Leontyne Price—I was just wondering, what's the difference between a diva from Mississippi and one from, say, Marietta, Ohio? Can you imagine being a little black girl in Mississippi and saying, "I want to sing opera"?

GN: They probably didn't say it. They probably wouldn't think to say it, because, God knows, they had no role models. I mean, they had Marian Anderson, but that was all.

NG: So maybe somebody else said it for them, or thought it for them. "You should sing opera."

GN: Maybe, if they were middle-class.

NG: I don't know what middle-class might have meant to black people in Mississippi.

GN: In Mississippi, if your father was a preacher, or if your mother taught school, or she was a nurse, or something like that, that made you middle-class.

NG: I don't know, when you think of middle class—Atlanta has a middle class because they have big houses, they have cars. The Kings were middle-class; Daddy King bought all of his children automobiles so they wouldn't have to ride on segregated buses. One of the funniest things about Martin Luther King, Jr., is that he came to public notice in an engagement over riding a city bus that in all probablity he never rode in his life, because Daddy King bought them cars because he didn't want his children being insulted.

GN: Isn't that something?

NG: And so probably one of the first times, if not *the* first time, that he was ever on a public bus was after the Montgomery Bus Boycott.

GN: And that's what they say, that the middle class led the Civil Rights Movement.

NG: Yes. And so when you think about Leontyne, I don't see a sharecropper, but I'll bet it was a struggle. It was a struggle to do music lessons. It was a struggle for her mother to believe in her voice. And yet these Mississippians come out and they say, "We're larger than life."

GN: James Earl Jones is from Mississippi. Richard Wright.

NG: Richard Wright was so angry.

GN: Richard Wright was a strange character. I don't know if there are any expatriates now running around in Europe. I assume there must be. I met a guy up in Finland who claimed he was an expatriate. But I'm wondering, what kind of group would be there now. Would they just be nuts or would they be talented people [*laughing*]. Because that's something I told you I'm thinking about. I just don't know what the culture is. I have one or two friends over there, but I don't know what kind of culture I would be entering as far as expatriates.

NG: Would you go to Scandinavia?

GN: I don't think so. I would think I'd end up in maybe London or over in Vienna. I have a long-term friend who lives in Vienna, and newer-term friends in London. I'm thinking about it. I said when I finished this book

I would make all this clear, so I should probably just shut up until it's clear in my own head. But this country *has* changed to a degree, from what led to writers moving abroad—the Richard Wrights and the James Baldwins, and . . . who else? Frank Yerby?
NG: Oh! Chester Himes, Ollie Harrington, the cartoonist. Chip Delany.

GN: But now there is room for them. I personally may not like the shape of the room, the appointments in the room, but I cannot deny that there is room.
NG: There's room. We have a lot of athletes going abroad. And they're not going abroad running from racism, but seeking opportunity. So you'll see them playing basketball, playing baseball. Because they go to Europe. And they make a mark, so that they're then invited back to the United States at good prices.

GN: Like the men in the old Negro Leagues, who worked around the clock, who'd go to Cuba and play.
NG: Yes, and that was a loss.

GN: That was a huge loss. You know this thing about integration, and the whole celebration around Jackie Robinson—I had to do a lot of research on the Negro Leagues for *Bailey's Cafe*, and it dawned on me, why are people so happy about one man, when if they'd held out maybe a whole team could have joined the league. What is the big thing about one man—oh, we let one man in. Black baseball was not unorganized, it was simply unrecognized. They had their own tournaments, their own stadiums, the whole business. So you hold out and you say, well, no, you're not getting a Satchel, you're not getting any of these people, what you're going to get is our League. So we have this league, and you have your league, and the fans are going to start coming, white boys are going to try to get into the Negro League—you know, I got so upset, I don't know. Is it only me? Sometimes you feel that way. I mean, I didn't watch Star Wars or *E.T.,* and is it only me seeing things this way? And you hate to give up speaking, or to throw cold water all the time. The whole world is happy about this fiftieth anniversary thing.
NG: It is interesting because, actually, as you know, the Negro Leagues were outselling the white leagues in terms of tickets. The demise would have been of white baseball. I think that that's hard, Gloria. I do see what you're saying, but I think it's hard. I think it's easy for me to say, well, one man, this is not

right, this is not the right way to approach it, it's just not right. And yet, everybody was happy.

GN: Yes, everybody was ecstatic.
NG: And of course it killed Jackie. He died at the age I am now. It killed him. The expectations, what he had to hear on the field, and the pressure on his kids, it killed him. And everybody is, like, well this is really great. And yet, there was something magnificent about it. Because we live in the western world where one man died to save us all. So what do we have now? Two men. Two men died. We believe in that syndrome of one man standing for all.

GN: Oh, yes, we believe in that. Sacrificing children to integrate schools.
NG: Oh, sure. But it would have been interesting. God knows you would like to see a decent play or movie—see, I don't understand Hollywood. And I know you love movies, so . . . I don't understand why we haven't had a movie on Linda Brown.

GN: I love that photo—you have it in your house somewhere, that classic photo of this little black girl between the legs of the state troopers.
NG: It's in my bedroom.

GN: Incredible.
NG: The framer who framed that said to me (or, his wife said to me) "Oh, isn't she cute?" And it was the last time they framed anything for me. I said, "Cute? Cute? They're throwing fruit at this girl, they spat on this girl, she's trying to go to school, and you think that's *cute*?" I just went off on her. And she was like, "Oh, Miss Giovanni, I'm sorry." I was furious.

GN: There are some days when you've just got to say something. Some days you don't.
NG: That was one of those days. That little girl cannot be cute. That little girl was being driven crazy. See, I wouldn't have the heart—and I'm not saying you do—to say to her that this was not meaningful. I know it was meaning-ful. I just don't know that the world she's living in knows it was meaningful. And that's why I have "Thug Life" on my arm. I *know* that Tupac Shakur was meaningful. And I know that his death was even more so. It was not an acci-dental death.

GN: You thought it was arranged?

NG: I think he was assassinated.

GN: You think he was assassinated?

NG: Sure. You see, I don't think that black boys who play with guns shot at Tupac Shakur.

GN: Okay.

NG: I think the same people that killed Malcolm X—if you believe that then—

GN: —I just never saw Tupac Shakur on the same level as the Malcolm X's or the Kings.

NG: But he met the same thing, didn't he?

GN: He was very powerful among young people.

NG: Sure. So we who are meeting the same fate, we who are paying the same piper, have to be dancing in the same dance. We at least have to be in the building.

GN: Yes.

NG: Because we're paying the same piper. And to watch them start to hound this boy, you had to say, why is an old crazy bitch like C. Delores Tucker complaining about Tupac Shakur? What does she know about what he's doing? I couldn't believe that. What's Tipper Gore doing complaining about Prince? Tipper Gore said her eleven year-old daughter was listening to "Darling Nikki." What's her eleven year-old daughter doing listening to *Purple Rain*? What does she have, her own MasterCard, her own trust fund?

GN: Probably.

NG: Well, she shouldn't. The Gores ain't that damned rich. So if she's owning these things, Tipper and Al bought them for her. So what is she saying? We want Prince to shut up. We want Tupac to not rap. We don't want rap because it offends us, or we don't think our children should hear it. Why don't you control your children? But that's the same thing that we used to say in the old days. Do you want your sister to marry a Negro? How about talking to your f—ing sister? And leaving my brother alone. That's what I don't understand.

GN: But getting back to Tupac. So he was really that much of a force?
NG: I think he was.

GN: Among young people? Kind of like a cult leader, maybe, because I remember my nephew had his picture up in his room and all. So you think they assassinated him? But then there are other ways to contain somebody.
NG: Yes, but the best way is to kill him.

GN: They don't assassinate us all.
NG: You see, for you and me, and we're not important anyway, Gloria, but for you and me, people have to read us. Right? And that's a skill that's becoming rarer and rarer. And so we're not the threat that a young rapper who has something to say is. I'm not a big rap fan. I was a Tupac fan. Because everywhere that I went I was seeing signs of this young man. Kids that I respected would say, well have you heard this? And did you hear what he said? And when you keep hearing the same thing, you wonder, well, okay, what is this kid doing? And then you realize, okay, this is Tupac Shakur, this is Efeni Shakur's kid. His mother was a Black Panther. As he said, I'm the seed planted in stone. So he was supposed to have been dead. And then you realize, oh, this is Geronimo Pratt's godson.

GN: Is he? Geronimo Pratt? I don't know him personally, but I know his case.
NG: He's been in prison most of your life. So then you think, now wait a minute. This kid carries something with him. I'm not saying that you had to have all of that, I'm just saying that you weren't dealing with a fool. And the rest of the world knew that as well. He was beautiful. He was charismatic. If you look at *Above the Rim*—

GN: —or *Poetic Justice*.
NG: *Poetic Justice* was so terrible. Such a stupid, stupid movie. And the only thing that saved it was Tupac. But it was a dumb movie. But in *Above the Rim* he was wonderful. He was a thug, he was a gangster. And you think, oh wow, look at this young man. And look at this possibility. And somebody said, oh, no, that's a cherry tree; we need to cut it down. Because if that starts to flower, if that starts to grow . . .

GN: Well, there's an investment, I think, since the March, and you know it was ten million—one to ten million is how they calculated. They were scared out of their minds. So that's why I think that the church burnings began, in retaliation. It just blew their frigging minds. It seemed like the impossible, the American nightmare.

NG: Well, Morrison says that every time blacks do anything wonderful, the white reaction is something horrible. And she's right. And I hadn't thought about it, but you're right. The reaction to the Million Man March is the burning of the churches. Or the beating of a Rodney King. Or, the reaction to *Brown vs. Topeka* was Emmett Till. And then the black reaction was Rosa Parks. But every time we do something, whites retaliate in order to say, "We're going to put you back in your place." I don't think so. I don't think we want to be back in our places.

GN: No, because it's shifted. It's not where it was anyway.

NG: And this is what I like about black people; it's just like, well, okay, we're going to go on now. And it's very sad, this burning of the churches, because you have to condemn a people who would burn a church. That's damnable and it cannot be made up. So the white Christians are saying things like, we'll rebuild your church. You cannot rebuild these churches. These are hallowed places that you've tried to destroy. So what you're trying to do is to put a building back up to save your soul; so if there would be a God, then you would have your answer: but I tried. Can I fool you a little bit on this one, Lord? So, you went down to St. Helena's to work on *Sapphira Wade*. And that didn't work, but in the back of your mind you had *The Men of Brewster Place*.

GN: I had that in the back of my mind for a while, especially since my father's death. And I said to myself, now, in the historical novel, you're going to have a meeting of a black African woman with a white European male and a Native American. And I was using that to form a microcosm of the founding of a nation. Because that trio then goes sailing off to find Willow Springs. And I said to myself, how can I write about the union—no matter what kind of union it is—of the black female with the white male and the red male if I haven't done the black man, you see. So it was a blessing in disguise; it came down that way, because I dedicate this book to my father and yours. So it [*Sapphira Wade*] was not meant to be yet. And I have to do the next novel about cults; I want to come to terms with my past religion, this kind of thing.

NG: Oh, nice.

GN: And then *Sapphira* will be my seventh novel. The kick-ass novel is the seventh novel, and that's going to be her, wedged in there for the cornerstone. So every curse hides a blessing. And so having to leave St. Helena and the whole business, I've written this novel in record time. I had slated off like eighteen to twenty weeks, and the thing only took me four months. So that's the fastest I've ever written something. And it's not schlock, either; it may not be the Great American Novel, but that's OK. It's good solid work and it's not rip off work, not all of it! [Laughter] You know, sometimes I re-enter scenes that I had in *Brewster Place*, but now you re-enter that scene from the man's point of view. So it's a good teaching tool. It will hopefully do that. Because it's not a long book.

NG: That's great.

GN: Well, it was something that I could accomplish. My friends had said to me, you'll look back on this as being troubled times, but at least you can look back and say, no matter how horrible it got, this is what I did. And I didn't understand that at first when people told me, you've got to do your work, your work is your salvation. I didn't understand it, Nikki, but, yes, it turned out to be the case. Because if I hadn't worked those four months, I wouldn't have been fit to come here or fit to go anywhere except into a sanitarium or something.

NG: No, we can't lose you like that.

GN: No, I'm a fighter. It's hard sometimes, but I fight.

NG: Good for you.

GN: Well, how did we get onto that? You asked me about *The Men*?

NG: If you put a novelist and a poet in a room with a fireplace on a windy day, you're going to get a little bit of everything. It's perfect. I think that sometimes—and I look forward to reading *The Men*—some of our best work occurs because we're working on another level, an unconscious level. And I know your sister novelists, the two that I'm most aware of in terms of how they work or how they say they work, would be Toni [Morrison] and Alice [Walker]. And they both talk about characters coming in and taking over, things happening not when *you* want it to happen but when *they* want it to happen. I don't think poems are that spiritual, I don't know.

GN: Well, but maybe lines are.
NG: That could be.

GN: Or concepts are. Do you ever feel when you're inside of a poem that after a while it's bringing you somewhere and you're not there?
NG: Yes, you're letting it flow.

GN: Yes, you see, you say, "you're letting it flow." I would say, "it's flowing through me." You see the difference there? So, now, which are you? We've had this discussion before, haven't we? About who's doing it?
NG: Yes, about who's doing it.

GN: So you're saying, "I'm doing it," but me, I'm a bit more humble, I say "Thank god, here's the river, it's coming." But it's all—who knows? That's the bottom line. We truly don't know. We are people who work with magic. And sometimes it can get brutal, but I think it is always a little bit obscure, so we just reach for metaphors that make us comfortable, metaphors that come from how we've been socialized, to try to explain the inexplicable. I tend to just say, OK, it's magic. Thank you, God. I got blessed with Excalibur in my pen, or whatever. But I love the work, I do. Sometimes circumstances can make you hate the work, but after all is said and done, I would do it all again, all of the pain and all of the sacrifices. And I'll be doing more of it again, won't I? So I don't have to worry about doing *it* again. But that's waiting up the road, I tell you. And a little bit of joy. I would have loved to share this with you, Nikki, even just share Brother Jerome's piece. But I do love my work.
NG: Let me shift for a moment to technology. I don't see how you open your e-mail.

GN: I don't. I'm no longer on-line. Because people had hacked into my system. And it was my suspicion that they were sending things under my name, you know. You remember the thing I had with the government last year? So I said, fine, I'm just going to get my butt off the internet. For about three years I had enjoyed it tremendously.
NG: What is your take on technology? As a novelist, is this good or helpful?

GN: I find it to be helpful. I think it's going to introduce literature to a generation of young people who would not probably pick up the book. I'm not afraid of *Moby Dick* being on line. I'm simply afraid that people will stop thinking. And if they're going to read books on line that same process that they do reading a paper book will kick in. And for me I think that would be a good thing. It's here whether we like it or not. We could say, well is it good or bad, like it or dislike it. It's here. But no one is thinking about what this means as far as the government goes, that we are just inviting them into our lives big time. There's nothing in private that you can do. But as far as it endangering art, no. I think that the creation of a web page by a kid using his or her head, his or her creativity, can be positive. So it doesn't frighten my generation.

NG: I'm a little bit older than you.

GN: Just a little bit, not much! But we were talking about how there's this odd cut off between 1948 and 1955 and the difference in what we experience. I grew up with television just coming in. And because we were poor we didn't get one until I was about six or seven years old. And there wasn't a whole lot on there except *American Bandstand* and *Mickey Mouse Club*. And so you were going to see those two and then you were going to go to bed. And *Ed Sullivan* on Sunday night. And that was the gist of it. I did not grow up like these kids now, who have a truncated attention span. Because books were then just your form of entertainment. And television was indeed limited.

NG: There's a program that I've seen—I don't know if it's experimental or available—and you can use it with, for example, *Moby Dick*. And you can click on it and the whale is jumping and so on. So you're actually ending up watching this book evolve.

GN: That's scary, that's not what I meant.

NG: Because *that* is despicable, as I actually think MTV is despicable, because some things have to be in *your* head. And everybody should know—I mean, there's no way to depict Simon Legree. He should always be unseen. Whatever devils we envision he can become that. But even on the internet—I was involved in part of something called "The Ulysses Project." And I thought it was interesting, but how much of this can we really handle? The kids could click onto me, and find out what I thought about the poem. Or they could click onto four other people and find out what they thought. If they didn't know a word, they could highlight the word and the dictionary would tell them what the word means.

GN: This was all in real time?

NG: Oh, yes. It's an IBM program. And right now it is probably too expensive. But it's in real time and it's showing you how to read a poem. I would like to think that people read "Ulysses." I've enjoyed Tennyson, Eliot, all these people. And of course we love Langston Hughes. Somehow or other you don't want "What Happens to a Dream Deferred" to end up being a cartoon. Do you know what I mean?

GN: I understand. I think the saving grace, though, is the fact that they have even an urge to make it as a cartoon. See, I don't want to think of the death of creativity and so I am hoping that whatever part of the brain that these kids have deadened or had deadened for them by television and video games will come back even if they do something like that—turn a section of *Moby Dick* into a cartoon, turn it into a web page where you can go listen to Ahab or Queequeg. That keeps that section of the brain alive. I'm willing to accept the dumbing of newspapers or television better than I can accept the dumbing of the internet, because that's the last frontier, Nikki.

NG: You really think so?

GN: I really do. Let me tell you something. The aliens are already among us. So there's no place left to go in the real world. Because we are just beginning now to grasp the enormity of what this will mean. And while you better not say anything that you don't want heard by other people, I just feel it could be a new frontier. I really do. I would like to think that some young person could get intrigued enough by *Moby Dick* to try to make it into a cartoon. I'm not scared yet about that. I'm not. And I shouldn't probably be afraid about government snooping, because they have used every technology to snoop anyhow on what people are doing. I may go back on line. I'm still just a little bit excited. I'll tell you, e-mail I handle like I handle real mail. I look and say, uh-oh, I didn't write you. But I was real curious about your take on this whole phenomenon. Will you put your poems on the internet? You wouldn't do that.

NG: I don't know—my poems are on the internet.

GN: But other people put them there.

NG: Other people did and I don't object. I've given away my work. But I also need to get paid, and so we're going to have to find a way to compensate art.

But what I don't like about technology goes back to something as basic as the telephone.

GN: [*Laughing*] Where's that carrier pigeon, Ginney?
NG: Exactly. What I don't like is that we are more alone. We're having more and more information while we are enclosed in our homes. And even something as simple as our daily bread—there was a time that you had to go to the store every day to get bread or if you were poor, every other day. You knew your grocer, and he knew you. "How are you? How's your grandmother? Tell her I said hello now." You had communication. But now, we live in one of the most wired cities in America, Blacksburg, Virginia.

GN: Why is that?
NG: Because Virginia Tech has wired everybody to everything. And those who do it love it. You can order your food, your hardware, have it delivered, never have to see anybody, never have to interact with anybody. You of course are a novelist, and this is where I think the poet comes in. We stand in danger, as we can extend human reach, of losing human speech. Because we don't talk anymore.

GN: You're right. You know QVC? I was hooked into that for a while—
NG: —so is my sister.

GN: —and I guess for the same reason she was. People have created communities around consumerism. They have these long-term relationships with these different sales people. "Well, Jack, I loved that ring I bought." And it's like two or three o'clock in the morning. And so, yes, you're saying that less and less interaction is going to happen.
NG: Yes. And if I wrote science fiction—where is Octavia Butler when you really need her? But you can see that we're going to get to the point that nobody talks.

GN: No one will have to, will they?
NG: But there'll be a yearning for it.

GN: So that's where someone will pick up a pen—
NG: Or do something. But there will be a yearning for this sound that comes from the mouth that means something.

GN: Because human beings need interaction. We could have done this [interview] over the phone or done this by e-mail.

NG: Oh, we couldn't have done it through e-mail, Gloria, because I don't open mine! [*Laughing*]

GN: A lot of that stuff you get is probably from the university.

NG: Most of what I seem to get is from friends and fans. And so I'm always pleased because I have a lot of respect for my fans, but I can't get my work done and answer. I think it's so brave of you because so many people read you.

GN: Yes, but I would never use my real name. I was Gene Naylor at one point. One time I was One-Way.

NG: I think that human sound is essential. And so you really can see if we could do that and I would be able to write a book that Octavia Butler should write—you can really see that whoever could finally come up with the sound of the human voice—"I love you"—would be able to bottle it.

GN: But we do bottle it.

NG: Yes, we do. Wouldn't that be wonderful? And so people would be falling in love to the sound of this James Earl Jones type "I love you" and they would buy this because they wouldn't know how to speak.

GN: Oh my goodness, there is an Octavia Butler story called, I think, "Speech." And it's a world where people are losing the ability to talk.

NG: You're kidding!

GN: And so this woman helps out a little boy and a little girl or something because they still had the ability to talk and their mother had somehow raised them not to speak. She'd taught them not to let others know they have that ability. You should look that up.

NG: I will. Because I think there's a hunger for human beings—I think that's why QVC sells bad jewelry because people have a hunger to be in touch. Maybe all of this is the fault of television. You mentioned Mickey Mouse. What's the one thing we all have in common? M-i-c-k-e-y M-o-u-s-e. Why? What did they say? "See you real soon." Why? "Because we love you." And we all by watching the *Mickey Mouse Club* thought that a television should love us. Then Jim Bakker came along and said, "I love you. Send money." But we were already prepared by Mickey Mouse!

A Dialogue with Gloria Naylor

Charles E. Wilson, Jr. / 2000

Charles Wilson: The first question I want to pose is about the South. Had you traveled much in the region before you went in 1968 to start your seven-year stint with the Jehovah's Witnesses?

Gloria Naylor: I had, because my grandparents were from the South. After my ministry was done, I came to New York.

CW: How did you find life in the South as opposed to your living in the city when you traveled as a child?

GN: Well, what impressed me was that it was a much slower-paced life. But now that I am older I understand that life in any place other than New York is slower.

CW: You are right. The minute I arrive in New York I get this energy that starts to flow.

GN: People walk faster here. I enjoyed the environment in the South, especially the physical environment. The weeping willows and palmetto trees are lovely. And also I found that people are generally courteous, both black and white. My experience, mind you, was very different from that of my grandparents or parents. Things were tense in the sixties. But when I started going there in the seventies and eighties, the region had changed.

CW: Interesting. Regarding the seven-year work with the Jehovah's Witnesses, what was most memorable about that time? I know it's hard to name everything.

GN: One thing that the church taught me was to care about other people. Whether or not they cared about your message was irrelevant. But it opened me up out of my shyness. Because I had a cause that was greater than myself. So I could knock on a stranger's door and talk to that person.

CW: That takes a lot of courage.

GN: That takes a lot of courage. Or even the idea of having a greater mission in life. You overcome whatever reservations you might have about knocking on a stranger's door. I think that being with the church helped me to come out of my shell. And also they gave me values. Those things are important, even if you don't follow the tenets of a religion anymore. There are basic sound principles of how to treat your fellow man that stay with you.

CW: I'm glad you said that because your comments lead to another question I wish to pose with regard to values. What values did they strengthen that your parents first instilled, considering the fact that parents are our first teachers?

GN: Exactly. They taught that it was important that we decide for ourselves what our goals are. Once you decide for yourself, let no one dissuade you. We were taught that we had values. Our lives mean something. For them, we were to go on and acquire an education. It was important that you become a nurse, or teacher, or government worker—that you do something meaningful with your life and you don't let others make you feel inferior.

CW: That's interesting what you said about the ideas that they had for you. What did they initially think about your becoming a writer? I am recalling the interview you had with Toni Morrison several years ago in which you made a comment that you told your mother that you were a writer and would not have a steady job. What did your parents think of that initially?

GN: Initially, they were a little put off by that, because they knew that writers didn't make a living. You know, you had to do something else. They identified more with my being a teacher. During the first ten years of my writing career I did a lot of teaching. And they identified more with the fact that I was teaching at a university.

CW: Right. That is something they could respect.

GN: Exactly. But when my father saw the first copy of *The Women of Brewster Place*, he said, "I didn't know you had this in you." I said, "Well, Daddy, I've been writing all of my life." But they never took that seriously, and most people don't. The arts are a tough field if you're an American. There is no sort of government help. They have consistently gutted the budget of the National Endowment for the Humanities since the Reagan years. When I went to Finland for a writing conference, it just so amazed me that the government actually paid writers a stipend to do nothing but write, and this is a national program.

CW: But here in America, writing is not held in high regard.
GN: No, it is not. We don't hold our teachers in high regard.

CW: I can certainly relate to that. Both my parents are teachers in the public school system. You said regarding teaching that for the first ten years of your writing career you taught. Where did you first teach? I have a list of the places you taught at.
GN: My first teaching job came right after graduate school, and that was at George Washington University in Washington, D.C. They had a fellowship there that was what they called a sweetheart deal because you only had to teach one creative writing course that met twice a week and once a week you ran a community workshop. And the other time you could just write. And it paid a good salary.

CW: Were you there for long?
GN: It was a year's fellowship. You said you have my resume. How did you get my resume?

CW: On-line.
GN: It is on-line?

CW: As part of a contemporary authors' data base. It lists George Washington Unversity, Cornell, Princeton, and Brandeis.
GN: Oh, okay.

CW: And you have not taught in about . . . ?
GN: I haven't taught in about six years.

CW: Do you miss it?
GN: I'm beginning to miss it. I had burned out. I might eventually go back.

CW: Shifting gears just a little bit. What kinds of things energize you and what kinds of things drain you?
GN: Music energizes me, and I have very eclectic taste in music. I like certain operas. I like rhythm and blues. I like some jazz. What drains me is stupidity.

When people refuse to look beyond their tiny, little horizons and interpret the world through their small world view, that drains me. I don't have much contact with people like that. As I said, I don't teach, so basically I can sort of create my own environment.

CW: You are so lucky.
GN: Yes, I am very fortunate in that regard.

CW: One of your comments leads into the next question I have on my list. This is so ironic. How has success altered your personal life? Here, I am really talking about your privacy. I know you have to be very concerned about this. Has it made making close friends more difficult?
GN: The friendships I have are about twenty years old now. So they have been with me through a lot of ups and downs. They have been with me through a lot of vicissitudes, to a large degree. I don't need to make more close friends. I have a cadre of friends already. I'm always meeting people and making acquaintances, though. I have found that an unlisted phone number works just fine.

CW: I find that curious because I know that just in aging you tend not to make the friends you might have made earlier in life. And I think that in having some celebrity status, making friends would be especially challenging.
GN: Exactly. You always have to question why people wish to get to know you.

CW: You have to ask whether it is because of who I am or what I have to give. What personal accomplishments are you most proud of? This relates some with your writing, I would imagine.
GN: One thing I am most proud of is that I earned my graduate degree. I'm proud of that. I'm proud of the fact that I have stuck in here for over twenty years doing the writing.

CW: That is so true.
GN: You do academic work so you know how difficult it is to do.

CW: It is a very lonely and isolated life.
GN: It is. It is a very insular life. I got my undergraduate degree from Brooklyn College and finished *The Women of Brewster Place* in the same month. They happened in the same month. I felt a keen sense of accomplishment. I knew I could start something and stick with it.

CW: That's great. I have to ask you this, especially after having recently read some of your *New York Times* columns from the 1980s. Are you still a *Wheel of Fortune* fan?

GN: I am. But game shows have changed, Charles. I always did like a game show.

CW: You are exactly right. People have been into whole *Survivor* phenomenon. I did not watch that the whole time, and I'm probably one of the few who did not. The concept is fascinating to me, but I just could not be bothered with that. Now your company is called One-Way Productions?

GN: Well, I have dissolved One-Way Productions as of this year.

CW: I was just about to ask about the significance of that name. I just sort of felt that I would get your feedback on it. What projects are you currently at work on?

GN: What I'm working on now is a novel. You know *Mama Day*? There was a character in there called Sapphira Wade. And she was the one who had a mysterious means of obtaining land from Bascomb Wade. Well, in my new book what I'm going to do is follow Wade's journey from Norway and Sapphira's journey from Senegal. They meet in Savannah and they go off with a Native American group. It is a like they are going back to the birth of that community. I deal with issues of slavery, identity, and the masses.

CW: That is going to be fascinating. I can't wait for that because, I must tell you, my men's book club read *The Men of Brewster Place* the minute it came out. I've been a fan of yours since *The Women of Brewster Place*, as I expressed in my letter. We are twelve guys who get together once a month and we were just bowled over. For some of them, that was their introduction to you. These are not academic men; these were just people from the community. And they knew *The Women of Brewster Place* because of the television movie, of course. But this was one of the most dynamic sessions we had. So I just wanted to share that with you.

My next question was, what was school like for you? I am speaking of public school, high school, and college.

GN: Well, it was in high school that I really began to appreciate the written word. I had read all of my life, it seems. But I had read indiscriminately. And when my teachers realized that I was a reader they would give me books to read, and they were inevitably always the English classics. I remember when I was thirteen years old my seventh grade teacher gave me *Jane Eyre*. She said that every young girl should read that book. And I read it and enjoyed it and acquired a love for the English classics.

But I was also writing. I've been writing since I was about seven or eight years old. I thought that black people didn't write books because such books were not on our standard curriculum. And when the teachers gave me books to read, those books were the classics. So it took me until I was in college before I had the whole world opened up to me in Black literature, which was a wonderful, wonderful thing. It made me feel much less lonely than I felt when I read other works.

CW: Well, I can relate to that. That makes good sense.
GN: But I was a good student in high school and an excellent student in college because, like I said, I was twenty-five when I started college. So I was much more focused than my peers were.

CW: Where I teach, the average age for undergraduates is around twenty-seven. There are many returning students, which makes for a very dynamic intellectual environment.
GN: Yes, because they bring with them life experiences.

CW: Yes, and that is so vital. Now, you are the oldest of three girls. How did you find that? Did you sort of take advantage of being the one with the power?
GN: But with that power came responsibility. If they messed up the house while your parents were away, you got it when they got back home. "You are old enough to know better." I remember that was the mantra throughout my life. "Gloria, you are old enough to know better." You had to be responsible for the behavior of your sisters. Sometimes, my sisters felt, "Why should I listen to you? You are not my mother."

CW: Now, where do they fall in proximity to you? What are their ages?
GN: One is a year younger; one is five years younger.

CW: I'm the oldest, too, and I can relate to what you are saying. I have a younger brother who is almost ten years my junior. Graduate school and, unfortunately, miscarriage sort of separated us. But I went into being protective and feeling

that I wanted the little brat to get out of my way. Of course, now we are quite close. I'm thirty-eight and he is twenty-nine. The gap sort of closes as you get older. Are you still close with your sisters, as adults.
GN: Yes.

CW: Well, that is great.
GN: One of my sisters lives with me. My youngest sister lives with me. Because I have a brownstone here in New York we have a lot of room.

CW: I actually reacquainted myself with someone about two weeks ago from Richmond, Virginia: Martha Gilbert, whose niece rented from you up until a couple of years ago.
GN: Yes. That is right. Her name is Alice.

CW: I don't know her name, but I've known Martha for about ten years now. It was sort of fascinating that we were talking about this not long ago.
GN: My sister and I now occupy that part of the house. My mother wants to come back to New York.

CW: Where is she?
GN: My parents retired back in 1992 and they moved to Charlotte, North Carolina. And then we lost my father in 1993. So my mother decided she would come back to New York and live out her days here.

CW: That's great. It is so important to have family close to you.
GN: We are a close family. My mother will never have to go into a nursing home, unless she gets extremely ill. We believe in taking care of our elderly. Most of us do. There are some exceptions.

CW: My family is the same way and I am happy to hear of others who share the same values. How would you describe the writing life? We talked about it indirectly when we said it was an insulated life. Anything else you want to say about that?
GN: Would you zero in on a more specific question?

CW: Let's come at this a different way. What authors do you like to read currently?
GN: I read a lot of women writers. Louise Erdrich, Paule Marshall, Alice Walker, and, of course, Toni Morrison are some of my favorites. But what is

interesting, though, is that I've found I have less time to read than I would like to have.

CW: That makes sense.
GN: A woman sent me a novel that is quite interesting. It is about the death of a young black man in a small Mississippi town. He was dating a young white woman. But it's not a predictable kind of death. That's what I liked about the work. The author delves into deep issues.

CW: Now you commented about three years ago in your interview with Charles Rowell of *Callaloo*. In fact, you said that you are now forty-seven years old and you speak your mind. You are not like you were twenty years ago. It is indelicate to talk about age but, of course, I have that before me. And this year you turn fifty. How did that feel in terms of feeling more confident in who you are?
GN: Well, that confidence started to build in my forties. I found that I just can't agonize over what people think of me. And you know your time is shorter and you want to spend it as honestly as you possibly can. But I began to get much more confident in my forties.

CW: I can imagine that. When I was asking about the writing life what I was getting at was what is a typical work day like for you? Or do they just differ from day to day?
GN: My days differ from project to project. When I have my choice, I will work until twelve or one o'clock, go off and do other chores, because there is a tendency to burn out. Maybe I will read. But I can't read fiction while I'm writing fiction. I can read poetry. I can read biography, but it is hard to read fiction. Now that's my formal routine. Now when I was working on *Bailey's Cafe*, my nephew had come to stay with me. He is a teenager. I had to spend time with him. And then I would write at night, from ten until two in the morning.

CW: How did you find being a surrogate parent?
GN: It was hard. Do you have children?

CW: No, I don't.
GN: Raising children is a rough thing.

CW: I tell you, watching my peers who do have children, I'm so much more appreciative of what my parents did. You really see it from a different point of view. Yes, I understand how hard it is. That pretty much exhausts my list of questions.

GN: Now, where are you in the process of your book?

CW: I have drafted all of the summary chapters of each novel. I have done the literary heritage chapter and so I'm fleshing out the biographical chapter, which I hope to have done in the next couple of weeks.

GN: Isn't that wonderful.

CW: It has been an enjoyable project because, again, I've been looking at the works I really enjoy, which are your novels. I've been hooked on them since 1984 when I was in graduate school and discovered *The Women of Brewster Place*.

GN: Well, look at that.

CW: As I said in my letter, I teach something by you every semester. I teach African American literature and Southern literature, and my students rave about your works.

GN: A lot of writers don't like academicians, but I have always appreciated the critical writer. You are creating, too. You are taking raw material and trying to assign some sort of structure to it.

CW: When you were talking about engaging with your characters and nurturing them—for instance, you wrote letters to Willie and Lester from *Linden Hills*—you became quite attached to them. I found your response to Willa's decision to go back and reclaim her role as housewife fascinating.

GN: Yes, I was put out with Willa for two weeks. You see, I knew the ending of *Linden Hills*, but Willa didn't.

CW: I loved that.

GN: But that's the magic of the process: if your characters really live. You don't own them, and they are going to do exactly what they wish to do. Later, I realized that Willa's dialog indicated what she would eventually do. But I just chose to ignore it.

Index